ROBED REPRESENTATIVES

ROBED REPRESENTATIVES

HOW BLACK JUDGES ADVOCATE
IN AMERICAN COURTS

TANEISHA MEANS DAVIS

STANFORD UNIVERSITY PRESS

Stanford, California

Stanford University Press
Stanford, California

Library of Congress Cataloging-in-Publication Data
Names: Means Davis, Taneisha, author.
Title: Robed representatives : how Black judges advocate in American courts / Taneisha Means Davis.
Description: Stanford, California : Stanford University Press, 2026. | Includes bibliographical references and index.
Identifiers: LCCN 2025012691 (print) | LCCN 2025012692 (ebook) | ISBN 9781503640627 (cloth) | ISBN 9781503641341 (paperback) | ISBN 9781503641358 (ebook)
Subjects: LCSH: African American judges. | Judges—United States—States. | African Americans—Race identity. | Identity politics—United States. | Discrimination in justice administration—United States. | Justice, Administration of—Political aspects—United States.
Classification: LCC KF8785 .M43 2026 (print) | LCC KF8785 (ebook) | DDC 347.73/1408996073—dc23/eng/20250325
LC record available at https://lccn.loc.gov/2025012691
LC ebook record available at https://lccn.loc.gov/2025012692

Cover design: Gabriele Wilson
Cover painting: T. Ellis, *Equal Justice*

The authorized representative in the EU for product safety and compliance is: Mare Nostrum Group B.V. | Mauritskade 21D | 1091 GC Amsterdam | The Netherlands | Email address: gpsr@mare-nostrum.co.uk | KVK chamber of commerce number: 96249943

For my beloveds, Husby (Rayshun Davis) and Children:
I swear I couldn't love you all more than I do
today, yet I know I will tomorrow.

In loving memory of Duke Means Davis, the best fur child ever:
I'm glad all dogs go to heaven.

CONTENTS

Contents

PREFACE

The African proverb "If you want to know the end, look at the beginning" resonates with the completion of this project because its origins take me back to Ohio. During the spring semester of my senior year of college, a local police officer pulled me over. I was confused and immediately went into freeze-fight-or-flight mode at the thought of having to interact with a police officer in the middle of the night while alone. I racked my brain trying to figure out what I did wrong, and to be honest, at the moment, I wondered if I had even done *anything* wrong. The latter thought increased my anxiety.

I grew up hearing community stories about DWBs—Driving While Black incidents and racial pretextual stops. I did what we (read: Black people) are trained to do by our families and communities: "Both hands on the steering wheel at 10:00 and 2:00 or 9:00 and 3:00, and no sudden movements. Speak clearly and move slowly. Do not forget to make eye contact!" It felt like there was an invisible checklist that I needed to make sure was thoroughly checked off.

I glanced at my side mirror and saw the white male officer leave the police cruiser. He adjusted his ill-fitting uniform, placed his hat on his head, and strolled to my vehicle. One hand was on the pistol nestled safely in the holster attached to his belt. He immediately began asking me questions.

"Do you know why I've stopped you?"

"No, I'm not sure, but I know I wasn't speeding," I replied.

With sarcasm in his voice, he said: "No, but you were driving without your headlights on, and that's dangerous." He asked me a few other questions in the same condescending tone and then told me to sit tight while he returned to his vehicle to verify my information. After about ten minutes, the officer returned to my vehicle, reminded me of my mistake, and handed me my license, car registration card, and a $200 ticket.

After reflecting on the experience, I decided to go to the arraignment to challenge the ticket. Instead of encountering a white male judge as I had anticipated, the municipal court judge was a petite, middle-aged Black woman with gray hair and a warm smile. She asked what brought me to court that day. I remember taking a deep breath and then sharing my experiences from the night I was stopped. After I finished, she shook her head in disbelief and rolled her eyes. I think deep down she could believe it. Judges, perhaps more than other legal actors, are uniquely positioned to observe the documented pervasive bias in the criminal justice system (e.g., Baumgartner, Epp, and Shoub 2018).

After listening to me explain my experience, the judge took a deep breath and said, "This case is dismissed." Then she apologized to me because she could see that I was still deeply affected by my interaction with the officer and having to go to court. After chatting with the judge, who eventually asked me to share how the area was treating me and what I was studying in school, I showed her my license, registration, and proof of car insurance.

As I walked out of the courthouse, I was satisfied that I had been allowed to speak my truth, be listened to, and be understood and believed by someone in a position of power. I was also happy with the case outcome. This type of procedural and distributive justice is essential, especially for individuals from communities who have had troubled relationships with those engaged in criminal justice work, such as judges and police officers.

I have been an "academic" my whole life—studying things and researching people and places. Who was that municipal judge? How many judges like her were there in the world, making Black litigants feel like I felt, acknowledging and believing our testimony, giving us space in their courtroom, and deciding cases in profoundly right and justice-oriented ways? These questions, among others, sat with me for years and remain with me.

In graduate school, I learned that Black judges, especially those at the state court level, were rarely discussed in racial and ethnic politics literature or in law and court scholarship. The work focusing on Black judges was outdated (e.g., Smith 1983; Washington 1994), studied them superficially, or focused on Black federal judges like Thurgood Marshall and Clarence Thomas and not state court judges, like the judge who presided over my arraignment. This lack of scholarship is significant because state court judges are much more likely to interact with Black litigants, given that most legal cases in our system are handled by state court judges. In other words, the discipline that studies power and the areas of study where Black state court judges should be discussed often overlooked them as legitimate political actors worthy of scholarly inquiry.

Since interacting with the police officer in 2009, I have been interested in policing and justice. Ever since the Black woman judge who presided over the case apologized to me during my arraignment and then dismissed the charges against me, I have been interested in what it means for the justice system and for Black communities to have racial representation in courthouses across the country.

In *Robed Representatives*, I focus on the nature and significance of racial representation in the judiciary by addressing the primary questions raised following the substantial increase in Black judges in the post–Civil Rights era: Have American courts and justice been transformed purely by this racial diversity? Are Black people represented in these political institutions because of this diversity? This book is what I wanted to read after my encounter with the Black woman judge. This book addresses many questions that have gone unanswered in the literature even though Black judges have been sitting on the bench in large numbers since the mid-twentieth century. This work combines multiple methodologies and explores the interplay of identity, especially race, in judicial politics.

Robed Representatives, which engages with scholarship on representation, racial identity, group consciousness, and judicial behavior, offers new insights into Black state court judges' lives, experiences, perspectives, socialization, and behaviors. Moreover, the voices and narratives in the book reveal various unidentified manifestations of racial representation in the judiciary. Finally, the book demonstrates that only through research that considers the lives, identities, and behaviors of historically underrepresented judges will we arrive at a more comprehensive understanding of the importance and limitations of racial diversity in the courts and whether, how, and why Black judges represent Black interests.

ACKNOWLEDGMENTS

Philippians 4:13 lets me know that I can do all things through Christ which strengtheneth me. I am thankful to my Lord and Savior, my redeemer, Jesus Christ, who strengthened me to do everything that needed to be done to complete this book. I cherish the calling on my life and feel blessed by the amount and kind of grace and mercy I've been shown.

As a child, I loved school. I thank all my K–12 educators for pouring into me as a quiet, young student. My favorite class before college was Ms. Yolanda Torrence's African American History elective. In the class, she taught us about Black politics, life, and culture. The class remains the foundation for my academic and professional work, including this book project. I deeply appreciate Ms. Torrence for teaching a young Black girl about herself and her community.

I owe thanks to the many professors at the University of Pittsburgh and John Carroll University who taught me and helped me develop personally and academically as an undergraduate. Thank you! I am indebted to Elizabeth Stiles and Mindy Peden for being affirming amid my academic anxiety and helping me develop an appreciation for the discipline of political science. Thank you, Sara Schiavoni, for introducing me to the study of law and courts.

I participated in the Ralph Bunche Summer Institute (RBSI) in 2008. RBSI is an annual five-week program at Duke University that introduces rising seniors to doctoral study in political science and strengthens the pipeline for underrepresented groups in the discipline. I'm grateful to Dr. Paula D. McClain for directing the program and investing in Bunchees, Dr. Scott de Marchi for making statistics fun, and the teaching assistants Jessica J. Carew, Niambi Carter, Pat Horn, Monique Lyles, Efrén Pérez, Eugene Walton, and Candis Watts Smith for their early support and mentorship.

I went to Duke University for graduate school. I'm grateful for all the professors in Political Science and beyond who taught, supported, and encouraged me while I pursued my graduate degree as a young mother. I'm incredibly grateful for the faculty on my doctoral committee who gave constructive feedback on my written work: Kerry L. Haynie (Chair), Guy-Uriel Charles, Christopher D. Johnston, Jack Knight, and Paula D. McClain. Thank you, Richard (Dick) Engstrom for modeling how scholars can apply academic skills to real-world problems to bring about policy changes and address inequities. A special thank you to Kerry L. Haynie and Paula D. McClain for believing in me, mentoring me, guiding me, and fostering a rich and dynamic intellectual space for the critical study of Race, Ethnicity, and Politics. I appreciated your mentorship during graduate school and appreciate that I still have both of you in my professional corner.

I was fortunate to spend two years at the Carter G. Woodson Institute for African and African American Studies at the University of Virginia while finishing my graduate degree. I am particularly grateful for Deborah McDowell's leadership of the program, as well as to Maurice Wallace, the Woodson faculty, and the faculty I interacted with from the Politics Department. I am incredibly grateful for the 2014–2015 and 2015–2016 cohorts and their support and collegiality that helped me cross the finish line.

I began my academic career at Vassar College. I am immensely grateful for the collegiality and friendship of faculty across the college, especially colleagues in Political Science and Africana Studies. I am fortunate to have close senior mentors and friends. Thank you for your support and mentorship, Candice Lowe-Swift, Quincy Mills, Shona Tucker, and Eva Woods-Peiró. Thank you to my colleagues who read parts of the manuscript and provided invaluable feedback and encouragement: Andrew Davison, Luke Harris, and Samson Opondo.

To Katie Hite, my dear mentor, colleague, and friend, thank you for showing me how to successfully juggle being a mother, scholar, teacher, and committed community member. I appreciate your advocacy, laughter, generosity (thank you for all the mandarins!), and love you have shown me and my family. Onwards and upwards, my friend! To Quincy Mills, a dear friend and mentor, thank you for welcoming me and for your support, continuous mentorship, and friendship. To Luke Harris and Samson Opondo, thank you both for always being available for a quick chat or a more extended conversation over a meal. I have appreciated your commitment to helping me develop and succeed as a junior scholar in the department. Thank you to the junior women in the VC Department of Political Science (Arpitha Kodiveri, Claire Sagan, and Mallory Whiteduck) for your friendship, and my dear friends and work buddies over the years, especially Leroy Cooper, Adam and Lisa Lowrance, Jasmine Syedullah, Kirsten Wesselhoeft, and Kimberly Williams-Brown. Thank you for being part of my village and allowing me to be part of yours.

As a professor at Vassar, I have enjoyed educating and working with hundreds of students. I am forever grateful and indebted to the countless students I have had the privilege of teaching. Thank you for letting me experiment with ideas in the classroom and for being brave enough to critique the heck out of them. I feel blessed to have had research assistants/undergraduate collaborators who have supported my data collection efforts and research projects. Thank you, Ria Bhutani, Hayley Craig, Robert Downes, Andrew Eslich, Achal Fernando-Peiris, Tomas Guardia, Michelle Itkin, Phoebe Jacoby, Joseph P. Kelly, Simon LaClair, Kremena Mestanova, Kaitlin Prado, and Katha Sikka for going above and beyond.

Within the discipline of political science, I have found community. I am grateful to the junior and senior women in the Law and Courts and the Race, Ethnicity, and Politics (REP) communities. I'm particularly grateful to the Junior Law and Courts Writing Group for their feedback on my in-progress work and to junior and senior scholars for their friendship, sponsorship, and support, including Christina Boyd, Rebecca Gill, Susan B. Haire, Gbemende Johnson, Laura Moyer, Rorie Solberg, and Susan Sterett. In REP, I have benefited from friendship, sponsorship, and support from numerous scholars, including Nadia Brown, Pearl Dowe, and Candis Watts Smith, and spaces for gathering, such as the Women of Color in Political Science pre-conferences.

I have benefited from critical feedback on the book. Thank you to my Book Manuscript Workshop reviewers Gregory Goelzhauser, Candis Watts Smith, and Isaac Unah. Thank you to audience members, fellow panelists, and discussants at various conferences over the years who have provided constructive remarks about the ideas and data analysis included in the book. Thank you to the African American Policy Forum's Summer Writing Retreat organizers and participants, including Devon Carbado, Kimberlé Crenshaw, Luke Harris, and Ezra Young. Thank you for your constructive feedback on my proposal. I don't think I will ever get feedback on a paper in a better place (a swimming pool in Negril, Jamaica). Thank you to Ronald Collins for your encouragement and willingness to provide feedback on the proposal and advice about publishing.

As a junior scholar, I've benefited from numerous pipeline programs over the years, including Ford Foundation's Fellowship Program, the Mellon Foundation's Summer Institute on Tenure and Professional Advancement (SITPA) program, and the Racial Democracy, Crime and Justice Network's (RDCJN) Summer Research Institute (SRI). In those programs, I was paired with a mentor and supported by various outstanding directors. Thank you, Gabe Sanchez, for supporting the completion of my SRI paper/project, and thank you to Jody Miller and Rod Brunson for leading the summer program and helping me strengthen my ties to the RDCJN collective. Thank you, Kerry Haynie, for leading SITPA on top of your various other responsibilities! I'm also thankful for the mentorship and support of Isaac Unah, who I was paired with during SITPA and who later served as my Ford postdoc advisor. Isaac is incredibly intelligent and quite humorous. For instance, when I asked his advice about hiring a humanities developmental editor, he responded with laughter, "Well, yes, to bring some humanity to the work." Thank you, Isaac, for your mentorship and sponsorship.

My work has been generously supported over the years. I sincerely appreciate Mark Hurwitz and the anonymous reviewers at the Law and Sciences Program at the National Science Foundation for supporting this research and data collection. Without the funding to field the surveys and travel, *Robed Representatives*, as it is currently written, would not have been possible. Thank you to the folks currently or formerly in Vassar's Grants Office, including Judith Dollenmayer, Gary Hohenberger, Christina Johnson, and Michal Woodbridge.

I'm a community writer/worker. Thank you to my National Center for Faculty Development and Diversity (NCFDD) writing crew and friends: Michael Bennett McNulty, Jenny Banh, and Kevin Jones. Thank you to the Vassar Women's Accountability Group, who welcomed me and supported my productivity over the years: Sarah Pearlman, Nancy Pokrywka, Jodi Schwarz,

Alison Spodek Keimowitz, and Shona Tucker. Thank you to Lissa Stapleton and Chinbo Chong, my former Zoom writing buddies. Thank you to Ms. Nadine at Easton's Nook (a NJ writing retreat space) for loving on me as I loved on my work. Your warm presence, delicious food including banana bread, and lighthearted approach to life are always just what I need when I'm trying to push through a writing block. Thank you to Ted Ellis for creating Black art and for granting me permission to use the art for the cover. Isn't she lovely . . .

Thank you to Stanford University Press for publishing books about identity and law. A special thanks to my editor, Marcela Maxfield. Thank you for your patience as I navigated life while finishing the book, for believing in me, and for guiding me through this process. This process was challenging at times, partly due to some health challenges and my struggle with imposter syndrome, and there were many days that I did not think that I could write a book, but I never felt alone or unsupported. Thank you, Justine Sargent, for your support toward final submission. Thank you to the various editors I have engaged with, including Judith Dollenmayer, Leanne Powner, and Sara Street. Leanne—thank you for the space to discuss my ideas, write through my anxiety and vulnerability, and develop as a writer.

Everywhere I've lived, I've found a spiritual home and leadership. In North Carolina, I appreciated Pastor Maurice Wallace's contemporary and engaging teacher-preacher style (the Wallace family and Cornerstone Community Church family). Thank you for your support over the years, even at different institutions! A special thank you to Ms. Doris Cross (Duke—RBSI), Ms. Mary Bogues (Duke—Center for the Study of Race, Ethnicity, and Gender in the Social Sciences), and Ms. Debbie Best and Ms. Danielle Marie Harris-Wright (University of Virginia—The Carter G. Woodson Institute) for the administrative support along the way and for nurturing me in a way that I've only ever received from Black women.

I'm grateful I have never felt confined to the "Vassar bubble." Instead, I have appreciated the community I'm part of in the Dutchess County area. Thank you to Shatiya Avent, Nyhisha Gibbs, Ms./Auntie Carmen McGill, Lennice Odums and the River Cities Athletics community, Brian Robinson, and my fellow antiracist activists in Arlington Partners Against Racism (On PAR!). I feel blessed to have family friendships as well. Deva Woodly and Gail Upchurch-Mills, thank you, my dear scholar-mamas, for being part of my family network in New York (and now beyond!).

Whodini asked: "How many of us have them? Friends." The answer to that question is easy for me—I do! Thank you to the PhDivas for the love, support, and friendship over the years: Gloria Ayee, Jessica J. Carew, Nura Sediqe, and Alicia Reyes-Barrientez. Thank you to the SITPA crew for friendship and accountability during the early assistant prof years: Yalidy Matos and Tacuma Peters. A special thank you to my friend from the Woodson, Ava Purkiss. I have always appreciated your warmth and generosity. Thank you to my RDCJN 2018 Cohort friends: Jane Daquin, Janet Garcia-Hallett, Susila Gurusami, Melissa Guzman, Marisa Omori, Ranita Ray, and Ebony Ruhland. Thank you, Kira Lawton, for your friendship. I appreciate our almost-monthly lunch dates! And I am so eternally grateful for my very best friends and sisters: Yalidy Matos, LaVonia Roane, LaTasha Smith, and Ecko Steadman. Ecko and LaVonia, we have been rocking and rolling since middle school. I love y'all. Yalidy, my academic wife and bestie, I love you, and you had better believe it is for life. I love being on this journey with you. LaTasha, I love you and am so happy to be your chosen sister.

Lastly, if you know me, you know I love my family and happily make the eight-hour drive home to Ohio multiple times each year. Thank you to my grandmother Bobbie J. Cox, parents Bridgette Means and Ralph Means, bonus dad Frank Davis, aunts and uncles from the Davis, Means, and Washington Families, and siblings (Daniel Greer, Tania Means, Serena Evans, Veyonce Wilson, V'Nina Wilson, and Nija Wright) for nurturing and loving me. To my husby, Rayshun Davis, thank you for choosing and loving me every time. Thank you for pushing me, holding me accountable, supporting me, and doing everything you do so that I can do everything I need to do. Your excitement for this project and belief in my ability to complete it has been palpable since day one. We did it! Thank you to Keyshaun Oglesby, whose presence in my life is a gift. To my little children, Javen, Raya, and Raegan Davis, your smiles and laughter, loud voices, messy faces and rooms, high energy, busy schedules, and big personalities bring me so much joy. I love you all.

ONE

BLACK JUDGES AND JUDICIAL DIVERSITY IN AMERICAN COURTS

> Judge Jackson, this is Joe Biden. How are you? . . . You're going to
> be more wonderful. I'd like you to go to the Supreme Court. How
> about that? . . . Well, I'm honored to nominate you . . . Well, you
> deserve it. You deserve it . . . No, I meant what I said. I think it's
> important. You are incredibly well-qualified and I think the court
> should look like the country. And I mean it. Thank you.
>
> **PRESIDENT JOE BIDEN TO KETANJI BROWN JACKSON**[1]

In February 2020, then-presidential candidate Joe Biden said, were he to become president, he would be honored to appoint a Black woman to the Supreme Court of the United States (hereafter SCOTUS).[2] Biden felt the bench should "look like the country" and that it was "long past time" to have a Black woman on the highest court in the nation given its more than 230-year existence. Two years later, after more than twenty-seven years on the court, Supreme Court Justice Stephen G. Breyer announced his retirement, leaving Biden with a vacancy to fill. Later that month, when asked who he was considering to replace Justice Breyer, President Biden affirmed his campaign promise to appoint a Black woman to SCOTUS: "While I've been studying candidates' backgrounds and writings, I've made no decision except one: the person I nominate will be someone with extraordinary qualifications, character, experience and integrity—and that person will be the first Black woman ever nominated to the United States Supreme Court. It's long overdue, in my view."

For weeks, political commentators and scholars alike hypothesized who President Biden would select. They did not have to wait long because just one month later, on February 25, 2022, President Biden announced that he would be nominating Ketanji Brown Jackson, a judge on the U.S. Court of Appeals for the D.C. Circuit, to SCOTUS to succeed Justice Breyer upon his retirement at the end of the court's session. Forty-two days later, in a split vote (53–47), the United States Senate narrowly confirmed Jackson to the Supreme Court as its 116th Associate Justice. The entire appointment, both the nomination and confirmation, was unprecedented and a historic moment. Biden's commitment to creating a judiciary that more accurately reflects the racial and gender diversity of the community is evident in who he appointed to the bench. His nomination announcement implies that race and gender matter in representation on the bench.

Despite the historic nature of Jackson's nomination, Biden's decision to name a Black woman to the bench came with significant controversy. The outcry seemed to be less about who specifically he named to the court and more about the idea that race and gender matter for the courts and then creating an entire pool of candidates with the marginalized identity characteristics to ensure that he eventually selected a Black woman. If judges' identities could matter for federal court outcomes, as Biden clearly believed, could judges' identities also matter in state courts, where most legal cases are adjudicated?

This is an important question to ask right now because racial diversity on state courts has increased in recent years, with Black Americans increasingly being elected and appointed to state judiciaries around the country (George and Yoon 2017). The meaning of this increased racial diversity for the representation of Black interests and for democracy remains unclear, however. Does having more Black state court judges mean anything for court processes and decisions? Existing scholarship about the significance of judicial diversity reaches mixed conclusions because studies have most often focused on case outcomes. Yet judges do more than adjudicate; they perform other important functions in the courtroom, courthouse, and community. This is the purpose of this book on Black state court judges. It addresses whether, and if so, how and why, Black judges represent Black legal interests in the decisions they make and the work they do as jurists.

JUDICIAL DIVERSITY AND BLACK REPRESENTATION
ON STATE COURTS

Black representation in state courts has a long history. Although Black judges were nonexistent in the South until the Civil Rights era, they were regularly present in states with large Black populations outside the American South, such as California, Illinois, New York, Ohio, and Pennsylvania, starting in the early twentieth century (Walton Jr. 1985, 220). Scholars writing about Black Americans and legal history, such as Hanes Walton Jr. (1985), Marvin D. Free Jr. (1996), and J. Clay Smith Jr. (1993), note that the legacy starts with Macon Bolling Allen and Robert Morris, two of the earliest Black Americans to hold judicial positions in the United States in the mid-nineteenth century.[3]

In 1848, Allen became a Massachusetts justice of the peace, a position similar to a notary public. During Reconstruction, he migrated south to South Carolina and was appointed a judge of the Inferior Court of Charleston (1873) and was elected as a probate judge in Charleston County (1876). Morris became one of the first Black jurists when he was appointed to the Boston, Massachusetts, Magistrates Court in 1852 (Walton Jr. 1985, x). Between the mid-nineteenth century and mid-twentieth century, fewer than fifty Black judges presided over state or federal courts (Smith 1983). This trend changed in the 1960s with the Black Civil Rights movement championing the representation of Black Americans in political offices and Congress's adoption of the Voting Rights Act, which (re)enfranchised Black voters. Additionally, scholars note some, albeit not consistent, conscious efforts by presidents, senators, and state political actors to diversify the judiciary, although this often came after external pressure or with electoral implications in mind (Goelzhauser 2011).

Two decades into the twenty-first century, racial and ethnic minorities comprise roughly 10 percent of the state judiciary and roughly 30 percent of the federal judiciary; the remainder are white.[4] After white jurists, Black judges are the largest racial group present in both state and federal judiciaries. Black jurists make up roughly 7 percent of state judges and 11 percent of federal judges. Figures 1.1,[5] 1.2,[6] and 1.3[7] indicate that Black American judges are concentrated in the Northeast and the South, although a number of Black judges work in the Midwest and on the West Coast as well. As of 2023, some of the states with the largest number of Black state judges continue to be Illinois, California, Louisiana, and New York. At the federal level, scholars find that these newer members of the judiciary bring important background diversity in terms of ideology and can influence jurisprudence on key twenty-first-century issues (Brazelton and Pinderhughes 2021).

Black Americans represent nearly 13 percent of the United States population. In comparison with figures for the overall United States population, in 2023, Black judges are still underrepresented in the country's courts. Despite this, the percentage change between the number of Black judges in 1960 and in 2023 is remarkable. Considering Black judges were virtually nonexistent before 1960, the fact that by 2023 the number has grown to nearly 1,000 is remarkable, and an increasing number of Black women are being selected for the bench (Moyer, Harris, and Solberg 2022).

Because Black judges have been appointed and elected in record numbers to both the state and federal bench in the post–Civil Rights era, court scholars imply that they, along with other underrepresented jurists, are "worthy of heightened analysis." Since the 1970s, scholars have shown an increased interest in understanding who these judges are, how they reach the bench, and what they do on the bench once they are there. That is, scholars have tried to understand Black judges' behaviors and decision-making and whether Black judges represent Black Americans and their legal interests.

A large and growing body of literature on Black judges now exists, but few of these studies systematically examine the backgrounds of Black judges, explore why Black judges might represent Black Americans' interests and respond to Black Americans' concerns, or identify whether Black judges represent Black Americans and Black interests.[8] This study seeks to address this deficit in our knowledge by examining the backgrounds and experiences of Black judges, whether they possess a racial group identity and racial group consciousness that would lead them to represent Black Americans' interests on the bench, and whether they behave in ways that demonstrate they represent Black Americans and Black interests.

THE CONCEPT OF REPRESENTATION

In politics, the concept of representation generally describes how political officials act on behalf of individuals or a group of individuals. Although the concept of "representation" was used long before the twentieth century (e.g., Burke 1774), Hanna Pitkin (1967) is often credited for her work on this sub-

FIGURE 1.1: Black state court judge population distribution, 2023.

Black State Court Judges - Total

Number of Judges

0 — 177

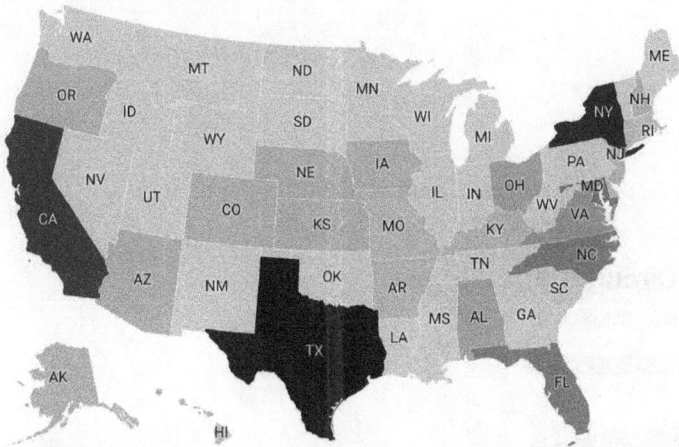

Created with Datawrapper

Source: State Court Organization Court Statistics Project.

FIGURE 1.2: Black federal district court judge
population distribution, 2023.

Black District Court Judges

Number of Black District Court
Judges

0 — 10

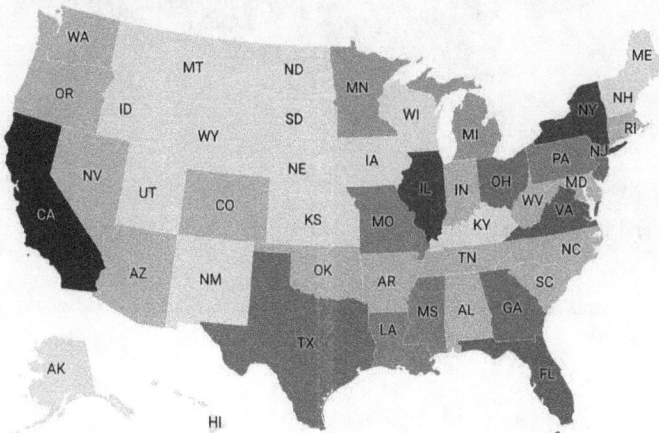

Created with Datawrapper

Source: Federal Judicial Center, Biographical Directory of Article III Judges.

Black Circuit Court Judges

**Number of Black Circuit Court
Judges**

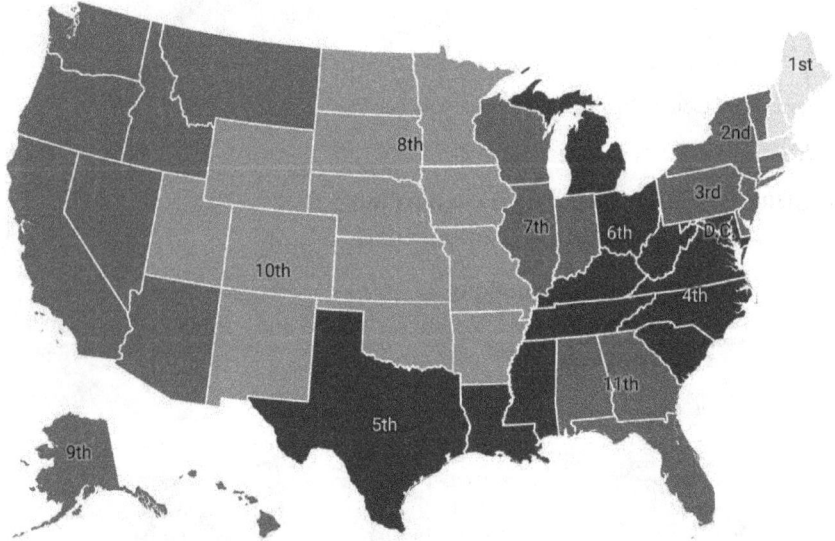

0   3

Created with Datawrapper

Source: Federal Judicial Center, Biographical Directory of Article III Judges.

ject. In her book *The Concept of Representation*, Pitkin articulates four theories of representation important to politics: descriptive representation, substantive representation, formalistic representation, and symbolic representation. Below I discuss the three types that have been particularly prominent in research on race and ethnicity as well as on democracies more generally: descriptive, symbolic, and substantive representation.[9]

Descriptive representation is the "making present of something absent by resemblance or reflection, as in a mirror or in art" (Pitkin 1967, 11). Thus, a racial group is descriptively represented when the institutions that govern it accurately mirror or resemble the community's important characteristics (i.e., race). For Black Americans, this means having Black Americans in positions of power within political institutions such as legislatures and bureaucratic organizations. In the judicial context, Black Americans are descriptively represented when Black Americans are elected or appointed as judges.

Pitkin (1967) describes symbolic representation as the ways a representative "stands for" the represented. That is, symbolic representation refers to the particular meanings that a representative has for those being represented. Symbolic representation is understood by the response to the representative by the individuals being represented. For example, this means seeing a representative and the political institution as legitimate and supporting and trusting in the political official's actions. For instance, Theobald and Haider-Markel (2009) find that Black Americans are more likely to perceive police actions as legitimate if Black police officers are present. Also, Scherer and Curry (2010) and Scherer (2023) find that Black Americans see courts with Black American judges as much more legitimate than courts with less racial diversity. This finding is consistent with Means and Unah (2024), who found Black Americans perceived Black judges to be fairer decision-makers than their white counterparts.

Finally, substantive representation refers to the content of the representative's actions when those actions are taken in the interest of the group being represented (Pitkin 1967, 209). Therefore, substantive representation is concerned with what political officials do on behalf of groups they are associated with and are charged with and held accountable for representing. For Black Americans, this means having political officials who behave in manners and pursue goals that respond to the group's needs and interests. Black Americans are substantively represented when legislators, for example, make decisions that adhere to, respond to, or are in accordance with the interests and concerns of Black Americans.

In brief, then, descriptive representation is concerned with a representative's presence, symbolic representation is concerned with the response evoked by the representative, and substantive representation is concerned with a representative's behavior. Each of these types of representation enhances democracy. Descriptive representation is important for individuals previously excluded from the benefits of democracy and for those who have been disenfranchised and oppressed. Additionally, descriptive representation is important in a democracy because the United States' power as a republican government resides in the citizens being represented in the government's decision-making bodies (Mansbridge 1999).

Scholars note that descriptive representation is also important for symbolic representation and substantive representation. Descriptive representation induces trust and legitimacy in political institutions and the government as a whole (Scherer and Curry 2010; Theobald and Haider-Markel 2009). For example, Mansbridge (1999) argues that descriptive representation increases the "attachment to the polity of members of the group" (628), and Black descriptive representatives affect the level of political engagement, especially voter turnout, among Black Americans, who tend to be politically empowered and more attentive to political affairs when they are represented by someone that looks like them (e.g., Bobo and Gilliam 1990; Gay 2001). Descriptive representation also induces and enhances substantive representation. Numerous studies of Congress, state legislatures, and local bureaucratic agencies show that Black politicians are much more likely than white politicians to provide Black people with substantive representation by behaving in ways that are beneficial to and advance their interests (e.g., Brown 2014; Haynie 2001; Nicholson-Crotty, Grissom, and Nicholson-Crotty 2011; Farrell, Ward, and Rousseau 2009).

THE CONCEPT OF REPRESENTATION IN THE JUDICIAL CONTEXT

While legislative and bureaucracy studies often use the concepts of symbolic, descriptive, and substantive representation to describe and understand the presence and behavior of Black political officials, court scholars have tended not to incorporate these concepts into their research. Ifill (1997) says, "Racial diversity on the courts is almost never discussed in the more forceful language of rights and representation. . . . Indeed, to describe judges as representatives is to invite hostility from both the bench and the bar" (97). The concept of representation in the judicial context is rejected by both judges and members of the legal profession more generally.

Several reasons explain why scholars tend not to use the concepts and language of representation in the judicial context. First, based on the nation's founding documents, including the *Federalist Papers*, the framers of the United States Constitution neither intended the court to be a representative institution nor judges to be representatives. Chief Justice of the Supreme Court of the United States John G. Roberts Jr. expressed this understanding at his confirmation hearing for Chief Justice:

> Judges are like umpires. Umpires don't make the rules, they apply them. The role of an umpire and a judge is critical. They make sure everybody plays by the rules, but it is a limited role. . . . Judges have to have the humility to recognize that they operate within a system of precedent shaped by other judges equally striving to live up to the judicial oath, and judges have to have modesty to be open in the decisional process to the considered views of their colleagues on the bench.[10]

Another reason scholars have not thought of judges as political representatives is that judges take an oath to be impartial as a condition to serving, and the dictates of the judicial profession require them to be guided by the law, legal principles and precedent, and case facts, and *not* group interests.[11] Related to this is the idea that judges are often viewed as a monolithic group; they are supposed to do the same thing because they have, for the most part, gone through similar processes to become judges in terms of legal training and then a history in the legal profession, usually as an attorney (Stumpf 1998). Many judges learn how to be knowledgeable and experienced judges through a "judicial socialization process" (Carp and Wheeler 1972, 359). Given this similar educational and professional background and socialization process, judges are thought to have developed a similar outlook that overshadows individual characteristics like race, gender, class, and religion. Conventional wisdom about the responsibilities and roles of judges and lawyers also influences how the concept of representation is used in the judicial context. The legal profession says advocating and representing are what lawyers do, and adjudicating is what judges do (Ewing 2000). It is therefore unsurprising that the concept of representation is not used as frequently in reference to judges as it is in reference to attorneys.

Finally, the lack of diversity in the courts is yet another reason the concept of representation is not often used in the judicial context. Until the 1960s, judges largely had similar educational, economic, and social backgrounds and were perceived as having similar interests, perspectives, and outlooks, largely as a function of their shared racial and ethnic heritages (Stumpf 1998; Goldman, Slotnick, and Schiavoni 2013). Prior to the Civil Rights movement, when the courts began diversifying significantly along gender and racial lines, both the federal and state judiciaries could largely be described as homogeneously white and male. Early-twentieth-century judges came "from a very narrow stratum of American society" and were "home-grown fellows who [were] moderately conservative and staunchly committed to the status quo . . . local boys who made good" (Carp and Stidham 1998, 261). Therefore, only in the last fifty years have racial minority (male and female) and white female judges increased their presence enough to make the judiciary more heterogeneous and thus peopled with individuals who have diverse educational, economic, and social backgrounds and distinctive interests, perspectives, and outlooks.

Despite resistance to the use of the concept of representation in the judicial context, the concept is now regularly used in studies of the court and judges (e.g., Bonneau and Rice 2009; Graham 1990; Hall 1995; Kastellec 2013; Segal 2000). These scholars generally, albeit implicitly, maintain that the concept of representation, as identified by Pitkin, can be applied to judges. This is similar to scholars who have adopted the language of representation in their studies of police officers, bureaucrats, and other nonelected officials, and other non-legislative contexts (Meier and Nicholson-Crotty 2006; Theobald and Haider-Markel 2009). This literature demonstrates that the bureaucracy also performs representational functions. For example, both minority healthcare professionals and minority teachers contribute to reduced minority-teen birth rates (Zhu and Walker 2013). Studies such as these demonstrate that the bureaucracy and individuals who are not elected to represent can still perform representational functions.

In *Robed Representatives*, I advance an argument about the concept of representation for judges. Although Pitkin's book (1967) does not feature in-depth discussions of the significance of employing the concept of representation when referring to judges and the courts, I contend that we *can* think about representation in the court context. The following section briefly summarizes my theorization of representation, and I fully explicate the theoretical framework undergirding this book about Black judges functioning as representatives of Black interests in chapter 2.

ADVOCATIVE REPRESENTATION:
THEORIZING REPRESENTATION IN THE JUDICIARY

Thus far, scholars have failed to recognize important dimensions of racial representation in the judiciary and that Black judges might engage in decision-making behavior in the interests of Black Americans. One of my central arguments is that, based on the perspectives and behaviors of Black judges, social scientists should expand conceptualizations of representation. In doing so, we are likely to enhance and advance our understanding of how institutions and their primary actors provide group-specific representation, even in the face of institutional designs intended to prevent representation of group interests. In this study I help expand our understanding of representation by advancing the theory of *advocative representation*. This theory considers the backgrounds, socialization, life experiences, and identifications of Black judges to understand them as representatives and their behavior on the bench as representation.

Advocative representation theorizes how representation can and does occur in public institutions with no expressed or widely recognized representation functions. As applied to courts, the theory posits that despite the constitutional and formal dictates about their roles, the legal and judicial socialization process of the judicial profession, and the conventional expectations regarding courts and judicial behavior, judges sometimes purposefully and nonpurposively behave in the interests of group interests. Thus, judges' behaviors can transform courts into representative institutions. Advocative representation can be best understood as a function of judges' racial socialization, salient group identities, and group consciousness. It can result from both intentional actions and unintended consequences related to a judge's presence in a court. Although this study focuses on Black judges and the advocative representation they may provide to Black people, the concept has broader application, as I explain in chapter 2.

BLACK JUDGES' BACKGROUND CHARACTERISTICS, SOCIALIZATION, AND LIFE EXPERIENCES

Underlying the belief that Black judges will have decision-making tendencies representative of Black group interests is the presumption that to some extent, Black judges have backgrounds and experiences that make them similar to each other and to Black Americans in the general population and different from their non-Black counterparts. Studies substantiate this belief by documenting important characteristics in Black judges' backgrounds that are not present in white judges' backgrounds (Shuman 1970; Smith 1983; Wilder and Ashman 1973). For instance, Black judges often experience racial discrimination; are active politically in local politics and in civil rights; have been employed in a prosecutor's office or served in the military at some point before becoming a judge; consider themselves liberals and identify with the Democratic party; and mostly train at Black educational institutions, especially Howard University.

Black judges, then, appear to have some distinctive background characteristics.[12] Unfortunately, this conclusion is somewhat problematic for several reasons. First, most studies that focus exclusively on Black judges are more than twenty years old, and the Black judges interviewed, surveyed, and researched for those studies were born before the Civil Rights movement (Shuman 1970; Smith 1983). Second, while they provide some evidence to suggest that current Black judges have distinctive backgrounds, many recent studies do not focus solely on Black jurists. Instead, researchers merge white female federal court appointees and racial-minority federal court appointees into one category and report the findings of the entire group as "nontraditional" minority judges, without considering the possibility of noteworthy distinctions within such a pooled category. Nevertheless, while scholars have examined the backgrounds and characteristics of twentieth-century Black state court judges and have evaluated the characteristics of twenty-first-century minority appointees to the lower federal courts, we still lack information on the backgrounds and experiences of twenty-first-century Black state court jurists and how those experiences compare to those of their predecessors. By examining their backgrounds and characteristics, this project seeks to highlight some of the life experiences of current Black jurists and how those experiences affect judges' work on and off the bench.

BLACK JUDGES' RACIAL GROUP IDENTITY AND
RACIAL GROUP CONSCIOUSNESS

Black Americans' political behavior is understood to be a function of a racial group identity and racial group consciousness (Dawson 1994; McClain et al. 2009).[13] For Black Americans, possessing a racial group identity and racial group consciousness involves perceiving a connection to other in-group members; perceiving that being Black or being perceived as Black has affected one's experiences in life and life chances; and believing that collective action is essential to accomplishing Blacks' interests and improving the group's status in America (Dawson 1994; Simien 2005; Tate 1994). Like most Black Americans, Black politicians, especially Black legislators, are also believed to have a strong racial group identity and racial group consciousness, although scholarship does not always demonstrate the connection explicitly (Broockman 2013; Smith 1983; Whitby 1997).

While scholars frequently imply that Black judges are connected to their racial group members, understand the interests of Black Americans, and act on their behalf while on the bench, this topic has generally been understudied with regard to Black judges. However, some early survey and interview data suggest Black judges possess a racial group identity and racial group consciousness (Shuman 1970; Smith 1983; Washington 1994). By "providing legal services to the Black community" and devising "a means of achieving social justice within the existing [political] structure" in their pre-bench careers, Black judges were perceived to be connected to the Black community and Black interests (Shuman 1970, 225). In his study, Smith (1983) used Black judges' civil rights activity to create an approximate index of Black judges' group consciousness. Smith (1983) concluded that because a substantial number of the judges in his study were contributors, workers, or officers in one or more of the prominent Black civil rights organizations, Black judges in the twentieth century could be understood as possessing a racial consciousness (123). Finally, Black judges interviewed by journalist Linn Washington (1994) alluded to possessing a group identity and consciousness by revealing they were deeply concerned about the dire conditions of many Black Americans; had personal experiences with racism as children, lawyers, and even judges; and believed racism was a central aspect of American society and the adjudication process.

Although some studies report Black judges have a sense of racial group identity and racial group consciousness, most of these studies focus on Black judges who sat on the bench in the mid-to-late twentieth century and were heavily involved in the Civil Rights movement; thus they are quite dated—thirty to forty years in some cases, or a full generation. Judges who are active on the bench today may differ from the judges who were sitting on the bench in the mid-to-late twentieth century. Scholars such as Smith (2014b) already note generational differences among Black Americans regarding their perceptions and outlook on life. Researching the racial group identity and racial group consciousness of Black judges will determine whether current Black judges identify with and feel connected to other Black Americans, endure racialized experiences like many of their Black counterparts, perceive racial discrimination to be an issue affecting the Black community, and feel compelled to behave with the group in mind while on the bench.

BLACK JUDGES' JUDICIAL BEHAVIOR ON AND OFF THE BENCH

Political scientists largely acknowledge and understand that Black politicians, especially legislators, feel connected to the Black community and other Black Americans and are intrinsically driven and motivated to advance and respond to Blacks' interests (Broockman 2013). Court scholars, however, have rarely made this argument. Two theories have primarily been advanced to explain why Black judges' decision-making will likely reflect that they are concerned about and responsive to Black Americans' interests. One theory is that Black judges, like other Black Americans, are likely to have personally encountered and experienced inequality and racial discrimination, and this experience with discrimination makes them sympathetic to individuals and claims involving discrimination (Farhang and Wawro 2004, 301; Steffensmeier and Britt 2001, 752). The other theory is that Black judges will generally support disadvantaged and oppressed populations when they appear in court because Black judges are likely to be liberal and see themselves as liberal (Welch, Combs, and Gruhl 1988, 127; Segal 2000, 140). I concur with scholars who say experiencing racial discrimination and being liberal can help explain why Black judges might have distinctive decision-making behavior in favor of Black Americans. But, in addition, I argue that socialization and racial group identification and connection are also likely to be important for Black judges' behavior because of the established connection between Black Americans and Black politicians' group identity, group consciousness, and political behavior.

There is also some evidence that Black Americans and Black interests are improved or increased with Black judges (e.g., Kastellec 2013; Chew and Kelley 2008; Scherer 2004). For instance, some Black judges are even-handed in their decision to incarcerate both Black and white offenders as compared to white judges (Abrams, Bertrand, and Mullainthan 2012; Welch, Combs, and Gruhl 1988). Additionally, some Black judges are sympathetic to defendants and rule for the accused, prisoners, and plaintiffs in racial harassment, employment discrimination, and death penalty cases more frequently than white judges (Kastellec 2013; Tiede, Carp, and Manning 2010).

Most scholars studying the nature of representation in the judiciary focus almost exclusively on the final case vote. For criminal cases, many have examined whether Black judges find defendants guilty or not guilty and the length of the sentence they give to defendants. For civil cases, scholars have focused on whether Black judges vote liberally in cases dealing with Black issues (i.e., in favor of litigants expanding, protecting, or promoting equality, civil rights, and civil liberties). Scholars have largely overlooked activities beyond final case votes, which limits our understanding of whether and how Black judges represent Black interests.

Judges make decisions the entire time they are on the bench. For instance, depending on the level and type of judge, judges can determine what cases they hear, what they say during judicial conferences and in interactions with other judges and lawyers, what they write in their legal opinions, whether they issue felony indictments in criminal cases, what evidence will be permitted during trials, what issues arise during jury selection and how to address those issues, which witnesses are approved, whether a plea deal or bail is appropriate, what bail amount and restitution is proper, whether a jury sentence is fitting for the crime committed, what can be said by lawyers and witnesses during trials, and what jurors should take into account or not consider when making their decisions. Judges also control the courtroom and the actors in it, hire court staff, provide the commentary during sentencing, and so on. Given these activities and responsibilities, judges' behavior and discretion are clearly not limited to their final decision in cases. Moreover, Black judges' decisions and behaviors are not limited to their adjudication duties. Instead, assessments of representation by judges should consider the many other decisions judges make off the bench, including initiatives they start and support, and how they engage with their colleagues. This book does this. By expanding what might qualify as "representation" in the judicial context, I anticipate finding that Black judges represent Black Americans and Black interests from the bench in several different ways overlooked by other scholars.

DATA AND METHODS

The questions central to this project about the socialization, experiences, identities, and behaviors of Black judges help us to answer the primary question undergirding this study about whether Black judges might represent Black legal interests. Moreover, I will address a secondary question: how and why do Black judges represent Black legal interests. Answering these questions requires multiple data analyses, qualitative and quantitative. The primary data sources utilized are in-depth semi-structured interviews with and surveys of Black judges.

To understand Black judges' backgrounds, socialization, life experiences, identities, and behaviors, I conducted semi-structured face-to-face interviews with Black state judges. Elite interviewing is an appropriate methodology for this study because Black judges are treated as experts about the topics discussed (Leech 2002). No one can address the topics covered in this book better than Black judges themselves. I interviewed a total of thirty-two Black state court judges who served in Illinois, Louisiana, Nevada, New York, North Carolina, Ohio, and Virginia. These states were selected because of the large number of Black judges working in them and access to the location for research purposes. I recruited judge participants for this study by calling and emailing them. Contact information was gathered from court administration websites.

Fifteen of the judges interviewed were male and seventeen were female. I interviewed judges between February 2013 and September 2020, and the interviews typically lasted one hour, although some lasted several hours. (Table A.1 in the Appendix contains non-identifying demographic information about the judges interviewed for this study.) In the interviews, I asked my respondents about their background, upbringing, life experiences, identity, and behavior, and their perspectives on topics in law and courts, such as judicial selection, public opinion about judges and the courts, and judicial roles. The interviewee names in this book are pseudonyms, and I have been careful to remove all identifying references to protect the confidentiality of the Black judge participants in this study.

Finally, for this project, I incorporate data from an anonymous survey of Black judges that I fielded between August 2019 and August 2021. Using a database that contained contact information for all sitting Black state court judges as of June 2019, I sent hard copies of a twenty-nine-page survey to all the Black judges in the database—roughly one thousand judges. Of these, 276 surveys were completed and returned in the stamped envelopes provided. I include 270 surveys in the analysis because these were the judges who confirmed being Black/Black-American. This is an incredible response rate, especially in the midst of a global pandemic. The survey contained closed- and open-ended questions organized around thirteen categories. (See Figure A.1 in the Appendix for location information about the judges surveyed, and Table A.2 in the Appendix for background information about the survey respondents.)

PLAN OF THE BOOK

This book engages with scholarship on representation, Black socialization, racial group membership, identity and consciousness, and judicial decision-making and behavior, and offers new insights into their application to Black judges. In the empirical chapters of this book, I draw on the interviews and surveys described in the previous section to thoroughly examine Black judges' backgrounds, experiences, identities, and behaviors. In doing so, I capture rich details about Black judges' upbringings and identifications, as well as myriad manifestations of and avenues for representation in the judiciary that are understudied in existing law and courts research.

Before delving into the empirical data for this book, I start by presenting my theory for why and how Black judges might represent Black interests. Chapter 2 introduces and advances the book's theoretical framework—advocative representation. I start the chapter by demonstrating that, thus far, scholars have largely failed to recognize essential dimensions of representation. As a result, existing theories of representation cannot fully explain why legal actors such as Black judges, who are highly socialized and are neither expected to nor charged with representing group interests, might still represent group interests. Then, I advance my theory of advocative representation to explain representation that occurs in public institutions with no expressed or widely recognized representation function and by actors with an identity-to-politics link and significant group attachments. In the context of this book on Black judges and Black representation in state courts, advocative representation is best understood as a function of Black judges' salient group identities and group consciousness and results from both these jurists' actions and the consequences of their actions, which align with Black judicial interests.

I have divided the book into two parts around the two primary guiding questions. Part 1 (chapters 3 and 4) addresses why Black judges are likely to represent Black interests; it focuses on Black judges' backgrounds and identities to assess whether Black jurists exhibit an identity-to-politics link. Part 2 (chapters 5–8) addresses whether and how Black judges represent Black interests by focusing on Black judges' actions and behaviors on and off the bench. Together, parts 1 and 2 will demonstrate whether Black judges have an identity-to-representation link and how it can impact their work.

Chapter 3 focuses on the paths by which Black judges arrive at the bench. Using surveys and interview data, I examine Black judges' backgrounds and life experiences. The chapter's primary argument is that Black judges' lives and paths to the bench are quite varied, yet there are important commonalities both with each other and with the general Black population. In any event, Black judges' backgrounds and trajectories to the courts afford them experiences that deeply influence and inform their identities as Black people and judges. This chapter finds significant social, educational, and professional characteristics and thus experiences in the backgrounds of many Black judges sitting on state courts. This chapter's findings are significant for the theoretical framework spelled out in chapter 2, which necessitates an identity-to-politics link for advocative representation to occur, by demonstrating the identity and socialization components of the theory.

The findings of chapter 3 lead directly to the primary arguments advanced in chapter 4, mainly that Black judges' socialization and life experiences are likely to lead them to develop a strong racial group identity and consciousness. Surveys and interviews with Black judges reveal that the factors that have helped many Black Americans develop and preserve a strong racial group identity and consciousness are present in their own lives. This chapter, which gives voice to Black judges' identities, demonstrates that Black judges self-identify as belonging to the "Black" racial group and feel connected to other Black

Americans and the Black community. Additionally, they perceive racial discrimination as one of the primary issues affecting the Black community and are mobilized to protect and represent the interests of Black people and help Black people realize equality and progress. The chapter concludes that many Black judges possess a strong and deep racial group identity and consciousness. They see themselves as important for Black communities and people. I argue that these group attachments and views about their role in the political system are consequential for their judicial work.

Whether Black judges can be viewed as representatives in the courtroom is the focus of chapters 5 and 6. In these chapters, using surveys and interviews with Black judges, I share the extent to which Black judges perceive of their behavior as representative of Black interests. Additionally, these chapters present the myriad ways that Black judges behave on the bench and, when available, the rationale Black judges employ to explain that behavior. Black judges illustrate that to best understand the importance of having Black Americans in the judiciary, scholars need to look beyond judges' final case votes. In short, this chapter presents evidence that many Black judges, both consciously and unconsciously, provide advocative representation of Black Americans in their behavior on the bench with regard to their courtroom hospitality (i.e., procedural justice), court proceedings, pretrial decisions, and case outcomes.

The last two empirical chapters, chapters 7 and 8, center on Black judges' behaviors in the courthouse and the community. I reveal some of the judicial activities Black jurists engage in when they are not sitting on the bench presiding over cases. The chapters argue that to fully assess representation in the courts, scholars must include judges' off-the-bench activities. Drawing on interviews, chapter 7 highlights Black judges' collegial relationships and interactions with their judicial colleagues, showing how Black judges' actions help their judicial peers develop cultural competency that can be helpful in their peers' adjudication of cases involving Black litigants. Chapter 8 draws on interviews and surveys, in addition to primary and secondary materials and archival data, identifying some similarities in Black judges' community activities and programmatic initiatives. Both chapters demonstrate that Black judges engage in advocative representation of Black interests when working with colleagues and in the community.

Finally, in the concluding chapter, I take stock of the collective findings. This leads to a discussion of this research's implications for representation and democracy. I reiterate my argument that, despite the general reluctance of legal scholars and professionals to use the term *representation* when referring to judges, we can and should consider many Black judges as representatives of Black interests and people, given their decisions and work. I conclude the chapter by discussing how institutions are being shaped by group interests, even those institutions that purport to be above group politics, and how transformation is taking place due to diversification. Ultimately, I demonstrate throughout the book how and why diversity matters in the courts and why we need to continue diversifying the judiciary, broadly speaking, to improve and ensure the courts are more representative, democratic, inclusive, and equitable spaces.

TWO

ADVOCATIVE REPRESENTATION
Theorizing Black Representation in the Courts

Persistent calls by Black communities and organizations for increased racial diversity have incrementally been answered since the 1970s, with Black state court judges being elected and appointed at unprecedented rates. Chapter 1 highlighted the existing literature on these Black political actors and how, despite decades of research, a question remains for us to answer: whether Black judges are doing what many imagined and hoped they would do. Are Black judges representing Black people and their interests, and if so, why are these judges engaging in this work when they are not selected for or charged with doing it? The goal of this chapter is to present a comprehensive theory of representation that can help us understand both why and how Black judges might represent Black interests.

When it comes to theorizing about Black judges representing Black interests, a significant segment of the law and courts scholarship stands in stark contradiction to the Black politics scholarship. The first body of work implies that Black judges are unlikely to represent group interests because, like all judges, they are constrained by precedent (i.e., the doctrine of stare decisis), the law, and the dictates and traditions of their rather-conservative profession, and most importantly, judges are not charged with or, broadly speaking, expected to represent group interests (Bailey and Maltzman 2008; Knight and Epstein 1996). Black politics literature suggests that Black judges are likely to represent Black people and interests because they are likely to have been racially socialized and have racialized experiences that lead them to possess a strong Black identity and consciousness that, ultimately, would impact their work (Dawson 1994). But the first body of literature lacks a nuanced understanding about what it means for Black judges to have salient social identities that could lead to the development of a collective group identity and consciousness, which are known to deeply shape Black people's attitudes and political behavior. The second body of literature overlooks what it means for legal actors like Black judges to not be charged with or expected to represent group interests and how the professions and institutions some actors work in constrain them and may make it difficult, if not impossible, for them to act on behalf of group interests.

Black judges, like all judges, may indeed be constrained by their institutions, be socialized to practice judicial restraint and not represent any group interests, face heightened scrutiny and be the subjects of reprisal, and not be charged with or expected to represent Black people (Means 2018; Means et al. 2023; Motley 1998). Nevertheless, I argue that many Black judges are still likely to represent Black legal interests. My argument is based on the theory of advocative representation, which I advance in this chapter. Advocative representation explains how and why *all* political actors, including Black judges, who are not expected to or charged with representing group interests might still represent group interests. The theory posits that despite institutional constraints, formal dictates, professional socialization processes, and conventional wisdom, political actors like Black judges can by virtue of their own individual and collective identities and consciousness behave in the interests of groups that they belong to when decision-making opportunities arise. This theory maintains that opportunities *always* exist for political actors to represent group interests because all these actors have jobs and responsibilities that grant them some discretionary authority.

Discretionary power affords actors opportunities to make decisions that hew most closely to their intrinsic preferences and interests. Consequently, responsibilities are also sites whereby actors can make decisions that result in consequences that I argue, if aligned with a particular group's interests and preferences, should be considered manifestations of representation. By considering as representation the consequences of an actor's actions if they are in line with the preferences of a group, this theory helps us incorporate numerous actors who have traditionally and typically been excluded or at least marginalized in research on representation because they lack a formal charge and expectation to represent. Though not specific to Black judges, this theory provides a useful and much needed framework that can explain and help us better understand how and why this group of political actors might represent Black people and their interests in state courts across the country.

The chapter will proceed as follows. First, it will discuss the concept of representation and present the leading theories of representation most often employed in political science to study Black political representation and discuss why and how those theories are inadequate for a study of Black judges and representation in state courts. Then, it will delineate the theory of advocative representation, including its primary components. The chapter will then move to explain how the theory is relevant, useful, and necessary for this particular project on Black judges. The chapter will conclude with several expectations about Black judges' identities and behavior that stem from the theory. These expectations are the basis for the subsequent empirical chapters of the book.

THE CONCEPT OF REPRESENTATION IN POLITICAL SCIENCE

"Representation" is a core concept in political science. Political theorists have written about the concept for centuries, leading to "many overlapping and sometimes inconsistent meanings" (McLean 1991, 172). Hanna Pitkin (1967) is often credited for her pioneering work that made the concept of representation less elusive by highlighting how it is multifaceted. In her seminal book, *The Concept of Representation* (1967), Pitkin suggests representation is fundamentally about bringing present something that otherwise is not present, but she regarded this general definition as being too abstract: "Political representation is as wide and varied in range as representation itself will allow. The most that we can hope to do when confronted by such multiplicity is to be clear on what view of representation a particular writer is using, and whether that view, its assumptions and implications, really fit the case to which he is trying to apply them" (227–28).

As mentioned in chapter 1, Pitkin presented four types of representation that political science should be mindful of: formalistic, symbolic, descriptive, and substantive. Formalistic representation concerns how representatives get their authority to represent and how they are held accountable for this formal responsibility. Symbolic representation focuses on how people feel about the government and how individuals and institutions, for example, can stand for something else altogether. Descriptive representation is the "making present of something absent by resemblance or reflection, as in a mirror or in art," whereas substantive representation refers to "*acting* for others . . . the substance of the activity itself" (Pitkin 1967, 11–12).

Descriptive representation and substantive representation, along with their derivatives, are frequently used in research about legislative and bureaucratic contexts (e.g., Canon 1999; Tate 2004). For court scholars, the term *representation* has largely been avoided in both discourse and scholarship about judges and courts (Ifill 1997). Even in her book, Pitkin mentions the concept of representation applying to judges only a few times and in a limited way. For instance, she writes: "[Judges] are, of course, formal representatives in the sense that they do hold an official position . . . but if we ask what they are to do, in what sense they might correctly be called representatives, it is not a matter of rights or obligations, or of being a symbol of a descriptive sample" (1967, 116–118). Here, Pitkin reveals that applying the concept of representation to the judicial context is challenging when jurists are not explicitly tasked with directly representing a constituency, reflecting a group's interests, or being held accountable for representation.

Furthermore, courts have never been commonly regarded as representative institutions. The U.S. Constitution and *The Federalist Papers* say as much in their discussions of the role and responsibilities of the legislative, executive, and judicial branches of government. From these founding documents, it is evident that legislative bodies are deemed representative institutions, and legislators, especially members of the House of Representatives, are intended to represent the public opinion and interests of their respective constituents.[1] Courts, however, were generally not viewed as representative institutions in which group interests were expected to be advanced via the behavior of judges. In fact, the Constitution emphasizes the importance of judicial independence by being clear that judges are never authorized to represent group interests nor are they to be held accountable for representing (Article III). Thus, the conventional understanding by scholars and laypeople alike has been that judges are not and cannot be representatives if they are generally supposed to strive to be like legal machinery, embodying the rule of law and operating in accordance with established precedent without regard for group interests tied to social identities like race or gender, or even political ideology.

In the last twenty years, despite some resistance, the concept of representation has steadily been incorporated into studies of judges (e.g., Alozie 1988; Bonneau and Rice 2009; Graham 1990; Scherer and Curry 2010; Segal 2000; Kastellec 2013). Scholars generally, albeit implicitly, acknowledge that the principles of representation articulated mostly by Pitkin (1967) can be applied to judges.[2] This work rests on the idea that if they so choose, judges can respond to group interests and concerns.

STUDYING BLACK POLITICAL REPRESENTATION

Pitkin's (1967) argument about a link between descriptive and substantive representation has been empirically tested in various contexts and is frequently supported by work that examines and evaluates the behavior of groups often marginalized and underrepresented in government, such as racial and ethnic minorities and women (Brown 2014; Dovi 2002; Tate 2004). Scholarship documenting the connection between descriptive and substantive representation largely reveals that who is represented in political institutions matters to the policy-making process within the institutions and to the policies emanating out of the institutions. Substantive representation is often a result of descriptive representation, and this is especially true for Black political representation.

Although having Black political officials does not guarantee the substantive representation of Black people (Pinderhughes 1987; Swain 1995), scholars of Black politics have time and time again shown that Black political officials are often the ones substantively representing Black interests in government (Brown 2014; Haynie 2001; Tate 2004). Many Black members of Congress and state legislators represent the interests of Black Americans, thus providing substantive representation (Grose 2011; Minta and Sinclair-Chapman 2013). Haynie (2001) and Brown (2014) both find that Black state legislators are the primary advocates of Black interests, by introducing, debating, and backing legislation deemed important for Black communities and Black people. Similarly, by examining roll-call votes, bill sponsorship, and symbolic acts in which Black American legislators engage, Tate (2004) finds that Black members of Congress represent their Black constituents' interests. Similarly, drawing on congressional hearings, Minta (2011) finds that despite the decline of national attention to traditionally Black issues such as civil rights, having more Black congressmen and congresswomen in the U.S. House of Representatives and to a lesser extent in the U.S. Senate is responsible for keeping these types of interests on the congressional agenda.

Occasionally employing the language of representation, scholars also study the behaviors of Black judges, asking whether Black judges' decisions are favorable to Black interests. Unlike studies in the legislative and bureaucratic contexts, the results from studies in the judicial context are quite mixed, and scholars lack consensus regarding whether Black judges consistently represent Black interests. Some studies show Black judges exhibit distinctive judicial decision-making behavior, with their decisions being favorable to either Black American defendants or the Black community in general (e.g., Bonneau and Rice 2009; Chew and Kelley 2008; Collins and Moyer 2008; Hettinger, Lindquist, and Martinek 2004; Scherer 2004; Smith 1983; Steffensmeier and Britt 2001; Welch, Combs, and Gruhl 1988). Other scholars, however, find that Black judges do not necessarily represent Black interests and decide cases in ways that are understood to be antithetical to Black interests (e.g., Uhlman 1978; Spohn 1991; Walker and Barrow 1985; Sisk, Heise, and Morriss 1998; Segal 2000).

When explaining why Black descriptive representatives might represent Black interests in their decisions, scholars suggest that these actors possess a collective group identity and consciousness (Broockman 2013). The assumption is that because descriptive representatives share a politically significant trait (i.e., their race) and likely a common background (i.e., socialization), they will possess similar interests and act in favor of those interests. This assumption is grounded in literature from Black politics that finds Black people in the general population behave in the interests of their racial group in the political arena because they possess a racial group identity and collective identity that stems from similar socialization. Scholars presume that an identity-to-politics link exists for Black political actors like state legislators, but this link is often an assumption not subjected to empirically testing (see Brown 2014 as an exception).

Although Michael Smith (1983) and Susan B. Haire and Laura P. Moyer (2015) argued that Black judges on the bench following the Black Civil Rights movement possessed a racial group consciousness that might lead them to represent group interests, most of the scholarship on Black judges in the last three decades has put forth two primary arguments to explain why Black judges might represent Black interests. First, some assert that Black judges are likely to have personally encountered and experienced inequality and racial discrimination, which may lead them to behave in the interests of Black people in cases concerning discrimination (Farhang and Wawro 2004, 301; Steffensmeier and Britt 2001, 752). Another group of scholars argue that Black judges are likely to be liberal, see themselves as liberal, and make decisions that have a liberal tone (e.g., Welch, Combs, and Gruhl 1988, 127; Segal 2000, 140). While I concur with scholars who say experiencing racial discrimination and being liberal can help explain why Black judges might bias decision-making behavior in favor of Black Americans, I argue that scholars have not thought deeply enough about what Smith (1983) and Haire and Moyer (2015) argue: Black judges possibly possess a group identity and consciousness, and the possession of a strong group consciousness might influence their behavior.

STUDYING POLITICAL REPRESENTATION IN THE JUDICIARY

While using the concept of "representation" in studies of judges has normalized over time, law and courts scholars have largely transplanted wholesale Pitkin's theories of representation that were primarily designed for the study of representation by legislators. In doing so, they ignore the fact that, unlike legislators, judges are not authorized by constituents to represent their interests, are not charged with representing constituents' interests, and do not have constituents who hold them accountable in the same way that legislators do. To me, this is a danger; Pitkin's theories of representation cannot satisfactorily capture or fully explain representation in the judicial context. I developed the theory of advocative representation to do what the theory of substantive representation does not and cannot do: offer a way to think about how, why, and when political actors who are not charged with, authorized to provide, or held accountable for representation may represent some group's interests.

Advocative representation builds on the theory of substantive representation and yet departs from it by grounding a conversation about why political actors with discretionary authority might represent group interests in the race and ethnic politics literature. The theory turns the focus away from authorization and accountability to recognize and center judges' individual and collective salient social identities, which, I argue, are likely to influence their behaviors and lead to decision-making in political and legal spaces that are in line with the interests and preferences of members of their salient social groups.

The development of new theories of representation like advocative representation is not meant to discount nor dismiss the importance and utility of Pitkin's theories of representation. Nor is the development of new theories intended to invalidate previously identified theories. Pitkin's' theories are quite useful to think about and examine representation in the legislative branch, but even Pitkin recognized that her theories of representation were not the only theories of representation. She describes expecting and anticipating the development of new theories of representation because, according to her, there is not a "correct meaning of the word" *representation* or theory of representation, and it is scholars' job to "specify all the varieties of its application to various contexts" (Pitkin 1967, 8). My purpose for developing the theory of advocative representation spawned out of a pressing need. The theory of substantive representation could not be used to examine representation (i.e., judicial behavior) in a space like the courts and with public officials like judges because it focused primarily on spaces and actors charged with representing, and authorized and expected to represent. Similarly, other theories of representation that build on Pitkin's work are also not useful to study representation in the judiciary when they have been developed with a different political context in mind. Like Pitkin's theories of representation, newer theories do not take into account what representation might look like in institutions like the courts where actors do not have an express or widely recognized representation function and are constrained by the law and professional dictates.

THE THEORY OF ADVOCATIVE REPRESENTATION

As a theory, advocative representation posits that despite formal dictates, socialization processes, institutional constraints, and conventional wisdom, political actors represent the interests of particular groups when their actions are in line with the collective interests of the group. The theory can be best understood as a function of actors' salient group identities and group consciousness and as manifesting itself in actors' intentional and unintentional actions and decisions. Building on the principal-agent concept of acting on behalf of an individual or group, advocative representation primarily has to do with the behavior and activities of an actor (Pitkin 1964, 338).[3] Furthermore, unlike other definitions of representation, advocative representation is not concerned with official charges, authorization, and expectations, nor is it concerned with political actors viewing themselves as representatives.

The theory has four core components, which are described in the following four sections of the chapter: (1) an individual that represents ("The Representative"), (2) people or interests to be represented ("The Represented"), (3) the manifestations of representation ("The Representation"), and (4) the impetus for the representation ("The Representational Impetus"). By expanding the boundaries around who can be a representative, who and what can be represented, what qualifies or counts as representation, and why representation may occur, this theory helps us understand how and why actors commonly thought to operate outside the bounds of politics and official representational roles, such as judges, may represent group interests.

THE REPRESENTATIVE

The first component proposes that all individuals with decision-making abilities and discretionary authority working inside institutions of power can act as representatives even when their primary role is not to represent. As mentioned previously, in the United States, those charged with "representing" have traditionally been elected officials like state legislators and members of Congress (Pitkin 1967). This is unsurprising because these political actors are indeed selected by a constituency to act in accordance with the interests of the constituents they are expected to represent and charged with representing. Moreover, these actors see themselves as representatives of group interests. These legislative actors are, in other words, authorized by and accountable to constituents. Because these elected actors are who comes to mind when considering who representatives can be, theories of representation have narrowly defined representatives as primarily these types of political actors, who are explicitly selected to represent.

The theory of advocative representation suggests that there are few political or legal actors who are outside the bounds of who can be representatives. The theory deemphasizes whether political actors' formal role is to represent and instead argues that how actors behave is key to determining who are representatives. Advocative representation maintains that representatives can be anyone with discretionary authority, a type of power that affords political actors the ability and opportunity to make decisions (Tyler and Mitchell 1993). In this theory, actors become representatives not because of their official title, not because of their formal role, and not because of what they are expected to do, but because of their behavior within an institution. Their actions, if aligned with what a group prefers, are considered representation work (i.e., actions that lead to consequences that align with group interests), and this work is what makes actors representatives. Thus, legislators can be representatives, but representatives can also be staff members, judges, and other political actors with discretionary authority to make decisions that bring about consequences that could be in line with a group's preferences and interests.

THE REPRESENTED

Second, advocative representation focuses on who is represented, which most theories of representation have defined as a constituency that resides in the jurisdiction of a representative and has the ability to participate in selecting who represents them (Pitkin 1967). What is represented is the interests and public opinion of the constituency. In the legal context, "the represented" has typically referred to clients who hire a representative to advocate for them in a court of law.[4] Again, what is represented is the best interests of the client. Thus, in the political arena, "the represented" most often refers to individuals who ask for and expect representation, and what is represented refers to their interests.

Advocative representation redefines who can be represented by submitting that *all* individuals are capable of being represented irrespective of whether those individuals ask, expect, or even consent to being represented. What determines who is represented is an actor behaving in a manner that is consistent with and in favor of their interests. The represented, therefore, can be any group or individual—voluntary or involuntary—because advocative representation is fundamentally based on representatives' behavior rather than the represented's desire to be or knowledge of being represented. Advocative representation maintains that representation is not conditional on being authorized to represent or held accountable for representation, and that representation can occur without the knowledge and approval of the individual or group being represented.

THE REPRESENTATION

The third component of the theory centers on the manifestations of representation that can occur within institutions of power. Most scholars who study whether actors represent group interests focus on the final decisions actors make in their institutions or the final outcomes in their institutions. In legislative studies, most scholars analyze roll-call votes, but scholars now study legislators' agenda setting, sponsoring activities, committee assignments and work, and hiring practices (Grose 2011; Reingold, Haynie, and Widner 2020). In the courts, scholars have mostly examined judges' rulings and final decisions in individual cases (Collins and Moyer 2008; Manning, Carroll, and Carp 2004; Welch, Combs, and Gruhl 1988), although they also look at the importance of diversity in terms of judicial colleagues' behavior (Haire and Moyer 2015). These activities and decisions are only some of the ways political actors can represent group interests. Scholars should think more broadly and perhaps innovatively about what representation might look like in order to properly examine and reach conclusions about whether group interests are being represented in institutions of power. As a discipline, political science needs to consider new metrics, frameworks, or case studies to understand how representation could be working in practice.

Advocative representation maintains that *representation* can refer to *any* and all behaviors and decisions political actors make that lead to and result in consequences that speak to, center, and further a group's interests in their institution of power. Advocative representation underscores the fact that most actors possess a great deal of discretionary authority and have opportunities to decide how they will act in their spheres of influence. Because institutions vary in terms of their abilities and powers, what representation is in one institution is likely to differ significantly from what it is in a different institution. Furthermore, manifestations of representation are likely to vary even within the same institution, owing to the fact that most actors shoulder multiple responsibilities.

Take, for example, representation in the medical field. *Representation* might primarily refer to doctors' decisions regarding treatment, but it might also refer to their decisions regarding where to practice medicine, how to interact with patients, the type of research they conduct, who they hire to work alongside them, their office aesthetics, the programs and initiatives they lead, and so on.[5]

For instance, considering that Black interests in the medical context include being descriptively represented in the medical field and having doctors who are respectful and allow for clients to have some agency and self-determination, Black doctors can be viewed as representing group interests when they work in clinics near Black communities or where Black community members can easily access them, engage their Black clients respectfully, are attentive to their clients' ideas about their health care and treatment, and hire Black nurses and medical staff. If the Black doctors' behaviors and decisions are done in ways that align with Black medical interests, advocative representation would insist that the doctors are functioning as representatives and that Black people and interests are being represented.

A similar argument can be made for judges. In courthouses, *representation* might refer to judges' final decision in the criminal and/or civil cases they preside over. *Representation*, however, might also include judges' decisions regarding their volunteer activities; how they interact with litigants, attorneys, and their judicial colleagues; the things they do in their courtrooms and courthouses; who they hire to work alongside them; and so on. Again, if judges' behaviors and decisions result in consequences that align with a particular group's interests, then advocative representation maintains that the judges are functioning as representatives and a group is being represented. Regardless of what the specific behavior and decisions are, what the theory of advocative representation considers to be most important is that the behavior leads to consequences that are in line with the judicial interests of the group being represented.

In addition to focusing on representatives' literal actions and behaviors, most theories of representation take into account intentionality (Hobbes, Rogers, and Schuhmann 2005; Pitkin 1967). Pitkin (1967) notes that substantive representation entails these types of intentional actions: "When we act for someone else we may not act on impulse; we may not risk what others have at stake 'just because we happened to feel like it.' We are expected to act as if we would eventually have to account for our actions. Thus, we ought to have reasons for what we do, and be prepared to justify our actions to those we act for, even if this accounting or justification never actually takes place" (118). Here, Pitkin suggests representation requires intentional acts on a group's behalf. But unlike substantive representation and other theories that focus on intentionality and purposeful behaviors, advocative representation does not concern itself with whether a behavior was deliberate and intentional or unconscious.

For advocative representation, what makes representation count as representation is actions that lead to consequences that are in line with the desires of a particular group. On one hand, actors might recognize the interests of a particular group, feel compelled to represent those interests, see justification and an opportunity to do so, and then behave in ways that are in line with the group's interests. This is consistent with advocative representation. Political actors behaving without thought and intention, however, and their unconscious behavior being in line with a group's interests are also consistent with advocative representation. In other words, advocative representation acknowledges representation resulting from actions that are both intentional and unintentional. Regardless of intentionality, what is most significant when it comes to manifestations of representation is that an actor with discretionary authority and decision-making responsibilities makes decisions and acts in a manner consistent with the interests of a group.

THE REPRESENTATIONAL IMPETUS: AN IDENTITY-TO-POLITICS LINK

The final component of the theory focuses on why political actors might represent group interests. For some representation theorists, representation results from authorization (i.e., being given the authority to act on behalf of an individual or group of individuals) and accountability (i.e., an expectation of representation and being held to account for their [in]actions). Pitkin (1967) writes about representation being the result of intentional actions and responses to external pressure: "One represents whatever guides one's action," and "[a] judge who represents group pressures is a judge conceived as responding to group pressures, through whom such pressures act" (117–18). In this way, representatives act in response to external pressure and have to "find out what the majority of [the individuals being represented]" want and then act in accordance (McLean 1991, 195).

The theory of advocative representation, however, argues that actors may represent simply because of who they are and the fact that, because of their individual and collective identities, they share perspectives and interests with their social group members and behave in ways that align with those group members' preferences because they know them and share them. Advocative representation fundamentally speaks to actors being intrinsically motivated to act in the interests of groups in which they belong. This motivation is best understood as a product and function of an individual's salient social group identities and group consciousness. It is not about representatives being coerced or otherwise "responsive to pressures and popular demands" (Pitkin 1967, 117). There is also no "finding out" what the interests of a group are to represent them. Advocative representation suggests that because of their common backgrounds, socialization, and personal and vicarious life experiences, some political actors have ingrained within them deep understanding and knowledge about their group's interests and needs, and that, at times, they act in accordance with those interests in the political arena when it is pertinent to do so.

Advocative representation is predicated on the existence of an identity-to-politics link for most people, even political actors, and the belief that individuals with an identity-to-politics link will represent their group members via their intentional and unintentional actions and behavior in the political arena mainly because their behavior is done with the group's interests consciously or even subconsciously. The literature in political science is clear—to understand the political attitudes and behaviors of Black people and other racial groups, we must consider and account for a collective group identity and consciousness. That is, an identity-to-politics link has been established for some groups in society, including Black people (Dawson 1994; Jardina 2019; Sanchez 2006). Although understudied in the literature, political actors such as Black judges may possess salient identities that influence their decisions in their spheres of influence. Like their counterparts in the general population, political actors may also have an identity-to-politics link.

THE IDENTITY-TO-POLITICS LINK AND IDENTITY FORMATION AND DEVELOPMENT

The identity-to-politics link refers to the idea that people develop individual and group identities related to salient social characteristics and that these identities influence their politics—their political attitudes and behavior. Some people make decisions and behave with regard for the interests of one or more identity groups they belong to in their spheres of influence because they share a collective identity and because they see their group status as politically salient (McClain et al. 2009). Social identity is a complex concept, and the formation of identity is embedded in and shaped by social, cultural, historical, economic, and political contexts (Sanchez 2006). Henri Tajfel, a social psychologist known for his path-breaking research on social identity theory, defines social identity as "that part of an individual's self-concept which derives from his knowledge of his membership of a social group (or groups) together with the value and emotional significance attached to that membership" (1978, 63). According to Tajfel, then, social identity has two components: an affective component and cognitive component.

Thus, individual and group identity fundamentally involves the positioning of one's self in a society. Groups are "a psychological reality that exerts greater or lesser attractive force upon its members" (Campbell et al. 1960, 306). Because social identity groups share a common trait, it is often the case that group members also share some interests. But belonging to a social identity group such as a racial group does not always or automatically result in group members behaving in the political sphere with the group in mind because it does not always mean they will develop a group consciousness. Social scientists have determined that coherent and rather uniform and homogeneous group behavior like that of Black Americans happens only when the identity is particularly salient to the individuals and the identity has been politicized. Identity matters for politics only when it is relevant, and "the higher the identification of the individual with the group, the higher the probability that he will think and behave in ways that distinguish members of his group from non-members" (Campbell et al. 1960, 307).

A four-stage process gets individuals from their social identity to group-inspired political behavior. The identity-to-politics link focuses primarily on identity development, or "the process of defining for oneself the personal significance and social meaning of belonging to a particular" group (Tatum 1997, 16). Because *Robed Representatives* focuses on Black judges and argues that they possess an identity-to-politics link that is a racial one and that they are likely to represent Black interests because of their collective group identities and consciousness, the following discussion primarily focuses on the identity-to-politics link as it relates to race, especially for Black Americans.

Step One: Group Membership

Group membership refers to the "assignment of an individual into a particular group based on characteristics that are specific to that group, in accordance with widely held intersubjective definitions" (McClain et al., 2009, 473). Group membership, therefore, is an ascribed identity or demographic classification. Scholars note that ascription is often done automatically and unconsciously (Allport 1958; Gaertner and Dovidio 2005). Though categorization is a basic human need used to make sense of the world (Tajfel et al. 1971), grouping people is not inconsequential and harmless; in the United States, group membership has long determined access to resources and power, who is discriminated against and how, and citizenship and the privileges and rights that stem from citizenship.

Group membership has more often than not referred to classification into socially and politically relevant social identity groups based on characteristics like gender and age. But because the United States is a racialized social system with a prevailing racial hierarchy, "race" has been and continues to be one of the most salient social identities in the country (Bonilla-Silva 1997; Smedley and Smedley 2018). According to McClain and Tauber (2019), race refers to the grouping of "people of various phenotypes, skin colors, and physical characteristics for political and social purposes" (18). This grouping is not scientific; as a social construction and invention, race was "institutionalized beginning in the 18th century as a worldview, a set of culturally created attitudes and beliefs about human differences" (Smedley 1997, 1), to justify the ongoing and future discrimination, inequality, and treatment of non-white individuals and to disrupt and inspire disunity among people with intertwined economic interests (Omi and Winant 2014; Painter 2010). As a social construction and not a genetic or biological fact, what race has meant and what racial categories have existed since the invention of race have been influenced by social and political contexts and have changed over time. In a country like the United States, race and racial group membership becomes the "aspect of identity that is the target of others' attention, and subsequently of our own" (Tatum 1997, 21).[6] Race is always salient for individuals once it becomes salient for the society in which they live.

Step Two: Group Identity

Group identity "refers to an individual's awareness of belonging to a certain group and having a psychological attachment to that group based on a perception of shared beliefs, feelings, interests, and ideas with other group members," in addition to perceptions of discrimination shared with other group members (McClain et al. 2009, 474). In this stage, individuals begin to identify with and see themselves as part of a group that is distinct from other groups. This happens early in life for racial minorities and often leads to the phenomenon Tatum (1997) uses as the title for her book: "Why are all the Black kids sitting together in the cafeteria?"

In psychology, group identity is a critical component of social identity theory; ascription lacks any intrinsic meaning, but it matters because group identity is often derived from group membership, with group membership influencing how people are perceived (Tajfel and Turner 1979). Being viewed and treated like group members over a long period of time often results in individuals feeling that they actually belong to a particular group and that their self-concept reflects or should reflect their group membership. This can lead to consciously or unintentionally privileging or favoring the ingroup over the outgroup.

Often derived from ascription, racial group identity is a multidimensional construct that includes "an awareness of *and* identification with a racial group based on feelings of in-group closeness" and is comprised of "physical, psychological, sociopolitical, and cultural elements" (McClain et al. 2009, 474). Most individuals base their racial identity on their racial group membership, but some also base it on their interests, culture, and connection or closeness to their group members (McClain et al. 2009). Group identification is often measured by an individual's feeling of being close to the group they belong to (Jardina 2019; McClain et al. 2009).

For Black Americans, possessing a group identity requires the development of a personal racial identity (Cross 1971, 1991; Cross and Fhagan-Smith 2001). Over three decades, psychologists William E. Cross Jr. and colleagues developed and refined the model of Black identity development, also known as the psychology of Nigrescence, which focuses on the process and progression of identification of individuals developing a Black identity.[7] Cross's model necessitates a deep understanding of Black Americans' backgrounds and lived experiences, especially as youth.

In addition to understanding Black Americans' own identity, racial group identity involves believing that being Black has deeply affected one's life experiences and chances and that because of their racial group membership and experiences, there is an inherent connection to Black people and to Black communities. Since the mid-twentieth century, survey data repeatedly shows Black Americans identify with the racial group and feel close to other group members (Dawson 1994; Gurin, Hatchett, and Jackson 1989; Simien 2005; Smith 2014a; Tate 1994).

Step Three: Group Consciousness

Group consciousness is "in-group identification *politicized* by a set of ideological beliefs about one's group's social standing, as well as a view that collective action is the best means by which the group can improve its status and realize its interests" (McClain et al. 2009, 476). Although related to racial group identity, racial group consciousness is distinct and refers to racial group members understanding the common and specific history and set of shared experiences that unify the group, recognizing the group's status in society and the racial hierarchy, and believing that collective action is necessary for improving the status of the group. To this last point, a strong sense of group consciousness often compels group members to act in ways that benefit the group they belong to intentionally and sometimes even unintentionally (Austin, Middleton, and Yon 2012; Chong and Rogers 2005). Possessing a racial group identity, or belonging to and feeling a connection with a racial group that is socially stratified, can result in the development of a racial group consciousness (McClain et al. 2009, 476). Scholars such as Miller et al. (1981) also suggest that group consciousness can be activated by a perception that one's group has been or is discriminated against in society because the group attributes its status in the social hierarchy to systematic and institutional oppression.

Individuals with a strong sense of racial group consciousness often come to see their own fate as inextricably linked to the fate of their racial group because members of the group are distinguished by society based on their group membership, and this in turn mobilizes them to respond collectively to issues they view as systemic and detrimental to the well-being of the entire group (Dawson 1994). This concept of linked fate conflicts with the standing assumption that people make political decisions based on their own self-interests and helps us understand why members of certain groups (e.g., Black and Latino/a/x

Americans) might consider and take into account the interests and needs of their group members when making decisions (Sanchez and Masuoka 2010). With racial group consciousness, there is typically agreement about issues that are important to the group, and there is usually some consensus around what is needed to address those issues. Additionally, there is usually some desire for collective action and commitment to addressing the group's concerns.

Step Four: Politics

The final stage of the identity-to-politics link is *politics*, which refers to individuals' political attitudes and behavior. The identity-to-politics link suggests that group cohesion or solidarity and a strong sense of group consciousness motivate the political preferences and behaviors of group members (Olsen 1970; Verba and Nie 1972). Group members often make decisions and behave cohesively, even if unintentionally, in ways that are meant to improve the status of the group and that reflect what most people in the group prefer.

Racial group consciousness is one, if not *the* best explanation for the political attitudes and behaviors of Black Americans (Shingles 1981). Black consciousness helps explain, for example, the partisan affiliation of Black people. Research on party identification that does not take race into account suggests that Americans with a high socioeconomic status and a high level of education are significantly more conservative and supportive of the Republican Party (Green, Palmquist, and Schickler 2004). When taking race into account, this trend does not hold for Black people the way it typically holds for other racial groups, especially white Americans. Specifically, wealthy Black Americans are more like their less wealthy Black counterparts than they are like wealthy white Americans in their partisanship, political attitudes, and political behavior. Essentially, racial group consciousness helps us understand why it is that despite increasing intra-group class differences, Black people have remained practically solid in their support for the Democratic Party and liberal political candidates since 1964 (Haynie and Watts Smith 2010).[8] Moreover, racial group consciousness also helps explain Black Americans' voting behavior, support or opposition to particular pieces of public policy, perceptions of political institutions, preferences for descriptive representatives, approval or disapproval of the way a particular politician is performing in office, and even interest in the political arena and political affairs (e.g., Bobo and Gilliam 1990; Shingles 1981; Tate 1991). The reason for uniformity, according to Dawson (2001), is that

Black people's networks and institutions "help to reinforce a sense of group identity and group political consciousness and propagate a racialized view of the world in response to the racialized environment within which African Americans seek to build their lives" (xii).

Ultimately, Black Americans in the general population are shown to generally possess a racial identity-to-politics link, and this is true irrespective of class. Scholars assume Black political actors are like their counterparts in the general population, arguing that these actors represent Black interests because they too have an identity-to-politics link, especially a racial group identity and consciousness. This theory is, however, understudied and underdiscussed in the literature on Black political elites, especially Black judges. Moreover, the theory about Black judges' group identity and consciousness has not often been subjected to *empirical* tests. These are important points because one of the arguments advanced in this book is that Black judges represent Black interests because they possess an identity-to-politics link.

THE IDENTITY-TO-ADVOCATIVE REPRESENTATION LINK

Advocative representation contends that political and legal actors are likely to represent group interests because they possess a collective identity and consciousness that result in them having similar perspectives and preferences, which inform, influence, and determine their decisions in situations where they exercise discretion. In other words, this theory suspects that an identity-to-politics link exists for many actors and that advocative representation is a significant by-product of such a link for actors who wield discretionary power. I argue that possessing a group identity and a strong sense of group consciousness leads actors to behave in ways that benefit the groups they belong to, even if the actors are not expected to or charged with representing group interests (i.e., no accountability or authorization). An identity-to-politics link, is therefore, a necessary precondition for advocative representation to occur. I suspect that such a link exists for many political and legal actors and, therefore, advocative representation is something that we might see happening often. There are also reasons why it may not.

One major reason that would explain why some actors might not act in consonance with their group's preferences and interests is the institutional environment in which they find themselves working, especially if the actors belong to a group historically and/or contemporarily marginalized and their group interests would change the status quo. In other words, institutional constraints might limit the ability of political and legal actors with strong group identities and consciousnesses from representing their group's interests, at least beyond certain boundaries.

In his study of Black state legislators, Haynie (2001) discussed institutional constraints faced by Black political actors: "One of the many ironies of African American politics is that in seeking to formulate and enact policies that address the particular needs and interests of the Black community, African American legislators must operate in a political system and within political institutions that are biased against drastic or revolutionary change, and where the advocacy of Black interests may be incongruent with both policy successes and professional advancement" (4). Haynie highlights the specific reality of Black political elites, but he also indicates the general reality of working in some political and legal institutions. These institutions function in ways that perpetuate and prevent disruption to systems that maintain deep inequality by making it difficult, if not impossible, for actors with strong group identities and with a great deal of discretion to make decisions that align with their group and thus transform sites of power. But I would argue that this likely applies only if the group being descriptively represented is a marginalized group and its group interests would disrupt or significantly change the current system. Such interests are rarely willingly given space in institutions of power, so political and legal actors with these interests may find it difficult, if not practically impossible to make decisions that their group would prefer.

Advocative representation is one potential by-product of an identity-to-politics link for political and legal actors, but not all political and legal actors will represent their respective group's interests, given institutional constraints. And to be clear, not all actors will actually possess an identity-to-politics link; the strength and extent of this link is an individual-level variable. Both these expectations—that an identity-to-politics link exists for many political actors and that political actors who are not charged with or expected to provide representation will in fact represent group interests because of their own collective identities and consciousness—require empirical testing.

Figure 2.1 depicts how advocative representation extends the identity-to-politics link by one step, with the final step being advocative representation. This figure is inspired by an illustration in Candis Watts Smith's book *Black*

FIGURE 2.1: Identity-to-advocative-representation link.

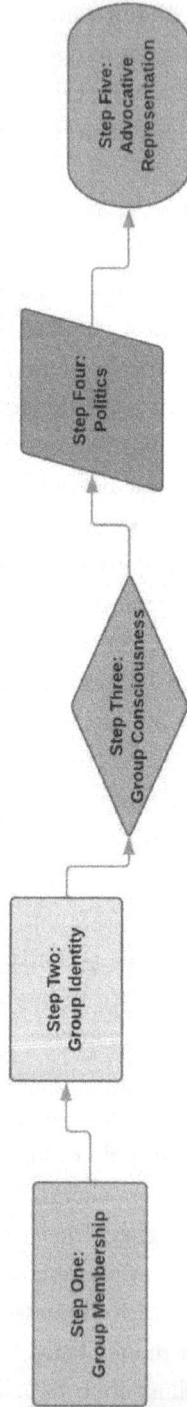

Step One: Group Membership

Step Two: Group Identity

Step Three: Group Consciousness

Step Four: Politics

Step Five: Advocative Representation

Source: Author.

Mosaic: The Politics of Black Pan-Ethnic Diversity (2014a). To test the theory of advocative representation and whether a political actor represents some group interests, scholars must first establish an identity-to-politics link.

BLACK JUDGES, ADVOCATIVE REPRESENTATION, AND THE REPRESENTATION OF BLACK INTERESTS IN THE JUDICIARY

The primary questions in this book are whether Black judges represent Black people and their interests, and if so, why are they engaging in this work when they are not selected for or charged with representing? The theory of advocative representation articulated in this chapter is a useful framework for examining and better understanding how, when, and why Black judges might represent group interests. For Black judges, this theory predicts that, despite institutional constraints, Black judges will represent Black interests in their institutions of power when there are opportunities to do so because they possess an identity-to-politics link. In other words, there are two parts to the argument, which correspond to the expectations for the project: (1) Black judges are likely to possess a strong group identity and consciousness, and (2) Black judges are likely to represent group interests by making decisions (that have consequences) that align with the interests of the broader group because their decisions are informed by their salient group identity. In other words, there is likely to be an identity-to-politics link for Black judges and thus an identity-to-advocative-representation link.

The argument about Black judges representing Black interests is consistent with the view that judicial decision-making is influenced by numerous factors and that at times there are no significant precedents for judges to follow and the law is unclear (Hall and Brace 1992; Klein and Mitchell 2010). In those moments, judges are unconstrained actors who are generally able to make decisions that align with their own ideologies and attitudes and their own personal inclinations (Segal and Spaeth 2002). Moreover, the way they view and evaluate cases, facts, and the law and interpret the Constitution can be influenced by their social attributes, such as age and gender (Davis, Haire, and Songer 1993; Manning, Carroll, and Carp 2004). According to a state court judge quoted in Carp et al.'s study (2020), this perception about judges being unconstrained is often the case: "We're where the action is. We often have to 'shoot from the hip' and hope you're doing the right thing. You can't ruminate forever every time you have to make a ruling. We'd be spending months on each case if we ever did that" (361). The freedom to "shoot from the hip" seems both necessary and plausible, given the strong principle of due process, the desire for decisions to be made in a timely fashion, and the fact that state judges make "hundreds of millions of decisions each year" (Carp et al. 2020, 360).

Assuming Black judges, like their colleagues, are often unconstrained and have discretionary authority, why might they represent group interests? Based on the theory of advocative representation, the primary expectation is that they will represent Black interests and Black people because they possess a strong racial group identity and consciousness, which are likely to exert some influence on their politics and political behavior. That is, I expect Black judges to have an identity-to-politics link that leads them to behave in Black Americans' judicial interests. This expectation builds on scholarship previously mentioned in this chapter from Black politics and Black Studies, which shows that the political behavior of Black Americans in the general population is a function of a strong racial group identity and racial group consciousness (Dawson 1994; Chong and Rogers 2005; Gurin, Hatchett, and Jackson 1989). Though I suspect that they do, whether Black judges actually possess a racial group identity and consciousness is unclear.

But do Black judges represent group interests, and if so, how and when? I agree with Pitkin (1967), who argued that one of the most important questions when studying political representation is "What *reasons* can be given for supposing someone or something is being represented?" (italics in original; 1967, 10). The primary expectation in this project concerning whether Black judges represent Black interests is that they will. Simply put, advocative representation predicts that, despite institutional constraints, conventional wisdom, professional dictates, and not being authorized or expected to represent Black interests, Black judges have discretionary authority and will frequently represent Black interests via the decisions they make as judges. This expectation builds on studies in political science that demonstrate that, through their actions and behavior, Black political officials, such as legislators and bureaucrats and maybe Black judges too, perform various representational functions.

Though advocative representation leads us to expect that Black judges will represent Black interests, I recognize and acknowledge that they may not for the reasons Beverly Daniel Tatum (1997) articulated in her book about racial identity development and the precarious situation Black professionals like Black judges find themselves in as they work within predominantly white settings. Tatum writes: "Those whose work or lifestyle places them in frequent contact with Whites are aware that their ability to 'make it' depends in large part on their ability and willingness to conform to those values and behaviors that have been legitimated by White Culture" (84). Because Black judges are ambitious and driven and they do want to succeed in their profession (Jensen and Martinek 2009), they may intentionally, albeit grudgingly, choose not to do things like represent Black interests, which could make them targets of reprisal (Means et al. 2023).

Many Black professionals feel as though they have to balance conforming and being authentically Black in mostly white spaces (Tatum 1997). This is not easy; it often creates a tension within these legal actors that Haynie (2001) calls the "duality dilemma." This dilemma has been discussed at length as it relates to Black professionals such as Black legislators and Black Americans in the general population. For instance, *The Souls of Black Folk*, W. E. B. Du Bois's seminal book on what it meant (and continues to mean) to be Black in America, articulates a double consciousness or internal tension that many Black Americans live with in their day-to-day lives: "One ever feels his twoness—an American, a Negro; two souls, two thoughts, two unreconciled strivings; two warring ideals in one dark body, whose dogged strength alone keeps it from being torn asunder" (2017, 30–32). This tension that Du Bois articulates is consistent with the work of others writing about Black middle-class life (Anderson 2011; Cose 1993; Feagin and Sikes 1995; McGowen 2017), and is particularly true for highly educated Black men and women who find themselves working within the very institutions that have maintained inequality, such as legislatures and the courts (Alexander 2010; Bell 1973; Browne-Marshall 2013; Butler 2017; Stevenson 2014; Van Cleve 2016). Existing literature suggests that, while Black professionals might have strong group attachments to Black people, they might find it difficult to represent Black interests given the spaces they work in.

Judges who legitimize a racially biased system by adhering to and respecting the lay of the land are likely to find themselves in accord with the system and able to advance in their judicial careers, but those judges who wish to realize the promise of equal justice for all may find it difficult to do so and may find themselves targeted in reprisal (Means et al. 2023). According to Tatum (1997), "because racism is so ingrained in the fabric of American institutions, it is easily self-perpetuating" if you are not actively trying to rectify the situation via anti-racist work (11). To maintain the inequality, "all that is required . . . is business as usual" (11). Black judges, therefore, may find themselves feeling like Black legislators in the post–Civil Rights era, who had to "manage the precarious and difficult tasks of becoming integrated into . . . institutions while at the same time trying to transform them" (Haynie 2001, 8).

But Black judges might find themselves empowered in the way Black jurors often are to represent Black interests with the tools at their disposal. In 1995, Paul Butler, a former federal prosecutor, published a provocative article on racially based jury nullification. Butler realized that some Black jurors feel that, "for pragmatic and political reasons, the Black community is better off when some non-violent lawbreakers remain in the community rather than go to prison" (679).[9] In their role as jurors, Black people "are in a unique position to act on their beliefs [and vote their conscience] when they sit in judgment of a Black defendant" (Butler 1995, 700). They can, if they so choose, ignore certain case facts, precedents, and law (Butler 1995). In doing so, they arguably represent Black interests by ensuring that what is considered best for the Black community is done so in a nuanced way, calculating the costs to families, relationships, the economy, and the politics of keeping nonviolent community members around versus sending them to prison.

Butler (1995) says jury nullification "is perhaps the only legal power Black people have to escape the tyranny of the majority," but this idea overlooks Black judges, a numerous bunch, and the role they can and perhaps do play in the justice system as they also wield significant legal power. Though there are structural and even psychological constraints, the reality is that, like Black jurors, Black judges are well-placed inside the legal system as "insiders" to processes that can influence how people experience the system. From their vantage point, observing (in)justice as it happens in real time, they are likely to possess a distinctive knowledge and understanding of the issues occurring in the justice system and the racial dynamics at work in the court system. Given their position, Black judges are empowered and possess numerous tools that they can use to respond to the issues and determine what justice looks and feels like. Like Black jurors, they can "use their power in a politically conscious manner" (Butler 1995, 723). Because their position bestows upon them a great deal of authority, discretion, and power, Black judges have the ability, the opportunity, and the means to take corrective and collective action. Such power and discretionary authority should be seen as a tremendous opportunity to represent Black interests. The theory of advocative representation as articulated in this chapter leads me to suspect that they will.

CONCLUSION

The theory of advocative representation articulated in this chapter broadens the current conceptualizations and understandings of "representation," especially substantive representation, by calling attention to and including actors commonly thought to operate outside of or, at most, at the margins of representation. As a theory, advocative representation compels us to think more deeply and broadly about the possibility and likelihood of representation occurring in a wide range of institutions of power not necessarily deemed to be representative of group interests. The theory helps us understand how and why actors who are not necessarily charged with or expected to represent groups may function as representatives as a result of their behavior. A necessary precondition of this theory is the existence of an identity-to-politics link for political actors with discretionary authority and power, just as there is often an identity-to-politics link for many Americans in the general population.

Here, I have argued how advocative representation is useful to examine how and why Black judges might represent Black interests. Again, this theory expects that (1) Black judges will possess a strong racial identity and consciousness and therefore, an identity-to-politics link, and (2) those group identities will lead them to make decisions that benefit their racial group when opportunities arise despite not being authorized or accountable for representing. In other words, I suspect an identity-to-representation link exists for Black judges. The following empirical chapters will test these general expectations because, while an identity-to-politics link has been established in the general population and among some elites such as Black legislators, we do not know if the link exists among elites that have been highly socialized like Black judges. Moreover, it is not clear that identity matters for Black judges in a way that influences their behavior and leads to representation of Black legal interests.

PART I

_Establishing an Identity-to-Politics Link
for Black Judges_

THREE

ROOTS OF THE ROBE

*The Backgrounds, Life Experiences, and
Socialization of Black Judges*

Being Black in America, in the South, are you kidding me? Everything you do is affected by your race. Everybody who comes in contact with you is conscious of what your race is. You are treated accordingly. I just can't say enough about that. You Black in the South . . . whew. You grew up in Ohio? You Black in Ohio too then! (*Laughs.*) But see, now, my experiences are much different than yours because you are much younger, and you are a female. So, times have changed.

    JUDGE WILSON, a Black male judge from the South

I think coming up poor you have a different perspective than someone who's affluent, who had an easier road to hoe. I'd like to believe we are more compassionate if you come from humble backgrounds. I think that we are generally more desirous of working hard and maintaining the positions we have, and we are probably a little more understanding of the perspective of people who come from similar backgrounds.

    JUDGE HUNTER, a Black male judge from the South

Well, we, my family was obviously not wealthy. They weren't even close to wealthy as a matter of fact. When we were kids, I think it would be fair to say that we were what we now call low-income.

I had a mother and father who were married to each other, who loved each other, who slept in the same bed with each other every night, loved their children, and wanted to see their children succeed. Who believed in education. Now, my mother did not graduate from high school 'cause she got pregnant with my older sister, which was a rarity back then, but that brought that to a screeching halt. Her senior year, she had the baby. She had to find a job so she could take care of her. My father, on the other hand, earned a scholarship to the [college] but was unable to take it because it was just him and my grandmother and it was the Depression and he had to go to work and get a job and help take care of my grandmother. But both of my parents were voracious, avid readers. All of us became excellent readers and I think that tremendously aided my academic success because I was a very good reader. So, I came to this job, but I tell people this all the time, with this knowledge and belief but for the grace of God I could be some of those people standing in front of my bench, but for God's grace and mercy. And I try to remember that.

JUDGE JOHNSON, a Black female judge from the Midwest

Racial identities and group attachments, which are known to influence Black people's perspectives, attitudes, and even political behavior, are established and reinforced through childhood and adulthood socialization and life experiences (Dawson 1994).[1] The extent to which Black judges have group-based experiences and have been socialized in ways that have led them to develop strong racial identities and group attachments is unclear and is the focus of the present chapter and the subsequent chapter. In this chapter, I examine Black judges' backgrounds, socialization, and life experiences. The following chapter centers on Black judges' identities and group attachments. Together, these chapters enable me to assess whether Black judges have an identity-to-politics link and explain why they might function as representatives of Black judicial interests.

Drawing mostly on a survey with more than 250 Black state court judges, I examine the social, political, academic, and professional background characteristics and experiences of current and recent Black state court judges, highlighting their life experiences prior to joining the bench and how this group has been socialized.[2] In-depth interviews with thirty-two Black judges complement the survey date; the rich details and illustrative examples help us make sense of their lives and how they have been socialized.[3] This chapter anticipates that, like Black Americans in the general population, Black judges' biographical and background characteristics along with their life experiences highlight group-based treatment they have experienced and shed light on their socialization. I argue that Black judges' socialization during childhood and adulthood via their biological and chosen families and communities, along with their pre-bench life experiences, such as personal and vicarious encounters with anti-Black discrimination, will be consistent with the socialization and experiences of most Black Americans.[4] Like most Black people in the United States, Black judges will have had similar racialized life experiences and will have been racially socialized by the people and institutions around them.

The data analysis in this chapter reveals that substantial diversity exists among Black judges' backgrounds and life experiences. Nonetheless, the findings show that many Black state court judges from around the country have common familial, community, educational, and career characteristics, backgrounds, and experiences. Between their childhoods and pre-bench careers, Black judges were exposed to and gained a heightened understanding of the significance of race and politics; the relationship between race, power, and inequality; and the importance of collective activism and engagement in the political and legal system. These commonalities underscore and are indicative of the racial socialization many of them have had as well as their embodied experiences with racism. Black judges' socialization and experiences highlight how they are not all that dissimilar from most Black Americans in the general population, which leads me to suspect that just as Black people's racial socialization and life experiences lead them to develop strong Black identities and group attachments, the same may be true for Black judges.

The chapter proceeds as follows. First, I briefly discuss the racial socialization of Black people in the United States generally. Then, I review the limited academic scholarship and other writing on Black state court judges' backgrounds, life experiences, and socialization. Next, after discussing the data and methodology employed in this chapter, I draw mostly on the survey data to present Black judges' social, political, academic, and professional backgrounds and their life experiences. In doing so, I highlight Black judges' childhood and adulthood socialization and group-based treatment and how both compare to the socialization and treatment of Black Americans in the general population. I conclude the chapter by first highlighting this chapter's contribution to the fields of law and courts and race, ethnicity, and politics by sharing background details about a group of jurists that are often assumed but understudied. Then, I discuss potential implications of Black judges' socialization and life experiences for their identities, group attachments, and behavior, which I argue are significant for determining whether an identity-to-politics link exists among Black judges that leads them to function as representatives of Black judicial interests in their capacity as state jurists.

RACIAL SOCIALIZATION FOR BLACK AMERICANS

Socialization is the process of learning and transmitting knowledge and ways of being that shape individuals' identities, perspectives, beliefs, and actions. In the United States, racial socialization is the set of transmission processes by which people come to establish and crystallize their individual and racial group identities, values, and behavior.[5] Racial socialization occurs throughout one's life and is heavily influenced by institutions and people, such as parents, family, schools, curricula, religion, peers, media, work, and the legal system (Tatum 1997).

Racial socialization generally describes the multidimensional process by which children of a racial group come to learn the perceptions, values, identities, attitudes, and behaviors of their racial group and then develop a psychological connection and attachment to the group. This process is particularly salient in child rearing within Black households and communities. Black families and community members exhibit not only a general commitment to fostering Black pride and joy in the nation's Black youth but also attention to teaching these young people about Black political history, culture, and heritage (Boykin and Toms 1985; Thornton et al. 1990). Moreover, this socialization often includes education around survival, and in particular, instructions regarding how to survive encounters and experiences that they are likely to have in the future, such as discrimination and being in mostly white spaces, and how to interact with political and legal institutions and actors that profoundly affect Black people and Black communities, such as the police (Brunson and Weitzer 2011; Hughes 2003; Hughes and Chen 1999). These features within Black people's racial socialization are adaptive and protective, and many are a result of racism and racialization processes in this country. All these features figure prominently in the interactions between Black family and community members, especially in intergenerational transmission by adults to children.

Occurring implicitly, explicitly, informally, and formally, racial socialization is central to and has important consequences for the development of Black people's self-concept and identities (Greene 1992). Self-concept defines what we know and think about ourselves individually and in relation to others and "frames experience and motivates action" (Oyserman 2001, 502). According to Spencer (1988), identity, however, is composed of an awareness of group membership, self-concept, self-esteem, responsibilities, internal and external expectations, privileges and disadvantages, and perceptions of future goals and development. Both self-concept and identity are often modeled after or are in response to what one experiences, witnesses, and learns from the institutions and people in close proximity. Because self-concept and identity are thought by some scholars to be enduring and stable throughout one's life, changing only slightly under ordinary circumstances (Campbell et al. 1960), most scholars see the most critical moments for self-concept and identity development to be in childhood, especially the formative years, and early adulthood. Family and community are two of the primary influencers (Spencer, Dobbs, and Swanson 1988).

The socialization that occurs within Black families and communities helps Black people develop, fortify, and strengthen a strong individual and collective group identity and consciousness (Spencer 1988). Racial socialization reinforces individual identity (i.e., Black people seeing themselves as Black), and it also creates and strengthens collective group identity (i.e., Black people seeing themselves as members of a racial group). In addition, socialization among Black people helps them develop group attachments by reinforcing the preexisting sense of "us" versus "them" that exists in the United States. Moreover, socialization instills in individual group members a sense that "us" is a group that must work together for survival because it is systemically disadvantaged by virtue of being in the group, or being perceived to be in the group (Dawson 1994).

I speculate that Black jurists, like most Black Americans, were racially socialized in their childhood and early adulthood by their families and communities. I suspect that they spent a lot of time in predominantly Black environments such as their K–12 schools, residential neighborhoods, and organizations. While in those spaces, I presume that they were exposed to racial and political messages. Additionally, I suspect that throughout their life, they witnessed and engaged in activism on behalf of Black people and racial issues. I also venture that for Black judges, growing up and living in the United States means that they were exposed and subjected to group-based treatment common among Black Americans such as racism and discrimination. All these speculations are grounded in literature that shows this type of racial socialization happens within most Black families and communities, and racialized experiences such as racial discrimination are one of the most common experiences that bind Black Americans to each other irrespective of class (Abramson 1977; Hughes and Chen 1997).

EXISTING UNDERSTANDINGS OF BLACK JUDGES' BACKGROUNDS AND LIFE EXPERIENCES

As mentioned in chapter 1, very few Black judges worked in state or federal courts prior to the mid-twentieth century as a result of racism in the legal profession. Nonetheless, Black periodicals and journals incorporated descriptions of Black legal actors such as judges and lawyers (Walton Jr. 1985). These periodicals would share, for example, Black judges' biographies, noting their backgrounds and paths to the bench with hopes both to inform Black people about their Black counterparts doing important work and to inspire young Black readers. One example is *Jet*, a weekly Black periodical, that has published numerous write-ups about prominent Black legal and political figures. One of the first was in the periodical's October 31, 1968 (vol. 35, issue 4) publication. Page 11 featured a write-up about the Honorable Ollie Bivens, who became the first Black judge in Flint, Michigan's history. Darren Walker, the current president of the philanthropic Ford Foundation, remarked in a recent interview for an NBC news story that being featured in *Jet* historically was significant for Black elites: "Until you made it in The *Jet,* you haven't made it in the African American community."[6] Despite the attention Black judges received when featured in Black periodicals, for the most part, Black judges do not often feature prominently or adequately in the scholarly research and popular discourse on state judges.

As the discipline that devotes significant attention to studying the actors who make political and legal decisions, unsurprisingly, political science has often overlooked Black judges in its studies of judges until it became all but impossible to do so (i.e., when Black judges increasingly reached the bench following the Civil Rights movement). This is reflected in general descriptions of (white) state court judges. As mentioned in chapter 1, Carp and Stidham (1998), for instance, described state jurists as generally being "overwhelmingly

older, white, male and Protestant. They tend to be home-grown fellows who
are moderately conservative and staunchly committed to the status quo. They
believe in the basic values and traditions of the legal and political communities
from which they come. State judges, then [have] the distinction of being local
boys who made good" (260–61).

While this description accurately reflects the reality that men and judges
from elite backgrounds are disproportionately represented on state courts, this
description renders invisible the women and racial minorities who also sit on
the state bench. In particular, Black judges have sat on the bench since the
mid-twentieth century, albeit in larger numbers in the post–Civil Rights era.
Carp and Stidham do not appear to be considering the backgrounds of Black
judges and their paths to the bench, which, based on the biographies of the
nation's first Black women and men judges, such as Jane Bolin, are likely to be
distinctive.

Although overlooking the nuances in the backgrounds of Black judges is
common in studies on race and judging, some scholars encourage a biographical approach to the study of judicial decision-making and argue that backgrounds are significant because they might help explain judges' behavior on
the bench (Haire and Moyer 2015; Smith 1983; Washington 1994).[7] In their empirical work on Black judges, scholars and journalists have drawn on surveys
and interviews with the judges on the bench during the time when they were
written, mostly in the two decades following the end of the Civil Rights era
(Wilder and Ashman 1973; Shuman 1970). This scholarship creates a window
into Black judges' backgrounds and lives and how they were socialized, but
these studies are long outdated.

The most substantial work on the backgrounds and socialization of Black
judges is Michael David Smith's classic book, *Race Versus Robe: The Dilemma
of Black Judges* (1983). When Smith interviewed Black judges in the two decades following the end of the Civil Rights era, most of the judges sitting on
the bench at the time of their interview were between forty-five and sixty-
four years of age (Smith 1983, 32). Out of the 185 Black judges Smith surveyed
and interviewed, more than half were from working-class backgrounds with
mothers and fathers who were not well-educated and who worked outside the
home. One-third said they came from middle-class backgrounds, and less than
10 percent of his respondents reported coming from upper-class backgrounds
(Smith 1983, 33). Most of the judges were trained at historically Black colleges

or universities (HBCUs), with a sizeable proportion being trained at Howard University Law School. After earning their degrees, most of the Black judges started their careers in legal offices, with many of them being affiliated with all-Black law firms because of employment discrimination, and they were interested in representing mostly Black clients whom they perceived as being under- or ill-represented. These judges largely classified themselves as active in civil rights prior to and after becoming judges, as members, financial contributors, and officers of civil rights organizations. Moreover, these judges noted encounters with discrimination and the difficulty that came with being Black during the Jim Crow era, when racial segregation was legal and racial violence was incessant. One of Smith's arguments is that these characteristics and backgrounds related to Black judges' childhood and adulthood highlight that they were racially socialized in ways that would lead them to have a strong Black identity and group attachment to Black people. And, to be clear, their socialization was influenced by not only their parents and those living within their childhood home but the community and neighborhood in which they lived, the schools they attended, the jobs where they worked, and even the time period in which they lived.

Since Smith's study was published in 1983, no other scholarly study has examined and emphasized the backgrounds of Black state court judges. Recent scholarship focusing on Black judges' backgrounds and characteristics focuses on judges appointed to the federal courts in the post–Civil Rights era, comparing white female and racial minority appointees to white male appointees. This work reveals many interesting commonalities among racial and gender minority appointees that distinguish them from white male appointees, including their class background, pre-bench career, and history of political activism (e.g., Goldman, Slotnick, and Schiavoni 2013). I am, however, cautious about arguing that what Goldman, Slotnick, and Schiavoni find in their studies apply to and describe Black state court judges' backgrounds, characteristics, and socialization. For one thing, their results often aggregate racial minority and white women judges, obscuring Black judges' specific backgrounds. More importantly, Black federal judges may differ significantly from Black state court judges. Although federal court appointees regularly come from state court benches now, federal and state jurists may be different populations entirely (Goldman, Slotnick, and Schiavoni 2013, 39). Thus, while scholars have examined the backgrounds and characteristics of Civil Rights–era Black state court judges (Smith 1983) and they have evaluated the characteristics of racial- and gender-minority appointees to the federal courts (Goldman, Slotnick, and Schiavoni 2013), it is not clear what the background and experiences of Black state court jurists sitting on the bench more than fifty years after the end of the Civil Rights era are. Thus, the extant literature generally fails to consider recent and current Black state court judges' life experiences and how they have been socialized.

DATA AND METHODS

In general, biographies for most state court judges are not publicly available.[8] This dearth of data makes it difficult to understand state court judges' lives prior to and outside their judicial career. Because judges themselves are best suited to tell their life stories and share details from their background, I draw on interviews and surveys with Black state court judges to understand their backgrounds, socialization, and salient life experiences.

I mostly present findings from the 270 surveys completed by Black state court judges from across the country between August 2019 and August 2020.[9] I also incorporate illustrative examples from the in-depth interviews conducted with thirty-two Black state court judges between 2011 and 2019.[10] This mixed methodological approach is consistent with the work of Smith (1983). Combining interviews and surveys is also valuable because I am able to practice methodological triangulation and reach a more comprehensive understanding about Black judges' life experiences and socialization (Flick 2004).

The data analysis section has been divided into three consecutive time periods deemed significant for socialization: childhood (0–18 years), young adult (18–25 years), and adulthood/pre-bench (25+ years). In what follows, I will present judges' backgrounds and life experiences from these different time periods.

BLACK JUDGES' CHILDHOOD SOCIALIZATION: FAMILY AND COMMUNITY

State and federal judges, as well as other political actors, have often come from middle-class and wealthy families, leading Tate (2004) to conclude that the "economic and social elite" are overrepresented in government (26).[11] Black members of Congress and judges, however, are generally less wealthy than their white counterparts and come from poorer families (Smith 1983). In this study, I find that despite economic prosperity and higher educational attainment for many Black Americans during the late twentieth and early twenty-first centuries, many of the Black judges surveyed come from nonaffluent families. Table 3.1 displays how the participants categorize their childhood socioeconomic class and their class currently.

Close to 60 percent of respondents said their families were either poor (23 percent) or lower-middle-class (34 percent). However, approximately two-fifths of the survey respondents said that they grew up in middle-class families (43 percent). Based on data from the U.S. Census and U.S. Bureau of Labor Statistics, Black judges' childhood class backgrounds are not significantly different from those of the general Black American population.[12] Note, however, that Black judges' self-reported net worth and class as adults stand out as being significantly higher than the net worth of the average Black American family in the general population.[13]

The perceptions Black judges have of their family's socioeconomic class are consistent with the highest level of education completed by their parents.[14] As Smith (1983) found of Black judges in the late twentieth century, I found many Black judges grew up in households with parents who were relatively well-educated. Twenty-two percent of their mothers and 13 percent of their fathers had a bachelor's degree as their highest level of education. Twenty-two percent of their mothers and 23 percent of their fathers had a post-graduate degree such as a master's degree, law degree, business degree, medical degree, or doctoral degree.[15] In other words, close to two-fifths of respondents (36 percent) had mothers and fathers who were college graduates, and slightly more

TABLE 3.1: Black judges' class as children and adults.

	Childhood class categorization	Adulthood class categorization
Poor	38 (23%)	6 (2%)
Lower-middle-class	56 (34%)	11 (4%)
Middle-class	71 (43%)	222 (86%)
Wealthy	1 (<1%)	18 (7%)

Source: Taneisha N. Means, "Political Representation in State Courts Study, 2020" (2020).

than three-fifths of respondents (64 percent) had parents without college degrees. The education levels of Black jurists' parents are consistent with their parents' primary careers.[16] Moreover, their parents' educational backgrounds are generally comparable to the education levels of Black Americans in the general population, although Black judges' parents are slightly more educated than the average Black American's parents, especially when it comes to post-graduate degrees.[17]

Because many Black state court judges were raised by middle-class parents who were relatively well-educated and had reasonable incomes, one wonders about the extent to which any or many of them are connected to Black people generally, possess a sense of social responsibility for the Black community, and will heed Du Bois's (2017) call and challenge for educated Black people to be "the talented tenth"—a small group within the Black population that intelligently leads the racial group and works to address problems disproportionately affecting Black America. For some middle-class Black Americans, they may be mobilized to action by their awareness of persisting inequality and their own recognition that class status does not protect Black people from racism (Cose 1993; Claytor 2020; Frazier 1997; Lacy 2007; Pattillo 2013), or they may be demobilized because they see that the world has improved from the prior centuries and do not regard the remaining issues as vestiges and legacies of historical and continuing racial oppression.

According to scholars who study socialization, children are deeply influenced by the individuals living in their home because of close contact and frequent interactions. The significance of childhood class and parental educational levels and careers for Black judges' socialization is that few Black judges grew up in households that might be characterized as affluent. In fact, the findings show that more than half of Black judges grew up in a household they perceived as poor or working-class. Nonetheless, most judges shared that they were raised in a household with hard-working parents who were mainly employed in jobs outside the home, and many of the judges' parents were not well-educated formally, although a significant number had parents with college and post-graduate degrees. Because of the long history of race and economics in the United States, Black judges' socialization as children includes exposure to inequality, economic insecurity, and difficulty of social mobility. Moreover, I suspect that their own families' social and professional experiences afforded them opportunities to see that racism, racialization processes, and capitalism are inseparable. Cedric Robinson (2000) calls this intricate fusion "racial cap-italism": "The development, organization, and expansion of capitalist society pursued essentially racial directions, so too did social ideology. As a material force . . . racialism would inevitably permeate the social structures emergent from capitalism" (2). According to Jodi Melamed (2015), within a capitalist system like the one in the United States, "capital can only be capital when it is accumulating, and it can only accumulate by producing and moving through relations of severe inequality among human groups. . . . Racism enshrines the inequalities that capitalism requires" (77). Black judges' childhood class and their parents' educational backgrounds and careers suggest they were exposed to racial capitalism and inequality. Moreover, Black poor, working-class, and middle-class families emphasize the importance of community solidarity and support, including economic support and collective action (Dawson 1994).

Spending time in predominantly Black spaces was another commonality among the Black state court judges surveyed. Table 3.2 displays the amount and some of the types of contact Black judges have had with other Black people as children and adults. Close to 70 percent of all survey respondents (69 percent) reported that their childhood neighborhoods were more than 61 percent Black, and fewer than one quarter of them (23 percent) grew up in neighborhoods that were less than 40 percent Black.[18]

Richard Rothstein (2017) writes about the long history of segregation in the United States and the government's role in dividing the nation's residential and social spaces along color lines. *The Color of Law* "makes the argument that government actions to create a system of *de jure* segregation were explicit, never hidden, that they were systematic and, not so long ago, well known by anyone who paid attention" (243). According to a recent report from Jorge De la Roca, Ingrid Gould Ellen, and Katherine O'Regan (2014) racial segregation continues to be an issue in the United States despite overall segregation levels between Black and White people declining.[19] Furthermore, Douglas Massey and Nancy Denton (2019) find that it is not just about Black and white people living in different neighborhoods, but the fact that the environments and re-sources within Black neighborhoods are not comparable to the environments and resources within mostly white neighborhoods. While the cause of segre-gation has shifted over time, with modern segregation resulting mainly from white housing preferences and not explicit housing market discrimination, the result for many Black Americans, including Black judges, is that they grow up

TABLE 3.2: Black judges' contact with Black people as children and adults.

| | Childhood Contact | | Adult Contact | | |
	Percentage of Black families in childhood neighborhood	Percentage of Black students in childhood schools	Percentage of Black legal clients*	Percentage of Black families in adulthood neighborhood	Percentage of Black judicial colleagues
0–20%	46 (17%)	56 (21%)	45 (21%)	102 (39%)	156 (60%)
21–40%	16 (6%)	35 (13%)	26 (12%)	54 (21%)	63 (24%)
41–60%	19 (7%)	53 (20%)	107 (49%)	46 (18%)	23 (9%)
61–80%	34 (13%)	29 (11%)	21 (10%)	45 (17%)	11 (4%)
81–100%	146 (56%)	89 (34%)	20 (9%)	14 (5%)	9 (3%)
Other	2 (<1%)	2 (<1%)	N/A	N/A	N/A

*This applies to Black judges who worked as attorneys prior to becoming judges.

Source: Taneisha N. Means, "Political Representation in State Courts Study, 2020" (2020).

and live in segregated neighborhoods with large numbers of Black people. The significance of segregation and growing up in predominantly Black spaces is often borne out in the eventual racial group identities that Black Americans tend to develop (Cross 1971). Contact with other Black people is known to influence the development of a racial identity and a deep connection with other Black Americans, especially when such contact provides "positive cultural images and messages about what it means to be Black" (Tatum 1997, 55).

Because most students go to school in the community in which they live, Black Americans often experience segregation during their K–12 schooling that mimics the segregation in their residential neighborhoods. The same is true for Black judges surveyed; they reported spending their kindergarten through high school years in schools with large numbers of Black students. Table 3.2 displays Black judges' contact with Black K–12 peers. Thirty-four percent of Black judge respondents said they attended schools that were less than 40 percent Black, although the overwhelming majority of Black judge respondents (65 percent) said they attended schools that were more than 40 percent Black. Intense segregation of Black students increases inequality, hinders mobility, and stifles familial, community, and economic growth, but scholars also highlight how segregation can enhance and reinforce personal racial identity and group cohesion and inspire collective behavior among racial minorities (McGrew 2019).

Religiosity represents another commonality among Black jurists that, like educational segregation, influenced Black judges' socialization and who they were around as children. According to Kendra King (2010), "without a question, the most pivotal institution that spans the entire African American experience in America is the Black Church" (171). The Black church has been and continues to be an important organizational, independent space for Black politics and life (Smith and Harris 2005). Black judges in this study allude to this when reflecting on their religiosity as children and as adults. Many of the Black state court judges in this study reported that religion was important to them and their families during their childhood. Almost all of the respondents grew up in households with a religious affiliation (99 percent). The most common religious affiliations among the respondents were Baptist (45 percent), Catholic (16 percent), Methodist (12 percent), Episcopalian (6 percent), and Presbyterian (5 percent). Table 3.3 displays how important Black judges reported religion being in their lives as children and as adults. Slightly more than three-fifths of the respondents (64 percent) said religion was either very or extremely important to their lives as children, whereas less than one-tenth of the respondents (6 percent) said religion was not at all important to them as children. Table 3.3 also shows that religion continues to be important to Black judges as adult—68 percent said religion is currently very or extremely important to their lives. Thus, childhood and adulthood numbers are practically identical. Black judges' religiosity is consistent with the religiosity of Black Americans in the general population.

The actual messages received during religious services are important when considering how religion might act as a socializing agent and shape one's identity and behavior. Table 3.4 displays information about the frequency of political and racial messages that Black judges were exposed to in their child-

TABLE 3.3: **Black judges' religiosity.**

Religion was/is . . .	As children	As adults
Not at all important to their life	16 (6%)	15 (6%)
Slightly important to their life	30 (11%)	18 (7%)
Somewhat important to their life	51 (19%)	51 (20%)
Very important to their life	95 (36%)	83 (32%)
Extremely important to their life	73 (28%)	93 (36%)

Source: Taneisha N. Means, "Political Representation in State Courts Study, 2020" (2020).

TABLE 3.4: **Racial and political messages Black judges received during childhood.**

How often . . .	Did your parents/ guardians talk to you about race	Did your parents/ guardians talk to you about politics	Were politics discussed during religious services*
Never	9 (3%)	24 (9%)	56 (21%)
Rarely	32 (12%)	68 (26%)	88 (34%)
Some of the time	113 (43%)	108 (41%)	98 (38%)
Most of the time	67 (25%)	40 (15%)	12 (5%)
All of the time	43 (16%)	24 (9%)	6 (2%)
Other	N/A	N/A	1 (<1%)

*This applies to Black judges who self-identified as attending religious services.

Source: Taneisha N. Means, "Political Representation in State Courts Study, 2020" (2020).

hood homes and church institutions. Many of the Black judge respondents said politics were discussed during the religious services they attended, and participants were regularly encouraged to participate in politics. Scholars note that this type of encouragement and pressure within the Black church has helped Black people move collectively and in harmony in the political and social arenas (King 2010, 174). Table 3.4 shows that more than half of the Black judges in this study said politics were discussed, to some extent, within the religious services they attended. Additionally, more than half of the respondents (52 percent) said they received at least some encouragement to participate in politics during religious services.

Because many Black judges reported perceiving religion as important to their childhood lives and they were immersed in religious environments where politics were a regular topic and participation was routinely encouraged, we can speculate that they were socialized in ways similar to the ways many Black Americans in the general population are socialized via religion and church (Smith and Harris 2005). The Black church and Black politics have historically and continually been linked; in those spaces, Black people generally are known to be racially and politically socialized to be active politically in the world and collective-minded.

The messages Black judges received at church complement the messages they received at home. Black judges reported listening to messages about race and politics from their families, especially their parents or guardians. Table 3.4 shows that the plurality of respondents—slightly more than two-fifths of the Black judge respondents (41 percent)—said their parents/guardians talked about race all or most of the time. These findings are consistent with a 2019 Pew Research Center survey that found Black Americans are more likely than other racial groups to talk to family and friend networks about race and race relations.[20] While education, party affiliation, and age influenced how often white Americans, Latino/a/x Americans, and Asian Americans talked about race or race relations, Pew found that, for the most part, Black Americans, irrespective of education, partisan affiliation, and age, talked about race or race relations in the networks closest to them: their friend and family networks.

Frequency of conversations about race is just part of the story about the type of racial socialization within Black households and communities. Regarding the content of the messages Black judges heard about race, interview respondents said these conversations were often reflections or lessons about history and Black culture. Judge Ingram, a Black female judge from the North, said her close relatives and not necessarily her parents talked to her about race and being Black:

> My father's sister and her husband did because . . . [they] considered them-
> selves to be socialists. . . . So, what they would do with their kids, because
> I used to spend a week with them also every summer and my aunt's hus-
> band had five other kids before he got with my aunt, and a couple of them
> were around my age so we would all hang out together. But they would sit
> down and have lectures with us on a regular basis and be like, "Kids gather
> around, we want to talk to you." And they would talk to us about Africa
> and history and different things of that nature.

Judge Washington, a Black male judge from the North, said his father, who he described as a "race man," and his mother always talked to him about race and racism in the United States: "They always talked about racial issues, always talked about how politics affected African Americans in the community."

These messages about race, Black culture, and Black life from Black judges' families and community members highlight an upbringing that resonates across many Black judges regardless of location. These race conversations are significant for developing group attachments among Black people and helping them to develop an individual racial identity as well. Additionally, these discussions are often principal ways that Black Americans come to learn about the Black American experience. Moreover, the conversations represent a counternarrative to the harmful messages Black people often receive from school, society, culture, and media about Black people, culture, and life. These discussions also are Black peoples' truth around their experiences and their analysis of those experiences. Finally, as I mentioned previously, these talks represent ways that Black people help one another, especially younger generations, navigate and survive a society and space that is to a great extent shaped by anti-Black racism.

In addition to conversations about race, Black judges were also exposed to conversations about politics and political activism in their homes and communities while growing up. When asked to share how often their parents talked about politics, Black judges were clear that their families talked to them more

about race than about politics, but nonetheless, political conversations occurred (see table 3.4). Close to two-thirds of Black judge respondents (65 percent) said their parents/guardians talked to them about politics at least some
of the time, with 9 percent saying these conversations happened all the time.
This is consistent with the fact that 82 percent of Black Americans responding
to a recent national study said they participated politically in the prior twelve
months by discussing politics with family and friends.[21]

Many Black judges grew up in households with family members that were
not just talking about politics but were actively engaged in politics and doing
politics. Table 3.5 displays the contact Black judges had with politically active
people in their household alongside their own political activism as adults.[22]
Most respondents (76 percent) said their parents were politically active to
some extent, with the majority of respondents (53 percent) saying their parents
were slightly or somewhat politically active. Their parents' political activism
may have inspired their own activism because table 3.5 shows that, as adults,
roughly three-fifths of the Black judges surveyed are to some extent politically
active, albeit to a lesser degree than their parents.

Examples of Black judges' families' political activism are highlighted in the
interviews with Black judges when I asked them to share how their families
participated politically in their community and in the country. Judge Washington, a Black judge from the North, described how his father was involved
in campaigning for Black politicians and candidates for office:

TABLE 3.5: Black judges' contact with politically
active people and their own activism.

	Black judges' parents' political activism	Black judges' activism as adults
Not at all politically active	63 (24%)	106 (41%)
Slightly politically active	63 (24%)	39 (15%)
Somewhat politically active	77 (29%)	58 (23%)
Very politically active	42 (16%)	29 (11%)
Extremely politically active	19 (7%)	24 (9%)
Other	N/A	1 (<1%)

Source: Taneisha N. Means, "Political Representation in State Courts Study, 2020" (2020).

My father was politically active in one of the major [city] Black political clubs. That's the club that [a famous Black woman politician] belonged to. That's the club that so many of the Black judges came out of in [city]. He was very active. He was active in [a famous Black woman politician's] campaign, he was active in the campaign of many of the Black [politicians] who came through in the '60s and '70s. He was always very active; he was always very active and engaged.

While this judge's father was extremely active in politics, campaigning on the behalf of Black political candidates, it was much more common for Black judges in the interviews to mention that their parents exercised the right to vote and were excited about supporting Black political candidates who ran in their districts. This reflects what political scientists know about Black Americans' political behavior; when registered to vote, they turn out and participate in electoral politics and they are also the primary supporters of Black candidates for political office (Philpot and Walton Jr. 2007). Both Black judges' parents' political activism and their own activism are in line with the results of a recent study showing Black Americans in the general population regularly participate in political activity. The numbers in table 3.5 are consistent with the political participation and activism of many Black Americans who have worked for a candidate, political party, or some other campaign (8 percent); contacted an elected representative or government official about a policy (18 percent); contributed money to a candidate, party, ballot issue, or campaign (14 percent); worn a campaign button or posted a campaign sign or sticker (22 percent); and attended a protest march, demonstration, or rally (11 percent).[23]

Being around politically active people in their home and community as children is significant for Black judges' socialization because they learn the nature and value of participating in democratic politics and collective action. Growing up in an environment with strong signals that political knowledge and activism are important is likely to have influenced Black judges' views about political activism and the role politics plays in affecting their community. Moreover, a politically active community and home are likely to enforce a social norm around whether, why, and how Black people should participate in politics.

BLACK JUDGES' YOUNG ADULT LIFE AND SOCIALIZATION: UNDERGRADUATE AND LEGAL EDUCATION

Black judges, like most judges, are some of the most highly educated persons in the nation. More than 95 percent of the judges surveyed had earned an undergraduate degree and a law degree. Many of them also earned associate degrees, master's degrees, and doctoral degrees. Table 3.6 displays the types of institutions these judges attended for their undergraduate education and law school education. [24]

Some colleges that educated many of these Black state court judges as undergraduates are Morgan State University in Baltimore, Maryland; Howard University in Washington, D.C.; Spelman College in Atlanta, Georgia; Hampton University in Hampton, Virginia; the City College of New York; the University of Texas system; and the University of California system. This list reflects the fact that many Black jurists attended public institutions for their bachelor's degrees. Table 3.6 shows that slightly more than one-third of the judges surveyed (37 percent) attended public institutions. The list of frequently attended institutions also reveals that Black judges are continuing to be educated at HBCUs. In fact, one-fourth (25 percent) of all survey participants attended an HBCU for their undergraduate degree.[25]

Given the historical and continuing racism in higher education admissions, especially at private and Ivy League institutions, the racial hostility Black students often face on predominantly white campuses, the racial diversity within

TABLE 3.6: Black judges' undergraduate and law school education.

	Judges by undergraduate institution	Judges by law school institution
Public institutions	98 (37%)	127 (48%)
Private institutions	39 (15%)	94 (36%)
Ivy League	14 (5%)	6 (2%)
Liberal arts colleges	46 (17%)	—
Historically Black colleges and universities (HBCUs)	65 (25%)	33 (13%)
Other (e.g., military academy)	2 (1%)	4 (1%)

Source: Taneisha N. Means, "Political Representation in State Courts Study, 2020" (2020).

predominantly white colleges among students and faculty, and the increasing cost of higher education, attending public institutions and HBCUs make sense (Outcalt and Skewes-Cox 2002). These two trends are consistent with early studies of Black judges who mainly attended HBCUs and public institutions for their degrees (Smith 1983).

Table 3.6 displays the types of law school institutions Black judges attended. Similar to the trends among the institutions most often attended by respondents for their undergraduate degrees, 61 percent of Black judges surveyed attained their law degrees from public institutions and HBCUs. The plurality—almost half of the participants (48 percent)—reported attending law school at a public institution, and 13 percent attended an HBCU for law school. Some law schools attended by numerous participants included North Carolina Central University in Durham, North Carolina; Howard University in Washington, D.C.; and Georgia State University in Atlanta, Georgia. I would argue that the reason for these institutional trends is similar to what I stated above, which is that these eminent institutions with histories of producing bright legal professionals are often less expensive than other institutions and they are more diverse.

Black judges' choosing to attend an HBCU for their education deserves some special attention.[26] HBCU attendance before the end of the Civil Rights era is not entirely surprising, as these institutions were some of the only ones that would admit, educate, and financially support Black students. In addition, many Black students who attended predominantly white institutions (hereafter PWIs) faced hostile racial environments and campus climates unconducive to learning (Astin 1975). Racism at both the interpersonal and systemic levels and at the admission stage and even on-campus stage has led students to HBCUs because they served the increasing body of bright Black youth who wanted to be educated but simply could not or preferred not to attend other (i.e., predominantly white) institutions. After legal segregation in education ended in the mid-twentieth century and a number of institutions established affirmative action policies for admission, Black students began attending PWIs in larger numbers than ever before (Fries-Britt and Turner 2002). A significant number of Black students, however, continue to choose HBCUs for their education, including Black judges, as we see with the findings in table 3.6. The significance of these institutions for Black judges' and other Black students' socialization is connected to what they are known to do: to serve the educational needs of

Black students and the development of their individual and group identities as Black people (Fleming 2001; Van Camp et al. 2009).

In addition to attending similar types of institutions, extracurriculars during college represent yet another way Black judges' backgrounds are similar. During their undergraduate and law school years, Black judge respondents were active via membership in various types of extracurricular organizations that enhanced their personal and professional identities (Hughey and Parks 2012). One of the common experiences among the judges was their membership and participation in predominantly Black sororities and fraternities. The data show that more than two-fifths of them (43 percent) were members of one of the nine historically Black, international Greek-lettered fraternities and sororities that constitute the collaborative organization known as the National Pan-Hellenic Council. "The Divine Nine," as they are often affectionately called, have distinct organizations with unique histories, philosophies, and foci, but these five fraternities and four sororities are all generally interested in building community and solidarity among Black students/graduates; helping their members excel personally, academically, and professionally; and giving and being of service to Black communities and institutions where they are located.[27]

These organizations' histories are tied to why they continue to exist and how they are significant to Black judges' and other participants' lives. Timothy Wilson (1996) explains in "Cool Like That: Exploring the World of Historically Black Fraternities and Sororities" that these organizations filled "an emotional and social interest, rather than a curricular vacuum."[28] Systematic exclusion by white fraternities and sororities and institutions led to the creation of Black Greek organizations (Whipple, Baier, and Grady 1991). Though they are sometimes mistaken as mere imitations of white Greek-letter organizations, renowned writer and historian Paula Giddings is clear in *In Search of Sisterhood: Delta Sigma Theta and the Challenge of the Black Sorority Movement* (1988) that Black organizations center Blackness and were designed and created by Black students interested in personally bonding with similar students within and beyond their institutions. These organizations mean Black students have access to a group of peers who perhaps have had similar life experiences, are going through similar things during college, and who might eventually go through similar things post-graduation. Within these organizations, students feel a sense of connectedness and belonging, and they are mobilized to voice and act on their concerns regarding justice. Additionally, these organizations stress the importance of meeting the needs of their participants and also of the broader Black community, often raising money and donating time. Moreover, these organizations operate as sources of racial pride by highlighting the beauty and diversity found within Black people and culture. Finally, these organizations focus on networking and role modeling for younger generations. Thus, these organizations influence their participants' individual and group identities by emphasizing collective action and the importance of community among Black people inside and outside higher education institutions. The fact that almost one-third of Divine Nine participants (29 respondents) attended PWIs suggests that, in doing so, they were provided with benefits similar to those received by Black students who attend HBCUs.

Another common college experience among the Black judge respondents was through their affiliation and participation in Black student groups, which I suspect parallel the reason Black judges who attended PWIs participated in Black Greek life. Close to three-fifths of respondents (58 percent) reported participating in a Black student organization during their undergraduate years, with more than four-fifths of Black judges having participated in such organizations while attending a non-HBCU institution (i.e., PWI). For students attending PWIs, these Black student organizations provide a social, cultural, and intellectual space, helping Black students to think through what it means to be a Black student and how they can survive and thrive in spaces that were designed without them in mind (Guiffrida 2003; Harper and Quaye 2007). At the undergraduate level, in most cases, the student organization the respondents belonged to was called the Black Student Union. Many of these Black student organizations appeared immediately following the Black Civil Rights movement, when students were admitted to PWIs in significant numbers (Robinson 2012). In the beginning, these organizations focused on demanding that institutions be more active in recruiting and retaining Black students and making the institutions more inclusive and integrated than they were. They have continued to push institutions to diversify the student body, faculty, and administration, and improve the climate for Black students at their campuses. They also provide an opportunity for students to engage in collective action around Black needs.

Just as they did in their undergraduate years, when Black judges went to law school, many of them participated in Black student organizations. Black judges reported belonging to Black student law associations, whose primary goals are to articulate the needs of Black law students and advocate for their interests within law schools and the broader legal community. The organizations are also interested in horizontal and vertical mentorship, networking, and connectedness among Black Americans in the legal profession, and some even work to ensure that Black junior and senior legal professionals are aware of and committed to the needs and interests of the Black community. Like undergraduate Black student organizations, Black law student associations donate time and expertise to vulnerable populations. For example, Black student law organizations often host legal clinics in communities without adequate access to legal resources, lending their expertise and support to people marginalized and often caught within the clutches of the criminal justice system, who are disproportionately Black Americans. These organizations are also important to the academic success of Black law students; as Meera E. Deo (2013) highlights, "Predominantly white law school environments are especially notable for being inhospitable and unfriendly, especially for students of color. Many law students of color create and join race/ethnic-specific organizations in order to receive support on otherwise unwelcoming campuses" (83). Although they are sometimes critiqued as a form of self-segregation, Deo (2013) argues that these organizations, which many of the respondents in this study said they belonged to during law school, are important because they represent a safe space for marginalized students.

The significance of these Black organizations created for and by Black students in undergrad and law school is clear: these organizations are often meant to be uplifting, supportive, affirming spaces for Black students within educational institutions. Like HBCUs and Black Greek-letter organizations, Black student organizations encourage and enhance identity development, social connections, leadership opportunities, networking, and collective voice and action. Additionally, within these organizations, Black-identifying students often find a space that celebrates and acknowledges the diversity that exists within the Black community.

BLACK JUDGES' ADULTHOOD SOCIALIZATION:
PRE-BENCH ADULT LIFE, POLITICS, AND CAREER

The years between graduating from law school and joining the bench represent a significant stage in the lives of Black state court judges. During this period, law school graduates establish themselves in their careers and communities and build strong reputations within the legal community that they can later draw on as they seek judicial service. I saw this with the judges I interviewed and surveyed, who reported working in the legal profession honing their legal skills.

There are few formal requirements to becoming a state court judge. Nonetheless, like many state court judges, Black judge respondents often followed similar paths. More often than not, Black judges were practicing attorneys prior to reaching the bench. In fact, more than four-fifths of respondents (88 percent) considered "attorney" as their primary career before joining the bench.[29] For the participants who had been attorneys and wanted to specify their type of practice (108 participants out of the 233 who identified being an attorney as their primary pre-bench career), the plurality—almost two-fifths of respondents (39 percent)—had been private attorneys, although a significant number had been prosecutors as well (31 percent). Thirteen percent of respondents had been public defenders, and 5 percent had been state or federal government attorneys.

As former attorneys, most of the Black judges surveyed have experience representing and advocating for an individual or group's interests. Their career facilitated the development of important analytical and oral skills and establishment of a strong reputation in the legal community and network. Both skills and reputation are important for individuals seeking judgeships. I would also argue that their close contact with the courts and legal system as attorneys gave them a vantage point to learn about its strengths and weaknesses. In the capacity they were working in, they were positioned to become acutely aware of some of the salient issues that plague the legal and justice system, including racism and classism (Butler 2010; Van Cleve 2016).

As attorneys, Black judges came to better understand the anti-Blackness at the center of the justice system because of their proximity to and location within the system as well as who they worked with and the stories they were privy to. Table 3.2 shows the percentages of Black legal clients that Black judges represented in their pre-bench careers. More than two-thirds of respondents (68 percent) said more than 40 percent of their legal clients were Black. As a result of long-standing racism within the criminal justice system, including with policing, prosecution, and adjudication, these percentages are not all that surprising because Black Americans are overrepresented among those who are stopped, arrested, prosecuted, and punished. Nevertheless, the numbers reflect the fact that prior to joining the bench, many Black state court judges advocated on behalf of Black clients inside the court system as their attorneys. A history of representing Black clients is likely to have enriched Black judges' connection with the Black community and positively influenced their group identity and attachments. Their experience representing Black legal clients also represents a form of racial socialization—by providing legal assistance and representation to Black clients, Black judges also witness racial bias at work firsthand and are likely to have an informed perspective about ongoing racial inequality in the legal system, which can serve as a factor that would strengthen their racial identity and group attachments.

To gauge their engagement in politics and commitments to issues related to inequality and civil rights, Black judge respondents were also asked about their political activities. Table 3.5 shows that most Black state court judges self-identify as being active in politics just like their family members from their childhood. Not only are they generally active in politics, but they report being active in various ways: as voters, campaign workers/managers, party officials, political candidates, political advisors, and financial contributors to political parties and candidates. Most of the judges say they did multiple things, including contributing financially to campaigns, working in campaigns, and voting. This is consistent with twentieth-century Black state court judges' political proclivities (Smith 1983).

Although the most common political activism among the respondents was participation in electoral politics by voting (94 percent), roughly half of them (49 percent) were involved in a political movement before becoming a judge. Many of the judges had been active in the Black Civil Rights movement, but respondents were also involved in numerous other movements in the late twentieth and twenty-first centuries, including the LGBTQ equal rights movement, anti-war movement, disability rights movement, environmental movement, voting rights movement, #BlackLivesMatter, workers' rights movement, women's rights movement, and children's rights movement. Of the judges who said they had been active in a movement before becoming a judge, three-fourths said they had been somewhat or very active, while only 1 percent said they had been extremely active. This activism highlights Black judges' similarity to their families, who they reported being active in politics during their childhood. Personal political activism, in particular, around issues and concerns of marginalized people is significant for Black judges' socialization. In such movements, Black judges would likely have developed an informed perspective about inequality, the value of solidarity, and the need for collective action. Engagement in political work meant upholding and protecting civil rights and liberties, especially those of Black people, reflecting Black judges' commitments and loyalty to the concerns of Black America and other marginalized groups.

BEING BLACK AND EXPERIENCING DISCRIMINATION

One aspect of Black judges' lives that does not fit neatly into a single time period and, in fact, extends across their entire life is their exposure to racial discrimination and racism. Repeatedly, Black judges noted that they had personally and directly experienced racial discrimination, and that it was a reoccurring experience.[30] An overwhelming majority—more than 90 percent of interview respondents and 97 percent of survey respondents—said that they had experienced race-based discrimination, often repeatedly. Thirty-nine percent of survey respondents said they personally experienced racial discrimination a few times a year; 18 percent said they experienced discrimination at least once a month; 13 percent said they experienced discrimination at least once a week; and 28 percent said they had experienced discrimination a few times in the past. Less than 1 percent of survey respondents said it happens, but they were not sure how often. Discrimination is, thus, by far one of the most common experiences in the backgrounds of Black judges and one of the shared experiences that bonds Black judges to one another and to other Black people in the United States. As surveys of the general Black population have often found, Black Americans report frequently experiencing discrimination in the United States.[31]

Some judges shared experiences with racial discrimination from their childhood. When asked about race affecting her life experiences, Judge Adams, an older Black female judge from the South, shared discrimination she remembered from her youth:

> There were very few Black people really, but enough of us that we had our own school, and my mother was a teacher there. I can remember us being maybe 8 or 9 and there was a water fountain, not the main one but the one kind of at the end of town. I went over to it. I don't even remember if I took a drink. Some little white boy who was about my age, he took issue with me at the water fountain and he pushed me and he said words to me too. That's one thing I remember. I used to walk to school sometimes too and I remember passing these little white girls and they would say, "Hey nigger."

Here, Judge Adams, a Black woman who grew up during segregation in the South, shares her personal experiences with discrimination and how it manifested as interpersonal, hostile verbal and physical attacks and violence and involved white children, both girls and boys, around her age.

Judge Wood, an older Black judge from the South, also shared a personal experience he had growing up during segregation. "I remember when I was a kid, when it came time to pay your taxes in Birmingham, you went down to the courthouse to pay your taxes. They had this beautiful park around the courthouse, beautiful, but Black folks couldn't sit in there. Black folks, we couldn't stop until we got to that courthouse and paid them taxes and came back out of there. That's within my time frame." Like Judge Adams's experience, Judge Wood's experience is partly a product of the time in which he grew up—during U.S. apartheid (i.e., Jim Crow segregation), when law explicitly permitted different rules for Black people and White people and treatment by race. According to Woodward (2001), Jim Crow laws that re-created or perhaps maintained the Black-white racial caste system were not inevitable after the Civil War and were not an immediate backlash against Black freedom, but instead they were part of a large system that over time was legitimized and legalized in legislatures and courthouses across the country. Both Judge Wood and Judge Adams grew up during the Jim Crow period, which was not that long ago, and with their statements, they highlight how they were socialized as Black Americans into a racialized social system. They understood all too well what the racial hierarchy was and what that meant in terms of the distribution of power and resources.

Similarly, Judge Taylor described his personal experiences with discrimination from his childhood:

> I grew up Black. Went to a colored high school. Many of the people who rode a bus past my house were going to a school different from the one I was going to, while I walked to school. The buses usually at the white school. When they would get a new bus, they would send the old bus to the Black school. Same thing with books. I guess I was in high school before I ever got a new book furnished by the state. We got the books from the white school. I've seen the discrimination in many ways. I'm a victim of it. So, I'm obviously very conscious of that.

Unlike some of the other experiences with racial discrimination that Black judges shared with me, Judge Taylor, a Black male judge from the South, highlights institutional racism, the type found within the practices and policies of institutions. Judge Taylor's statement emphasizes racist policies and practices related to busing and new educational tools that maintained disparities in the educations received by Black and white children. According to Vaught (2011), policies related to which students receive new books and other resources such as computers and tablets in a school setting help explain the racial achievement gap in education in the United States that has been sustained for decades and results in the continued undereducation of Black and Brown students. As Judge Taylor's statement shows, these students clearly recognize and experience this undereducation, and importantly, they attribute it to white supremacy and anti-Black racism.

While some judges described racialized experiences from their childhood, other judges described racialized experiences from their adulthood. Judge Thompson reflected on his personal experiences with exclusionary practices. He shared that he has had "experiences of being told, either directly or indirectly, 'You can't come in' or 'You can't go there.' Or you're at the end of a table and there's a conversation, and you aren't part of it." Judge Thompson's experiences highlight two important ways that systemic racism can be present and operate on an interpersonal level in Black judges' lives. First, being told where he could or could not be and being denied autonomy and agency over his body highlights the arrested mobility that Black Americans experience. External restrictions have always limited Black Americans' ability to move freely in physical, economic, and social spaces—and thus Black Americans' opportunities and access. The second scenario exemplifies racist social exclusion Black Americans experience despite their physical presence. The scenario highlights the undervaluing of his presence and potential contribution to the conversation, potentially leaving him with a sense of not belonging and inferiority and an erosion of self-esteem. Together, Judge Thompson's scenarios highlight his exposure to racialized power dynamics and contestation around Black Americans' intellectual value, agency, and autonomy.

Similarly, Judge Terry, a judge raised in the South, shared experiences with racial stereotyping of Black men as violent. "I have experienced women, white females, being afraid of me when I'm out in public, where they will move to the other side of the road when they are walking or turn on their panic alarm when I am walking through a parking lot approaching them." These experiences with racism highlight how Black men specifically, as well as Black people generally, are stereotyped as criminals and an immediate and grave threat to white safety (Welch 2007). The notion that Black people are "violent" grew out of scientific racism as well as challenges to and the denial of the humanity of Black people, such as the infamous *Dred Scott v. Sandford* (1857) U.S. Supreme Court case. Before the late nineteenth century, the stereotype helped to justify enslavement, and according to Welch (2007), the stereotype of Black people as criminals was used to justify the lynchings that took place after slavery ended. The stereotypical tropes were eventually used during the Civil Rights movement to try to dismiss claims of racism and inequality. Billy Hawkins (1998) suggests that stereotypical representations of Black men as violent brutes are manifested based on the "needs of the system of white supremacy" and often influence criminal justice policies and practices, including racial profiling. Moreover, these views influence the individual behavior of white people who act as pseudo-police officers or extensions of the law in communities by policing Black people (i.e., #BBQBecky; #CornerstoreCaroline; #PermitPatty). In noting that white women take obvious steps to avoid him, Judge Terry highlights the persisting stereotype that Black men are brutes who animalistically lust after white women and warrant social control interventions to maintain public safety.

Judge White, a Black female judge from the Midwest, shared a long story about being racially profiled by police with her brother in a Midwestern state while she was an acting prosecutor:

I can remember when I was a prosecutor and I was in the car with my younger brother who had been in an accident probably the year before, and his case finally settled. And what young people do, he went out and bought him a little Cadillac and everything. . . . And I was in the car with him and he got pulled over.

And soon as the police pulled up, they said, "Jackpot. Where are the drugs?" . . .

So, I was trying to like hide my face because I knew those two officers and they knew I was a prosecutor, and I wanted to see what they were doing.

So, [my brother] was like, "What are you talking about?"

They were like, "I know this is not your car. Did you steal it? You know, "Where did you get this car, Black boy?" And this was in the '90s. . . .

I was just sitting in the car with my head down, and they were like, "Is this your little bitch? Your whore?" I am not lying! . . . I couldn't wait for them to see my face.

They were like, "Step out the car."

And [my brother] was like, "What?" You know, "Why are you stopping me? If it's a speeding ticket, I have my license and I have insurance."

[They said,] "Step out the car. We are going to search your car."

[My brother] said, "I'm not giving you permission to search my car."

They said, "Well if we find something, we are going to write on the report that you gave us permission." And so, they were like "Step out the car! You too, ma'am."

When I stepped out, I said, "Hey, Officer."

When they looked up, they said, "Oh, Prosecutor—[her first name]!" And they were like, "Oh, we're sorry, we're sorry, let him go!

Judge White's experience and interaction with the criminal justice system highlight yet another example of Black judges being exposed to anti-Black discrimination and socialized in the United States. Moreover, this experience highlights for Judge White important features about our criminal justice system and the racial profiling and disrespect experienced by Black men in particular, but also Black women, in their encounters with law enforcement (Baumgartner, Epp, and Shoub 2018; Butler 2017; Ritchie 2017).

Judge White's particular experience with officers boldly sharing that they would falsify police records influences how much she trusts police officers' documentation and their testimony in cases she presides over in her court. She mentioned that, normally, officers would come to the prosecutor to get documents approved. After she had the incident with the two officers, "they never came back to my room to ever have charges signed. They just stayed away from me." In addition to raising questions about those officers' ethics, Judge White says the experience had a much bigger impact because she now "question[s] . . . other stuff that officers do."

Discrimination, irrespective of when it occurs in one's life and regardless of the specific act, can reinforce Black Americans' racial identity and group attachments. Indeed, discrimination is one of the few experiences that most Black people in the United States have in common despite the heterogeneity within the population, especially along class lines. Just as the racial identity of poor and working-class Black people is reinforced as a result of discrimination, the racial identity of middle-class and wealthy Blacks is also reinforced when their class status proves to be powerless to protect them from discrimination and prejudice. Scholarship by Feagin (1991), Pattillo (2013), McGowen (2017), and others highlights how middle-class Blacks experience discrimination in public accommodations and public spaces as well as residential neighborhoods when they reside in integrated or mostly white communities. Middle-class Black people's racial experiences often underscore the continued significance of race and reinforce a Black identity in a group whose professional and social networks are unlikely to be predominantly Black.

CONCLUSION

An identity-to-politics link for Black people typically stems from life experiences and socialization common to the racial group that leads group members to develop a strong racial group identity and group attachments, which work together to inform their perspectives, attitudes, and behavior (Dawson 1994; McClain et al. 2009). Racial socialization and group-based treatment are, therefore, two of the essential components of Black people's identity development. I speculate that just as racial socialization and racialized life experiences are essential components of Black people's identity development, they are likely to be essential components of Black judges' identity development.

The goal of this chapter has been to examine and analyze Black judges' familial, community, educational, and career characteristics, along with their embodied experiences, to understand their paths to the bench and how these jurists have been socialized throughout their lives. I argued that Black judges' socialization during childhood and adulthood via their biological and chosen families and communities, along with their life experiences, such as personal encounters with anti-Black discrimination, would be consistent with the socialization and experiences of most Black Americans. That is, similar to most Black Americans, Black judges would have had similar racialized life experiences and have been racially socialized by the people and institutions around them.

The backgrounds and life experiences of twenty-first-century Black state court judges are revealing and interesting for two reasons. First, a great deal of diversity exists within this group, from their childhoods to their young adult lives to their adult lives. Yet the results also highlight the similarities and characteristics that connect Black judges to each other and to Black Americans in the general population. Many of the background characteristics discussed in this chapter are often assumed but not actually known by scholars because a serious lack of data and scholarship on judges' lives exists. The significant contribution to the little knowledge scholars have about state court judges, especially Black judges, makes this chapter uniquely important.

The data examined in this chapter also provide support for my argument that Black judges' socialization is similar to that of Black Americans in the general population. The findings show that many Black judges have been racially socialized, like most Black people, since their childhood. The biological and chosen families and communities they belonged to, the undergraduate institutions they attended, the organizations and movements they participated in, and the political and professional work they did as adults highlight the racial socialization many of them experienced. Moreover, their embodied experiences via discrimination represent yet another way that Black judges have been racially socialized in the United States in ways similar to most Black Americans.

Between their childhood and adulthood, Black judges gained a heightened understanding of the relationship between race, power, inequality, law, and justice. Moreover, they learned and witnessed the importance of activism and engagement in the political and legal system, and even were politically engaged as adults. Finally, Black judges' socialization has helped them see community and collective work in action. Such socialization and characteristics highlight how Black judges are not all that dissimilar from most Black Americans.

Stages two (racial group identity) and three (racial group consciousness) of the identity-to-politics link rely on Black people feeling close to other Black people and having a psychological attachment to other group members. Scholars suggest that feelings of closeness, group attachments, and group consciousness develop from individual racial identity, common experiences and socialization that resonate with group members, knowledge about the group, and a willingness to work with others to address the plight of the group (Dawson 1994). The data analysis presented in this chapter indicates that the preconditions for stages two and three of the identity-to-politics link have been established. However, the extent to which Black judges feel close and connected to other Black people, possess a group consciousness, are knowledgeable about issues of Black America, and understand collective action as necessary to improving the status of the group remain to be seen and shown with evidence.

In the subsequent chapter, I focus on Black judges' identities and group attachments by highlighting the extent to which Black judges identify as "Black," see themselves as close and connected to other Black people and Black America, and feel mobilized to make a difference. Whether Black judges possess a racial group identity and consciousness and have group attachments are fundamental to understanding whether the group of jurists possess an identity-to-politics link, which may in turn lead to advocative representation.

FOUR

THE COLOR OF THEIR SOULS

Black Judges' Identities and Consciousness

> Opponents of [Clarence] Thomas's confirmation to the Supreme
> Court were not questioning the color of his skin. They were ques-
> tioning the color of his soul, his heart, his concern about the weak,
> the poor, minorities, and Native Americans.
>
> JUDGE A. LEON HIGGINBOTHAM JR., a
> former Black federal court judge[1]

> Being Black is something that I don't think you can separate your-
> self from. People who say they don't think about being Black are
> really delusional. It is something that affects everything—OK, a lot
> of what you do—something I had to learn to be proud of and not
> wear the badge of shame.
>
> JUDGE HALL, a Black female judge from the South

While Black judges have been racially socialized and have life experiences
comparable to Black Americans in the general population (see chapter 3), it is
not clear whether their socialization and experiences have led them to develop
a Black identity and consciousness. As judges who are part of the country's
political and legal elite, Black state court judges may have connections and a
consciousness that relates to their socioeconomic class or their profession and
not one that relates to their race. In this chapter, I assess whether Black judges

have developed a Black identity and the extent to which they possess a racial group consciousness. The epigraphs by Judges Higginbotham and Hall that open this chapter suggest that at least some Black judges think about their identities and consciousness. Both epigraphs underscore the significance of Black judges accepting their Black identity, having a sense of Black pride and joy, being concerned about issues facing marginalized groups, and dedicating their lives to repairing broken systems for the betterment of marginalized and oppressed people. All of this is potentially consequential for what these judges do once they reach the judiciary.

While the overarching question for the chapter is whether Black judges possess a racial identity and consciousness, the following specific questions guide this chapter's analysis. Do Black judges identify with being Black? To what extent do they feel attached to other Black Americans and Black communities? How, if at all, are Black judges connected to Black America and Black people? Do Black judges perceive treatment based on race as an issue for the Black community? To what extent do Black judges feel responsible for or compelled to address the concerns of Black people in their capacity as judges? Among others, these questions encompass the key issues that help scholars understand whether Black Americans possess a racial identity and consciousness (McClain et al. 2009).

Because many Black judges have racialized life experiences and have been racially and politically socialized throughout their lives, I anticipate that Black judges will likely have developed a strong racial group identity and group consciousness. Namely, Black judges will have an awareness of being Black, will feel connected to and maintain connections with other Black Americans, will understand racism as an issue affecting the Black community, will value the importance of racial representation and collective action, and will see Black elites and leaders as having a social responsibility to act in the interests of Black Americans. Analysis of the surveys and interviews with Black state court judges reveals that Black judges are not a monolithic group in terms of their identities and their group consciousness. Yet many of them share a strong Black identity and sense of group consciousness.

RACIAL GROUP MEMBERSHIP, IDENTITY, AND CONSCIOUSNESS

As I mentioned in chapter 2, when I described the identity-to-politics link and discussed the link's relevance for the theory of advocative representation, racial group membership, racial group identity, and "racial group consciousness are related but distinct concepts. McClain, Carew, Walton, and Watts (2009) disentangle these seemingly fused concepts. They define *racial group membership* as the "assignment of an individual into a particular group based on characteristics that are specific to that group, in accordance with widely held intersubjective definitions" (473). *Racial group identity* is an "awareness of belonging to a certain group and having a psychological attachment to that group based on a perception of shared beliefs, feelings, interests, and ideas with other group members" (McClain et al. 2009, 474). Finally, *racial group consciousness* is defined by McClain et al. (2009) as "in-group identification *politicized* by a set of ideological beliefs about one's group's social standing, as well as a view that collective action is the best means by which the group can improve its status and realize its interests" (476). While related, these are distinct concepts with their own meanings.

BLACK JUDGES AND RACIAL GROUP MEMBERSHIP, IDENTITY, AND CONSCIOUSNESS

In the United States, visible phenotypical characteristics like hair texture, nose shape, and skin color denote racial group membership. For Black people, similarities in phenotype result in perceptions of Black people as constituting a Black racial group, categorization as Black, and treatment as though they belong to a group (McClain et al. 2009). As a result, Black people have had similar racialized life experiences, and subsequently, have been racially and politically socialized by their families and communities to understand the way race works in America and in the lives of Black people. Over time, their experiences and racial socialization have led them to see themselves (i.e., to self-identify) as Black and as belonging to the Black racial group. Black Americans' self-identification has often led them to develop psychological attachments to other Black people and make political decisions that align with Black group interests (Bunyasi and Smith 2019; Gay, Hochschild, and White 2016). Since the twentieth century, survey data frequently report Black Americans possess a racial group identity based on Black Americans self-reporting that they are aware of the racial group, identify with the racial group, and feel close to other group members (e.g., Dawson 1994; Gurin, Hatchett, and Jackson 1989; Simien 2005; Tate 1994).

Because of their shared experiences and history within the United States, Black Americans have also developed a sense of racial group consciousness (Miller et al. 1981). They tend to feel the fate and future of other Black Americans is linked to their fate (Dawson 1994). They also perceive group solidarity and the collective action of Black people as crucial to improving the group's status. Consequently, Black people use the well-being of the entire racial group as a proxy for the welfare of the individual self when making decisions. This proxy-guided behavior often leads to the general homogeneity among Black Americans that political scientists note when assessing their political attitudes and political behavior. As mentioned in chapter 2, Black consciousness, for instance, helps explain Black Americans' voting behavior; views about public policies, politicians, and political institutions; and even interest in the political arena and political affairs (Bobo and Gilliam 1990; Gay and Tate 1998; Haynie and Watts 2010; Shingles 1981; Tate 1991).

Because Black people possess a strong group identity and consciousness due to their life experiences and socialization, and their consciousness influences how they make decisions in the world, scholars generally understand an identity-to-politics link to operate within the group. The extent to which Black judges possess such a link is mostly unknown because we know very little about Black judges' group membership, identity, consciousness, and politics. Few scholars have empirically assessed how Black judges identify themselves and whether they (1) see themselves as belonging to the "Black" group, (2) are connected to Black America and people, (3) perceive Black people as having a lower social status, and (4) are mobilized to collaborate with other Blacks for the betterment of the group. Nonetheless, it is presumed that Black judges would possess a strong racial identity and a group consciousness that would lead to distinctive judicial behavior.

The expectation has generally been that, because of their life experiences as members of a marginalized group and how they were socialized, Black judges would develop a strong racial identity and group attachments that would lead them to be responsive to the interests of the Black community. Unfortunately, studies that posit that Black judges possess strong racial identities and attachment do not provide much evidence to support their claim—the data necessary to test these claims is not readily available. Thus, few researchers have produced scholarship that focuses on whether Black judges possess a racial identity and group attachments.

Two studies, however, provide clues about Black state court judges' identity and consciousness. The first is Michael David Smith's (1983) monograph *Race Versus Robe: The Dilemma of Black Judges*, which draws on interviews and surveys with Black judges. By studying the civil rights activities of the Black judges, Smith created a "rough index of degrees of race consciousness" (123). Most of the Black judges he interviewed described some activity in the race equality movement. "Substantial numbers were contributors, workers, and most importantly, officers in one or more of the civil rights organizations. Almost all of them confined their activities to the more moderate National Association for the Advancement of Colored People (NAACP) and the Urban League," versus the Student Nonviolent Coordinating Committee (SNCC) or the Congress of Racial Equality (CORE) (Smith 1983,123).

Smith (1983) also demonstrated that Black judges were genuinely concerned about the conditions of Black Americans. His respondents were disturbed by the pervasive racial discrimination they perceived in the everyday lives of Black people, as well as the racial bias they admitted existed within the criminal justice system. Although at the time Smith's respondents agreed that they had witnessed some racial progress in the country during the previous twenty years (1960s–1980), many of them argued that the country had far to go to achieve racial equality. Their concern about the welfare of Black Americans and the quest for racial justice was pervasive in the lives, legal careers, and bench attitudes of Black judges (Smith 1983).

The respondents in Smith's study also shared personal experiences with racism. They described experiencing racial discrimination and racism as children, lawyers, and even judges. The significance of these experiences is that they resulted in the attitude they adopted regarding their behavior and their judicial role: "provoked by racial experiences, Black judges have adopted an attitude of judicial activism" (Smith 1983,125). That is, they report engaging in certain activities that reflect their connection to and concern with the Black community and their belief that racism exists in the world (Smith 1983). Based on Black judges' civil rights activities, experiences with racism, and thoughts about the social status and treatment of Black people, Smith concluded that many of the Black judges sitting on the bench in the late 1970s and early 1980s had a racial group consciousness.

The second study that hints at Black judges possessing a group identity and consciousness is Linn Washington's book (1994) on Black state and federal judges working in the early 1990s. Drawing on in-depth interviews and biographies, Washington shed some light on Black judges' racial identification, their perceptions of and experiences with discrimination, and their connection to other Blacks. Though Washington never developed a Black consciousness index like Smith (1983) did and did not explicitly discuss Black judges possessing a group identity and consciousness, the biographical narratives he shares imply that Black judges possess a group identity and racial group consciousness.

In Washington's book, one biographical chapter focuses on the life of a Black former federal court judge, the Honorable A. Leon Higginbotham. Higginbotham shares experiences he had before becoming a judge and his perspectives on injustice. One personal experience that he had with racial discrimination highlights how race affected the treatment and embodied experiences of Black judges growing up during Jim Crow:

> [Charles] Elliot was the president of Purdue in 1944, the year I entered as a sixteen-year-old freshman. There were only a dozen Black students when I entered Purdue, which at the time had about six thousand white students. All of the Black students lived in a separate house. We slept in the attic, which had no heat. After two winter months of going to bed every night wearing earmuffs, four pairs of socks, and sometimes a jacket, I decided to go talk with the university's president. I felt we should at least have heat, and I asked President Elliot if we could have a section—a segregated section—of any dormitory on campus that had heat. Elliot looked me in the eye and told me the law didn't require the university to allow colored students in a dormitory. He told me either to accept things as they were or leave—leave immediately.

This disturbing narrative that Higginbotham details where he experienced anti-Black racism and thought about racial injustice mirror many of the stories in Washington's book.[2] Like Higginbotham, the dozens of other Black judges interviewed for Washington's project indicate that they identify as Black, see themselves as connected to other Black people, have experienced racism and are aware of racism, and make decisions that they hope will benefit the group

(Washington 1994). They, therefore, imply that they possess a racial group identity and consciousness.

Judges in Washington's study and Smith's study were born in the early to mid-twentieth century, lived during the Jim Crow racial apartheid era, and were active in fighting for Black civil rights via their professions and their political activities in social movements. Their socialization and experiences led them to develop a strong Black group identity and consciousness. Because their socialization and experiences as Black people are both somewhat similar to and yet different from the experiences of Black judges currently sitting on the bench, we must assess whether Black judges today differ from their predecessors when it comes to possessing a group identity and consciousness. Do Black judges today possess a strong group identity and Black consciousness like their Black judicial predecessors and like Black Americans in the general population? Or do Black judges today generally not possess a strong racial group identity and consciousness?[3]

On the one hand, Black judges might not possess a group interest and consciousness. Societal changes have occurred that influence how Black people today, including Black judges, experience and navigate the world, such as subtler forms of racism, growing class divisions in Black America, and the removal of institutionalized explicit legal racism. Consequently, Black judges today might not see themselves as being connected to many other Black people, especially lower-income and less educated Black people. More importantly, they might not see racism as remaining an issue affecting the entire group, or they may attribute disparities to other sources (Smith 2014b).

Another reason Black judges might not possess a group identity and consciousness is that Black judges differ from Black Americans in the general population in potentially consequential ways. Unlike the Black masses, they are an elite population academically, economically, socially, and politically.[4] On some measures, middle-class and better-educated Blacks express less racial consciousness and are less connected to Black America. Therefore, Black judges might not possess high levels of racial group identity and group consciousness. W. E. B. Du Bois cautioned us about the growing class divide in Black America. He warned that such a gap could lead to the slow erasure of connection between wealthy and poor Black people and a lack of Black social responsibility and willingness to commit to and engage in collective action among well-off Black Americans. To this point, he noted in a speech that one population he encountered that vexed him were "sharp young persons, who received the education given very cheaply at Fisk University, with the distinct and single-minded idea, of seeing how much they could make out of it for themselves, and nobody else."[5] If Black judges are like the highly educated, middle-class, ambitious, self-interested young folks that Du Bois encountered, they may not feel close to Black people, be connected to Black America, feel concerned with issues that affect the larger Black population, or feel obliged to behave in ways that would indicate they have a sense of group consciousness. That is to say, Black judges might not possess a strong sense of group identity and consciousness.

Finally, Black judges differ from other Black elites. Black judges self-select into a recognized conservative discipline (i.e., the legal profession); some legal scholars suggest the legal field opposes extreme progress and resists change and significant reforms due to the internalization of the norms of their discipline (Bodenheimer 1947, 222–26). As a result of belonging to their profession and being socialized in that environment, Black judges may experience substantial attitude and identity changes that may lead to low levels of racial group identity and consciousness (Erlanger and Klegon 1978).

Yet Black judges might possess a Black group identity and consciousness like Black Americans in the general population and their Black judicial predecessors. Black judges are, arguably, part of the Black middle class, given their educational attainment and professions. Evidence suggests that middle-class Black people, including Black political actors and Black American immigrants, have feelings of group identification and consciousness (Broockman 2013; Dawson 1994; Smith 2014a). The United States continues to be a racialized social system whereby race, regardless of class and gender, matters profoundly for Black people's life experiences and opportunities (Bonilla-Silva 1997). Discrimination persists and continues to be pervasive for Black people of all genders and socioeconomic classes. Because Black judges today have racialized life experiences and have been racially socialized in ways similar to Black Americans in the general population (see chapter 3) and in ways known to lead to the development of group identity and consciousness, we may find that Black judges have developed a strong group identity and consciousness. Black judges, an elite Black population, given their educational level, high net worth, and prestigious profession, may nonetheless feel close to Black people, be connected to Black America, feel concerned with issues that affect the larger

Black population, and feel obliged to behave in ways that would indicate they have a sense of group consciousness.

In sum, whether Black judges possess a racial group identity and racial group consciousness is unclear; the identity-to-politics theory and existing empirical work presents arguments for both questions. I suspect that Black judges have developed a group identity and Black consciousness. Despite their profession and their current socioeconomic status, I anticipate that they possess a strong Black identity and group consciousness due to their backgrounds, socialization, and embodied life experiences as Black people.

DATA AND METHODS

Black judges are best suited to provide insight into their group identities, attachments, and consciousness. Accordingly, in this chapter, I draw mainly on the roughly 270 surveys I used for the previous chapter.[6] Relying on surveys to examine Black judges' identities and attachments is consistent with the methodology scholars use to study racial group identity and consciousness among racial groups in the general U.S. population and even Black judges (Smith 1983).

I supplement the surveys with interviews. Surveys are often unable to capture sufficient depth and details. Washington (1994) and Smith (1983) found illuminating information about Black judges' group identity and group consciousness by interviewing Black judges in the decades following the end of the Civil Rights era. Consequently, this chapter also draws on interviews with thirty-two Black judges to give a better sense of their identity and consciousness and add context to the survey data responses. Thus, similar to the methodological triangulation practiced in chapter 3, this chapter combines qualitative and quantitative data to practice methodological triangulation to reach a more comprehensive and fuller understanding of Black judges' identities and consciousness.

BLACK JUDGES AND THEIR RACIAL GROUP MEMBERSHIP

Racial group membership among Black people involves them identifying as "Black" or "African American," the two most commonly used concepts to refer to Black Americans. Based on the U.S. Census's July 1, 2024, population estimates, Black people comprise 13.7 percent of the U.S. population.[7] This figure corresponds to the number of people living in the U.S. (U.S.-born and foreign-born) self-identifying their racial group as Black or African American.

The overwhelming majority of Black judges surveyed and interviewed for this study self-identified as Black or African American. Their self-identification happened in a variety of ways. In my outreach to and recruitment of participants, I noted that this research was about Black state court judges, and that was the one requirement to participate in the study. By agreeing to participate and then completing a survey or taking part in an interview, the participants acknowledged that they met the requirement (i.e., a Black state court judge) to participate in the research project.

Ninety-five percent of the Black judges surveyed said they were Black or African American. The remaining 5 percent of survey respondents reported being bi- or multi-racial with at least one of their races as Black or African American. The trend was similar for interview respondents, whom I asked to share the racial terms they use to describe themselves. Ninety-seven percent of the interview respondents said they were either Black or African American.[8] Judge Smith, for instance, said, "I am unapologetically Black." Judge Green, a Black female judge from the South, stated, "A little joke I've told: I was Black before I was a woman, a girl. Regardless of what gender I came out, I was going to be Black." Judge Wilson, a Black male judge from the South, talked about his self-identification resonating with how others categorize him racially:

> That's debatable. (*Laughs.*) More importantly, how does everybody else classify me? You know? Now talk to Tiger Woods, ask him how does he classify himself. He said, "Well, I'm Cablinasian." But it doesn't matter what he thinks, you know. How do people who look at him on T.V. think about him? He's Black! I'm Black! He can be all the other stuff he wants to try to be, but he is Black.[9]

In sum, the majority of the Black judges in this study identified themselves as being either Black or African American. Black judges acknowledge that they are aware of how others see them, seeing themselves racially as others see them, and openly acknowledging their racial group membership as a Black American.

BLACK JUDGES AND THEIR BLACK GROUP IDENTITY

The Black judges interviewed and surveyed in this study indicated that they are quite connected to Black Americans and Black America. To assess Black judges' psychological connection to other Black people and thus their racial group identity, I asked judges to share how important race was to their identity and the group they felt closest to. Their responses to these questions as well as the specific pronouns they used to describe themselves and Black people generally reveal whether they see themselves as members of the racial group. Moreover, I asked them about the organizations they participated in, their social activities, and the neighborhoods where they live. These questions about where and how Black judges spend their time can show how connected Black judges are to Black people, communities, and issues.

The Importance of Race to Black Judges' Identity

Black judges' classifying themselves as Black says very little about how important they feel being Black is to their identity. It might be the case that they simply identify as Black because that is how others see them and not because they see being Black as a critical part of who they are. When asked how important race was to their identity, strikingly, no Black judges surveyed said their race was not at all important. Eighty-five percent of respondents said race was either very or extremely important to their identity.[10] Table 4.1 shows Black judges' responses to this question alongside the responses of Black Americans

TABLE 4.1: Importance of race to overall identity.

How important is race to your identity?	Black judge survey respondents*	Black Americans in the general population**
Not at all	0 (0%)	— (8%)
Slightly	6 (2%)	— (5%)
Somewhat	33 (13%)	— (15%)
Very	95 (37%)	— (32%)
Extremely	124 (48%)	— (39%)

Source: Taneisha N. Means, "Political Representation in State Courts Study, 2020" (2020).

**Source*: Pew Research Center, "2021 Survey of Black Americans."

in the general population.[11] The results indicate that race is important for both Black judges and Black Americans in the general population, and race is also significant for how these two groups understand and think about their overall identity.

Black Judges Seeing Themselves in Community with Black People

Individuals can potentially belong to several groups, including a racial group, a gender group, a specific race-gender group, a class group, a professional group, and so on. But feeling close to group members is not always instinctive. To understand whether Black judges feel a sense of closeness to Black people, I asked Black judges to identify the group of people they feel *closest* to. Respondents could choose from identity groups such as their racial group and gender group, professional groups such as lawyers and judges, and other types of groups such as their class group. They could also fill in their response. The overwhelming majority (73 percent) of Black judges said they feel closest to their racial group. Other groups that judges feel close to include their gender group (6 percent, the majority of whom were women), their professional group (6 percent, the majority of whom were attorneys), and their socioeconomic class group (4 percent, the majority of whom were middle-class).

When talking about or referring to Black people, the pronouns someone uses can indicate the extent to which they see themselves as part of or separate from that group. If Black judges use terms such as *us* and *we* when talking about Black people, they imply that they see themselves as belonging and as group members. I asked Black judges to share how often they use *we* instead of *they* when referring to Black people. The majority (59 percent) said all of the time, 29 percent said most of the time, and 9 percent said some of the time. Less than 3 percent of respondents said that they rarely or never use pronouns such as *we* when referring to Black people as a group. These survey results are consistent with the interviews for this project.

Although I did not ask interview respondents how often they use *we* instead of *they* when talking about Black people, a review of the interview transcripts revealed that the vast majority of the judges used pronouns like *we* and *us* to refer to other Black Americans.[12] For instance, while discussing the underrepresentation of Black judges in his state, Judge Wood, a Black man from the South, said, "To a degree, we minorities/Blacks are responsible for a part of that. . . . We don't participate to the degree that we can to make a difference to make things change." In his statement, he not only uses the pronoun *we*, but he explains what he means by the term in case it was unclear. Additionally, later in his interview, while discussing why "Black folks" are afraid of going to the courthouse, he says that it is because "we associate the courthouse with bad things. Going to jail, getting lynched, taking your property—that is the historical view of Black folks and the courthouse. And rightfully so. But again, we have to change that." Another example came from an interview with Judge Allen, a Black female judge from the West, who said that she is mindful of the way "they describe and the way in which they label us." Here, Judge Allen is referring to Black people being stereotyped and talks about how that can be particularly harmful in the criminal justice system when legal actors might view litigants in ways that might be detrimental to their quest for equal justice.

Many of the Black judges interviewed also referred to the Black community as "my community," "our community," or "the community." This linguistic practice implies that they see themselves as a part of the Black community. For example, while discussing her electoral supporters, Judge Allen said the majority of Black Americans in her district supported her candidacy. When asked why she thought that was, she replied, "I think it was my relationship with my community." Taken together, Black judges' use of pronouns reveal that they feel a sense of belonging to the Black racial group and include themselves in that group.

Thus far, I have shown that Black judges see race as being salient to their identity and see themselves as belonging to the Black racial group. Moreover, they feel close to and connected with Black people as a group compared to other groups to which they belong. But what is feeling close to Black people if that is not borne out in the decisions Black judges make in their day-to-day lives? That is, one way that Black judges might demonstrate their connection with and to Black people and the Black community might be through the decisions they make about where and how they spend their time.

Black Judges' Decisions About Where to Live and Work

Where to reside represents a critical decision most adults have to make. Many individuals, especially those belonging to marginalized groups, do not often have much say in where they live because of pervasive discrimination in banking and redlining that leads to racial segregation (Pattillo 2005; Rothstein 2017). We might imagine, however, that Black judges, who mostly identify as

middle-class, are likely to live in the types of neighborhoods that they want because their financial resources give them increased access and options.[13] Therefore, their choice of residential neighborhood might be more indicative of who
they prefer to spend time with and live around. Regardless of why Black judges
choose their community, the composition of their residential area highlights
who they regularly see when they are home.

I asked Black judges, "To the best of your knowledge, what percentage of
the families living in your neighborhood are Black?" Table 4.2 displays the
racial composition of Black judges' neighbors, showing that a plurality of respondents (39 percent) said Black families made up less than 20 percent of
the households in their neighborhood. Approximately one-fifth (21 percent) of
Black judges report living in racially diverse communities where Black families
make up between 21 and 40 percent of the tenants. Based on these percentages, Black judges' adulthood neighborhoods differ significantly from their
childhood neighborhoods, with their current communities having fewer Black
families.[14] The data about their residential neighborhoods indicates Black
judges are not necessarily connecting with Black Americans as cohabitants in
residential communities since so many of them reside in areas with very few
Black families.

Outside of spending time in their residential neighborhoods, most adults
spend a great deal of time at work. Although they are not connecting with
many Black families in their residential communities, they may be connecting with colleagues who are Black via their chosen place of employment: the

TABLE 4.2: Diversity of Black judges' home and work environments.

	Percentage of Black families living in Black judges' neighborhood	Percentage of the judges working alongside Black judges who are Black
0–20%	102 (39%)	156 (60%)
21–40%	54 (21%)	63 (24%)
41–60%	46 (18%)	23 (9%)
61–80%	45 (17%)	11 (4%)
81–100%	14 (5%)	9 (3%)

Source: Taneisha N. Means, "Political Representation in State Courts Study, 2020" (2020).

courts. I asked survey respondents, "To the best of your knowledge, what percentage of your judicial colleagues are Black?" Table 4.2 displays information about the racial composition of Black judges' judicial colleagues. A comfortable majority of respondents (60 percent) said less than 20 percent of their judicial colleagues are Black. Sixteen percent of respondents said Black judges made up more than 40 percent of their colleagues.[15] We see that Black judges are not surrounded by Black Americans as judicial colleagues; however, Black judges are likely to encounter many Black Americans in their role as judges, given the race of litigants that come before them.[16] Thus, Black judges' connections to Black America and Black Americans might rely on their decisions about where to spend their free time.

Black Judges' Organizational Affiliations

Black judges surveyed and interviewed were asked to share which social and professional groups they belong to and to talk about how they spend their free time. Black judges' organizational affiliations are a way to see how connected Black judges are to Black America and people. If the organizations they belong to are predominantly Black organizations in terms of membership, their affiliations shed some light on Black judges' connection with people who share their racial group membership and identity. Moreover, the links say something about the amount and type of contact that Black judges are having with other Black people.

While their interests are undoubtedly varied, several organizations and types of organizations repeatedly appeared in the survey responses. For instance, just as Black sororities and fraternities were important to Black judges while they were in college as undergraduates and law students (see chapter 3), these Black Greek-letter organizations remain important to Black judges even after they have finished school; 117 Black judges listed a Black sorority or fraternity as one of the social organizations they belong to. Black judges report viewing these organizations as essential to the well-being of the Black community, given the community service work and mentorship they engage in, serving food in homeless shelters, visiting local schools to speak with Black youth, and hosting pop-up legal clinics. Through their respective organizations, Black judges describe how they maintain connections with Black America and people despite not necessarily living in majority-Black communities.

Community work, in particular, gives Black judges some insight about the status of and issues within predominantly Black neighborhoods. Judge Adams, a Black female judge from the South, for example, noted the importance of some groups she spends time with, including her Black sorority, for her connection to Black America: "I attend a Black church, [am] active in a Black sorority, in another city organization. I don't live in a Black community; I live in a mixed community. But I would say I am fairly well connected to the Black community." Black Greek-letter organizations also allow Black judges to engage with other college-educated Black Americans and develop a network of Black college-educated people. Thus, Black Greek-organizations help Black judges connect with the Black masses and Black elites.

Church is another type of social organization that is important in Black judges' lives. Just as Judge Adams said that the Black church is one way she connects to the Black community, Judge Martin, a Black male judge from the South, said his primary connection is through being a Black church member. "I'm heavily connected through the church. As I mentioned earlier, my [parent is] still a preacher, [they are] now in a higher position within the [church]." The church is not only a way Black judges remain connected to Black people, but judges also mention that their church attendance helps Black Americans feel connected to Black judges in case they see them in court. Judge Jackson, a Black female judge from the South, says, "With the Black community, I think there is a profound proudness that they feel when they see us at church in the community because it's someone that they know." Church makes connections possible for Black judges and other Black Americans.

Social organizations such as Jack and Jill of America and The Links, Incorporated, are primarily geared toward the Black middle class.[17] Twenty-four Black judges surveyed listed Jack and Jill of America as one of their social organizations, and eighteen listed The Links. According to Jack and Jill's website, it is "a membership organization of mothers with children ages 2–19, dedicated to nurturing future African American leaders by strengthening children through leadership development, volunteer service, philanthropic giving, and civic duty." It was founded during the Great Depression in Philadelphia, when close to two dozen women united to create an organization dedicated to providing "social, cultural and educational opportunities for youth." This organization's elite nature is clear from how one becomes a member and the cost associated with membership.

Membership in Jack and Jill is available via either legacy status or invitation. Prospective members require sponsorship from a current active member who is in good standing. Legacy status is granted to children who graduate from a chapter and whose mother is an active member in good standing. To become a member, one must pay the initial membership fee and then annual dues. The exact cost to join the organization depends on the local chapter. For example, in 2015, the initial fee to join the Houston chapter was $1,800 (according to the application form). Following that, members typically paid annual dues of around $500, as well as the fees for events and activities. Due to the cost to join and remain a member, the organization is viewed by some as an "elitist" association, available only to a very small segment of Black Americans.[18] Nevertheless, the organization is viewed by many as necessary for the Black middle class because it makes it possible to establish relationships and connections with people who resemble their cultural and societal tastes and proclivities.

While Jack and Jill is considered an elite social organization, The Links is regarded as a Black volunteer service organization. According to the organization's website, The Links is "an international, not-for-profit corporation, established in 1946. The membership consists of more than 16,000 professional women of color in 288 chapters located in 41 states, the District of Columbia, the Commonwealth of the Bahamas, and the United Kingdom." The organization's mission highlights its relevancy to Black identity; it describes itself as "one of the nation's oldest and largest volunteer service organizations of extraordinary women who are committed to enriching, sustaining and ensuring the culture and economic survival of African Americans and other persons of African ancestry." Like Jack and Jill, The Links provides Black women judges with an opportunity to improve Black communities while also helping them to connect with like-minded individuals.

Finally, twelve Black judges surveyed reported belonging to the National Association for the Advancement of Colored People (NAACP).[19] It is one of the nation's oldest and most renowned Black civil rights organizations. According to its website, its mission is to "secure the political, educational, social, and economic equality of rights in order to eliminate race-based discrimination and ensure the health and well-being of all persons." Its priorities have shifted over time since its founding in 1909; currently, it has six focus areas: federal advocacy, education, economic opportunity, criminal justice, health, and environmental and climate justice. Black judges belonging to the NAACP highlight their interest and investment in bettering and protecting Black lives and communities.

In the surveys, Black judges also shared that they belong to various professional organizations. The most common organization among the group of judges I surveyed was the National Bar Association (NBA).[20] Seventy-six Black judges surveyed said they were NBA members. According to the NBA's official website, the organization was "founded in 1925 and is the nation's oldest and largest national network of predominantly African-American attorneys and judges. It represents the interests of approximately 65,000 lawyers, judges, law professors and law students." This organization provides Black judges access to other Black Americans around the country who are interested and involved in law, adjudication, and legal education. In addition to their NBA membership, Black judges also reported belonging to local, state, and regional Black bar and lawyer associations and the American Bar Association. Judge Hall, a Black female judge, talked about her connection to the Black community that is made possible by the legal and political organizations of which she is a member: "I think I maintain ties with the Black political community primarily—Black political caucus, Black lawyers' association, those kinds of associations." Black legal organizations such as the NBA help Black judges connect with Black people who share their intellectual and career interests.

Insofar as they can, Black judges also spend time in their close friendship circle, which often reflects the connection they have with Black people. Judge Allen, a Black female judge from the West, made this point when reflecting on her desire to spend her free time with in-group members and how that has influenced her judicial career, including her evaluations. While discussing her judicial evaluation, Judge Allen reported that much of the criticism she received was about her not wanting to eat lunch with or spend time with white judicial colleagues and lawyers. In her evaluations, Judge Allen said her evaluators would write, "She prefers Black people. She only talks to Black people. She only goes to lunch with Black people. She only does this with Black people." In response to their criticism, she said, "It's amazing that they find that insulting when they live in a land where they go and do whatever with each other on a regular basis. The fact that I don't want to be a part of that is very troubling for them, and my social life I get to spend with who I want to spend it with and I'm not trying to assimilate into anything."

The significance of how Black judges spend their free time signifies their interest in connecting with other Black people, especially the Black middle class and Black Americans working in the legal system. Judge Allen's narrative even highlights the lengths some judges will go to for these connections and what she is willing to sacrifice (i.e., higher evaluations and white colleagues' approval and social acceptance).

Many of the social and professional organizations Black judges are affiliated with are predominantly Black organizations where members receive social, intellectual, and cultural benefits. Black judges like Judge Allen appear to turn to these organizations and their chosen friend groups to ensure that they do not feel isolated socially and professionally. The organizations, in particular, help members network with other Black Americans in their communities and beyond. Moreover, the organizations expose their members to interests and issues that affect the groups' members (i.e., Black Americans). For these reasons, these organizations and friendships address Black judges' desire for connection to Black people and issues. It is important to note here that the contact with Black America may not reflect much of the rest of Black America because these groups are a highly unrepresentative sample of Black Americans.

Black Judges' Engagement with and in Black America

Besides spending structured and unstructured free time with Black people, Black judges can also connect and maintain connections with Black people and the Black community by being intentional about the establishments and businesses they support. I asked survey respondents, "Generally speaking, how often do you make an effort to go to predominantly Black establishments and businesses such as barbershops, hair salons, stores, etc.?" Not one judge surveyed reported that they never make an effort to go to predominantly Black establishments and businesses. More than half the respondents (59 percent) said they make an effort either most of the time or all of the time. Thus, most respondents report making an effort to patronize Black-owned establishments and contribute to the Black economy. Intentionally choosing to support these organizations allows Black judges to express their desire for connection to Black culture and community, especially when, as a result of their wealth, they can technically shop wherever they want.

In interviews, Black judges shared that they are connected to other Black people by intentionally visiting predominantly Black institutions. Some judges noted in their interviews that being a civil servant (i.e., judge) has meant that they are connected to Black Americans, given that their jobs entail a bit of community activism and outreach. They choose to do that outreach in the Black community. For instance, Judge Jackson, a Black female judge, talked about valuing the community-engagement aspect of her job because she can connect with the community as well as be instrumental in the education of that community: "One of the things I like to do is to go to the schools. To see someone who looks like them, actually comes out and sits with them, and talks to them about the processes of the judicial system to them." Judge Jackson's statement indicates that she intentionally goes into the Black community to engage in intergenerational racial socializing and can be viewed as supplementing the formal education the community members receive about the legal system. Part of this engagement seems like role modeling, but the other part sounds like the dissemination of information that the judge deems necessary for their future and survival. This engagement appears to be at least partially in response to the fact that Black Americans are more likely than most other racial groups to have interaction with the criminal justice system; therefore, arming them with information about their rights and the processes of that system is critical to their existence (Alexander 2010). In doing this, Judge Jackson is contributing in symbolic and substantive ways to Black youths' socialization.

Similarly, Judge Martin, an elected judge from South, says he enjoys the community outreach he can do as a judge: "Just being a judge keeps me connected because I'm—because of how you—judges come into office, you always have to stay out there in the public, and attending events and just staying relevant to the people, at least keeping your name out there, and so I attend a lot of events both in the African American community and out of the African American community, but the point is I have to get out to these events, and so that keeps me relevant." Part of Judge Martin's message is that to retain his judgeship, he, like other elected Black judges, must remain seen and known in their communities to maintain electoral support. The other part of his message resembles what Judge Jackson says about prioritizing being visible and engaged in the Black community.

Finally, merely being Black American means that Black judges are often connected to Black communities and people via their families. Judge Terry, a Black male judge from the South, mentions this in his interview when he talks about the contact and connection he has with Black community members and the role socioeconomic class plays: "The only connections I have right now with other members of the Black community are with family members primarily, who would be probably classified in a lower economic group." Although not as connected to the Black community as other Black judges in this study, Judge Terry's remark makes it clear that it is hard, if not impossible, for most Black judges to be completely disconnected from the Black community due to their kinship ties.

This section demonstrates that Black judges have developed a racial group identity. Namely, they feel connected to Black Americans. More importantly, they find ways to connect with other Black Americans. Although their neighborhoods do not have large numbers of Black families, and they do not have many Black judicial peers, Black judges seek out predominantly Black spaces. Black judges' connections with Black Americans can strengthen their attachments to Black people and expose them to the experiences of other Black Americans and the issues facing their co-ethnics.

RACIAL GROUP CONSCIOUSNESS: UNDERSTANDING THE COLOR OF BLACK JUDGES' SOULS

Racial group identity and consciousness are, according to Bunyasi and Smith (2019), "rooted in the idea that when people believe that their racial or ethnic group membership influences their life chances, they are likely to consider the group when making political decisions" (684). I conceptualize a Black group consciousness as meaning that a person feels that their fate as a Black person is linked to the fate of the racial group, group solidarity is important, and collective action of group members can improve Blacks' social status.

Perceiving and Understanding Racial Discrimination and Bias in the Black Community

Perceiving that one's group has historically been or is contemporarily discriminated against in society can activate a group consciousness (Miller et al. 1981). Perceiving discrimination and bias against Black people indicates a belief about Black people's status within society and sheds at least some light on a critical factor that might be influencing that group's status. Accordingly, I asked survey respondents to share their perceptions about the nature and frequency of discrimination Black people face. The overwhelming majority (86 percent) said Black people are discriminated against a lot. The other 14 percent of respondents said that Black people are discriminated against somewhat. Interestingly, no respondent said that Black people were not at all discriminated against or were not discriminated against very much. Thus, their responses suggest consensus among the respondent judges about Black people generally experiencing discrimination based on race. Data from a recent Pew Research Center survey indicate that these judges' perceptions are consistent with what Black Americans in the general population believe about the prevalence of discrimination against Black people. Close to 80 percent of Pew Research Center's Black survey respondents said they think there is a lot of discrimination in the United States today against Black people.[21]

I also invited Black judge interviewees to share what they thought the primary issues facing the Black community were. Thirty of the thirty-two (or 94 percent) Black judges mentioned racial discrimination as one of the principal problems facing and affecting the group. Most of the judges interviewed indicate that discrimination within the criminal justice system is particularly pervasive. To this point, Judge Hall remarked that there are "so many opportunities for discrimination . . . and racial bias . . . to rear its ugly head and lead to disparities we see." This interviewee went into detail about racial bias in the judicial system:

> I think it's [racial bias] being completely ignored. I think the best example I've heard is if you have a tank full of fish and you woke up one morning and one fish was dead, you would take the fish out and examine the fish. But if you woke up one morning and all the fish in the tank were dead, you would then look at the water. That is how I look at our judicial system, and really every system in America, but you know, when you look at the disparities with the number of African Americans coming to the judicial system, they are sentenced more harshly and so on and so forth—you probably know those statistics and could go on forever—no one is addressing race. In fact, there is always this tremendous attempt to not talk about race. I don't know how you can address it if you don't talk about it. They don't want to talk about it.

Judge Hall's remarks indicate her view of bias in the system as both as systemic and unresolved.

Judge Smith, a Black male judge from the Midwest, discussed racial discrimination in the criminal justice system as a historical and contemporary issue. He described growing up in a segregated community in a Midwestern state and witnessing the disparate treatment of Black Americans by law enforcement officers:

> I recognize that a lot of the decisions that were made by police officers were based on race. And where I lived. And I saw it. I observed it. I never saw the police take any action against kids when I lived in [largely White area]. When I moved to the African American section of the city, in the segregated part of the city, I saw the police act unnecessarily. For essentially the same acts! . . . I told you, in [largely White area], the police respond one way. In the segregated community I lived in, the police responded a different way, which lets me know that officers do make decisions that are based on things other than objective factors.

Judge Smith went on to talk about how the issue of problematic policing he observed as a child continues to be an issue in his city more than half a century later, leading to some notable legal settlements for victims of police mistreatment and discrimination.

Like Judge Smith, Judge Martin talked about the racial issues he observed in the legal system. His perception of the prevalence of racial injustice and disparate policing being the primary issues in the Black community stemmed from what he witnessed playing out in his courtroom: "There are policing issues that disproportionately affect African Americans. In fact, that is the most prevalent issue right now . . . just how African Americans are treated in the judicial system and policing. . . . When I step into a courtroom . . . or dealing with traffic court, and I see 60–70 percent African American, I think, dang, 60–70 percent around here driving are not African American. Or, even in misdemeanor court with marijuana. It makes you wonder." Judge Martin insinuated that who he sees in court on any given day makes him "wonder" about racial bias in policing. This idea is similar to those expressed by Judge Terry, who described racial discrimination in terms of the arrests of Black individuals as an important issue facing the Black community. Instead of seeing this as a contemporary issue, Judge Terry provided some historical context, explaining how the problems of today are legacies of historical treatment: "I don't think the Black community has recovered from slavery and segregation, Jim Crow, or whatever you want to call it. . . . The vestiges of those practices are basically responsible."

All in all, many of the Black judges surveyed and interviewed for this project revealed their perception that discrimination and racism are prevalent and pervasive issues for U.S. Blacks. For some of them, their opinions about the amount and nature of racial discrimination faced by Black people resulted from their vicarious experiences, witnessing Black people in their families and communities being harassed and mistreated. Yet personal exposure and embodied experiences with discrimination help Black judges sense the frequency and nature of racial discrimination (see chapter 3).

Linked Fate Among Black Judges

Linked fate, or the perception that what generally happens to the group you belong to will affect your life, is by far one of the most common ways scholars assess the extent to which Black people possess a sense of racial group consciousness (Dawson 1994; McClain et al. 2009; Simien 2005).[22] Accordingly, I included a question on the survey that assessed Black judges' sense of linked fate. Table 4.3 displays the responses to this question alongside the sense of linked fate expressed by Black Americans in the general population in a recent nationally representative survey. The overwhelming majority of respondents (95 percent) said that what generally happens to Black people in this country will affect their life some or a lot, with the plurality of respondents (49 percent) saying "a lot." Interestingly, no Black judges (0 percent) surveyed said that what generally happens to Black people in this country will not at all affect their lives. Based on these percentages, the majority of Black judges clearly identify with and have a strong sense of linked fate with Black Americans generally. That is, Black judges believe that what happens typically in the country to Black people will have some effect on their personal, individual lives. Black judges' sense of linked fate is consistent with the sense of linked fate espoused by Black Americans in the general population (see table 4.3). This feeling of linked fate may motivate Black judges to be in solidarity with Black masses, including poorer and less educated Black people (Dawson 1994; McClain et al. 2009).

Since Black judges feel linked to other Black people, it was relevant to examine how Black judges think about Black solidarity in thought and action. I specifically asked survey respondents to share what they feel about Black solidarity and Black people working together, engaging in collective action to address the group's needs. When asked the question about Black solidarity, the

TABLE 4.3: Black linked fate.

	Response of Black judge survey respondents when asked "Do you think that what generally happens to black people in this country will affect your life?"*	Response of Black Americans in the general population**
No/No, not at all	0 (0%)	— (34%)
Yes	258 (100%)	— (76%)
Yes, not very much	13 (5%)	— (7%)
Yes, some	118 (46%)	— (58%)
Yes, a lot	127 (49%)	— (34%)

Source: Taneisha N. Means, "Political Representation in State Courts Study, 2020." (2020).
**Source:* Matt Barreto, Lorrie Frasure-Yokely, Edward D. Vargas, and Janelle Wong, "Collaborative Multiracial Post-Election Survey (CMPS) 2016" (2019), https://latinodecisions .com/wp-content/uploads/2019/06/CMPS_Toplines.pdf.

overwhelming majority of respondents (96 percent) said it was either very or extremely important for Black people to work together to address their needs, with almost three-quarters of respondents (71 percent) saying it was extremely important.[23] Notably, no Black judge respondents said that it was not at all important for Black people to work together to address their needs. Black state court judges from across the country, regardless of gender and background, generally agree that Black solidarity and Black people working together is important for the betterment of the group.

Black Judges' Views on the Responsibility of Black Elites to Represent Black Interests

Although most Black judges report feeling that Black people must be in solidarity and work together to address their needs, their perceptions of what role Black political and legal leaders should play are unclear. This point relates to the ideas promulgated by Du Bois (1903) in his essay "The Talented Tenth." In the piece, Du Bois argues that "The Negro race, like all other races, is going to be saved by its exceptional men" (33). Du Bois's vision is for the educated Black class to become leaders and assume influential and powerful positions in various sectors of society, such as the courts. For Du Bois, Black leaders have a responsibility to work on behalf of the group or at least with the group in mind.

With Du Bois's ideas in mind, I asked Black judges what they thought about Black leaders' social responsibility, including their own social responsibility, to tending to Black interests. Table 4.4 displays Black judges' responses to the questions about the social responsibility of Black political and legal leaders to advance the interests of Black people. The table shows diversity of thought among survey respondents regarding the extent to which Black judges have a social responsibility to protect and represent Black people as compared to Black political leaders.

When asked "To what extent do Black political leaders have a responsibility to protect and represent Black interests?," the overwhelming majority of respondents (80 percent) said Black political leaders have a great deal of responsibility to protect and represent the interests of Black people. I also asked them to what extent they felt Black judges specifically as a group have a social responsibility to protect and represent the interests of Black people. A plurality of respondents (44 percent) said Black judges have some responsibility to protect and represent Black people, and one-third of respondents (30 percent) said Black judges had a great deal of responsibility to do that work. It is also important to note the large number, one-quarter of respondents, who said Black judges have no responsibility at all (13 percent) or very little responsibility (12 percent).

The significance of Black judges' perceptions about the social responsibility of Black leaders, especially Black judges, is evident in the thoughts of one of the Black male judges I interviewed. Judge Brown, who was working in the Midwest, described belonging to a community of Black political elites and how they are and should be connected to the community:

TABLE 4.4: Black judges' perceptions of social responsibility of Black political and leaders and judges.

	Perceptions of the social responsibility of Black political leaders	Perceptions of the social responsibility of Black judges as a whole
No responsibility at all	1 (<1%)	30 (13%)
Very little responsibility	1 (<1%)	28 (12%)
Some responsibility	45 (19%)	99 (44%)
A great deal of responsibility	187 (80%)	68 (30%)

Source: Taneisha N. Means, "Political Representation in State Courts Study, 2020" (2020).

I strongly believe that when you are an African American lawyer, police officer, or political office holder, that you owe it to your community to make a difference . . . to something beyond you and your family. For example, if you come to this job and your only goal is to do just like those who have never suffered as African Americans have suffered and have never felt the pain of being discriminated against. Although you felt it, you are not going to now look with more informed eyes and ears than those who are not in our community. You are not an addition. You are not a substantive addition to solving the problem.

In Judge Brown's rich narrative, he powerfully articulates his perception that, in order to be a substantive addition anywhere, Black elites must pay a debt, and these leaders are under a moral obligation to Black people in general to work in ways that demonstrate that they are aware of Black political history and experiences in this country. This judge insinuates that Black leaders need to challenge and dismantle the deeply rooted, long-standing systems of oppression that have operated in ways detrimental to Black America and people. In other words, this judge is articulating his perception that Black judges and other Black elites have a social responsibility to advance and tend to the interests of Black Americans.

Black Judges Are Mobilized to Make a Difference

How Black judges feel about Black judges as a group might be different than how they think about themselves regarding social responsibility issues and addressing Black interests in the courts. For this reason, I also asked Black judges directly, 'To what extent do *you* feel responsible for protecting and representing Black interests as a judge?' The responses to this question mirror the answers to the question about Black judges in general. Seventeen percent reported feeling not at all responsible for protecting and representing Black interests as a judge, and 14 percent said they felt slightly responsible. The majority of judges (56 percent), however, said they felt either moderately or very responsible for protecting and representing Black interests. Fourteen percent said they felt extremely responsible. Therefore, slightly more than eight out of ten respondents said they felt some degree of responsibility for engaging in some representation work around Black interests.

This line of inquiry sheds light on Black judges' role orientation. According to Gibson (1978), role orientation is essentially a summary variable which defines for the role occupant the range of appropriate behavioral alternatives in any given situation. As such, role orientations are very similar to many of the situational intervening variables identified above and are almost identical to Rokeach's (1968) notion of "attitude toward situation" (A_s). Role orientations are also similar to Campbell's situational threshold. In order for an attitude to find expression in behavior, the behavior consistent with the attitude must lie within the range of acceptable behaviors, i.e., be defined as situationally appropriate. (917)

In other words, role orientation refers to judges' understanding and approach to their judicial responsibilities, including how they balance competing priorities. Scholars operationalize role orientation in their empirical studies in a variety of ways, including judges' perception of discretion (Gibson 1981). Whether Black judges see themselves as personally responsible for representation in the courts resonates with the concept of role orientation and sheds light on their understanding of their role in that position.

In addition to asking Black judges to share their perspective on their own social responsibility to advancing Black interests, I asked them how important they thought Black judges were for realizing Black equality and progress generally. I wanted Black judges to think less about "responsibility" and more about the role the courts and judges can play when it comes to improving the status of Black Americans. The overwhelming majority of respondents (85 percent) said they thought Black judges were very or extremely important for this work and objective, with 54 percent saying "extremely important." Black judges clearly see themselves and their Black judicial counterparts as playing a significant role in Blacks' advancement and betterment in the country.

Along these lines, I also asked Black judge interviewees to share whether (and if so, why) they thought the presence of Black judges could do anything for the justice system and the Black community. Twenty-seven of the thirty-two (84 percent) Black judges interviewed believed that their presence on the bench is essential to creating a better justice system. Their narratives reveal a consensus about Black judges having life experiences that influence their work as judges. Their words imply that for diversity to matter, Black judges should have a consciousness and allow their backgrounds, experiences, and consciousness to influence how they understand the cases before them and do the work of judges.

This is similar to what Judge Thompson talks about when he remarks on the importance of having Black judges who are aware and connected to the Black community, who come to the bench with a consciousness: "You want minorities coming to the bench who care. Who remember what they're part of. They may not have had bad things happen to them personally, but they saw family and friends, and they are aware of that. It doesn't mean everybody gets a get-out-of-jail card free, but everybody doesn't go to jail." What Judge Thompson insinuates in his narrative about judges remembering who they are and what they are part of resonates with the story told by Judge Moore, who explains why she feels it is crucial to have "conscious" Black judges present in the judiciary:

[One] challenge of having minorities, but if they are so assimilated, do they really give the diversity we are looking for? There's a difference in our culture, vernacular, so you have to be able to change the hats. The issue of race is becoming more challenging. The challenge is to phrase it so it's palatable. . . . Diversity is critical. If again, you know you get Clarence Thomas, just because you are Black, especially when you look at racism that is institutionalized, Blacks can be an instrument of perpetuating that racism because they don't want to rock the boat, they don't want to be perceived as the angry Black person; they don't want to be perceived as the "Black" judge. So, diversity if you understand why you are here. So again, this is the concern with the new generation [of Black judges]—do they understand that? And some may say, I'm not here to represent anybody. They might be like Charles Barkley, who says, "I'm just out here to play ball. That's all I'm doing." But I think it's bigger. That gets to the issue of purpose, and with that if you understand what your purpose is. I hope that while I'm here and when I'm gone, they gonna know that I was here.

Judge Wilson also shares his perspective on what it means to have Black judges on the bench who have some degree of consciousness and relevant life experience. In his interview, Judge Wilson remarked on how he can make proper, sound judgments because he understands the lives and circumstances of the litigants that come before him:

By appearing in courts, I saw sometimes minorities weren't getting a fair shake. Sometimes discretionary calls, discretionary decisions, and if the judge doesn't understand the life conditions that bring people into that courtroom, in my opinion, they aren't really able to ascertain a proper judgment. They don't know what you've been through. They don't know why you did what you did. Not knowing where you've been, they can't adequately address your decision-making process . . . you know, when you are on the bench, you aren't born a judge. You know, you have your own life experiences and everything that you've been through up through the time you become a judge. It is a part of your personality. So, it has to have an effect on who you are and the decisions you make. But you don't make your decisions based on race, but your life experiences enable you to make proper decisions, ideally.

These judicial narratives show how at least some Black judges vehemently disagree with the notion that Black judges and white judges are alike. Instead, they say their presence creates a judicial system that is more conscious. Their backgrounds and life experiences are vital to their perspectives and understanding about the world; this is why and how, with their presence in the system, Black judges can change the system that has been devoid of critical Black perspectives and knowledge. Their narratives reveal that some of them are mobilized and feel responsible for going to the bench to improve the justice system and help the Black community. Black judges appear to be mobilized to make a difference, an important aspect of racial group consciousness.

This section of the chapter highlighted data from the surveys and interviews with Black judges that reveal many Black judges possess a sense of racial group consciousness. Not only do Black judges understand racism as an issue affecting the Black community, but they even note discrimination in the system in which they work (i.e., the legal system). The data show that Black judges see their fate as linked to the plight of other Black people. This linked fate feeling might be what is leading Black judges to see Black solidarity as crucial for the betterment of the group. With their responses to questions about Black leaders' social responsibility and the role Black judges can play in improving the status of Black Americans, Black judges underscore the importance of Black solidarity and how they believe Black leaders are not exempt from working for the betterment of the racial group in society. Finally, the data highlighted that Black judges value the importance of racial representation in the courts, and they see judicial diversity as necessary for equal justice and improving the system.

CONCLUSION

This chapter addressed whether Black judges possess a racial group identity and consciousness The simple answer to this question is a definite yes for many Black judges. That is, the findings in this chapter are consistent with the projects of other scholars that suggest Black judges have a racial group identity and consciousness (Smith 1983; Washington 1994). Like their predecessors and the majority of their Black counterparts who are not judges, current Black state court judges see themselves as part of the Black racial group. Moreover, many of these judges express being connected to the Black community and feeling close to their group members. While some judges' community engagement projects, such as visiting predominantly Black schools and talking to Black youth, are what connects them to Black people, other judges reveal their connections to Black America and people are primarily through their families and friends, religious practices, recreational activities, and organizational memberships. That is, despite not living in a Black community and having only a few Black judicial colleagues, they find ways to maintain a connection with Black America, people, and political and legal issues.

Many Black judges also reported possessing a sense of Black consciousness. The factors that typically signify a Black consciousness were self-reported by Black judges, both interviewed and surveyed. Like the Black masses, Black judges believe discrimination against Black Americans is widespread and ongoing and represents one of the main issues disproportionately affecting the Black community. They also expressed feeling that their fate is linked to the fate and lives of Black Americans as a group. Moreover, many of them reported being mobilized to and responsible for improving the status of Black Americans. Black judges suggested they had a sense of obligation or felt compelled to go to the bench since they possess more "informed eyes and ears" (Judge Brown). Since they "come from the minority communities," "they are aware of the problems and the differences between the two communities" (Judge Taylor). Like their Black counterparts (Dawson 1994; Tate 1994), Black judges reported being mobilized to engage in behaviors on the bench that would help bring about political and social change. When asked what Black judges could do for the justice system and the Black community, the majority of them were clear that their presence on the bench could create a more empathetic, sympathetic, just, anti-racist, and responsive justice system. In other words, Black judges hold a strong belief that they can alter the criminal justice system and the legal system more broadly, which would go a long way toward improving the social status of the group.

Now, I turn to the primary question guiding part I of the book: do Black judges possess an identity-to-politics link? This question is significant because the advocative representation theory maintains that we can expect Black judges to represent Black interests on the bench only if they possess an identity-to-politics link. We know an identity-to-politics link exists among Black Americans in the general population (Dawson 1994) and is even suspected to exist among some Black political elites (Broockman 2013). The extent to which Black judges possessed such a link was unclear at the start of this project.

The data and analysis presented in chapter 3 and this chapter provide clear and definitive evidence for a link among many Black judges. Evidence shows a link between Black judges' racial membership, background and socialization, identity consciousness, and politics. Black judges are strong identifiers with their racial group, seeing and putting themselves in community with other Black people. This way of seeing themselves was introduced and then reinforced through their childhoods and adulthoods. Moreover, many of the judges espouse a racial, political identity and articulate feeling that their fate is linked to the plight of other Black people. They deliberately make decisions that help them remain connected or close to other Black Americans. When it comes to their perceptions of the role of Black leaders like themselves (i.e., legal leaders) and political leaders, they are clear that these leaders have some social responsibility for representing Black interests and improving Black America. Many of them reveal they possess a sense of racial group consciousness. Like Black Americans in general, many Black judges perceive racial discrimination as a significant issue facing the Black community and feel compelled to consider the well-being of marginalized people such as Black people in their capacity as judges. Moreover, their racial group identity and consciousness appears to be at least partly derived from their shared racialized experiences as people of color within America's racialized society and racial socialization (see chapter 3).

The theory of advocative representation argues that understanding why Black judges might represent Black interests in their capacity necessitates knowing something about Black judges' identities and whether a link exists between their identity and politics (i.e., identity-to-politics link). The previous chapter and the present chapter make it clear that Black judges do possess an identity-to-politics link. Whether Black judges' identity-to-politics link leads to decisions as judges that are representation is the focus of the next three empirical chapters, which center on Black judges' actions and decisions on and off the bench.

PART II

Black Judges' Advocative Representation
On and Off the Bench

FIVE

BLACK JUDGES' SELF-PERCEPTIONS AND PROCEDURAL JUSTICE

I explain. I do. I do a lot of explaining when I make decisions. "Wait, do you understand what that means?" And I'll say, "I can't give you advice, but I can tell you this is what X, Y, Z means. If you have more questions, ask your attorney; they'll explain it to you." But I try to make sure that they [understand] what happened before they leave. Because that's another thing, these cases don't take that long, and they come in, a lot of people [are] nervous. They're scared. They don't know. They're like, "It's my first time, I don't know." I don't expect you to know. "What questions do you have? I'm going to tell you as plainly as possible." And I do. There are some people that speak legally. I just don't.

JUDGE INGRAM, a Black female judge from the North

Between 2009 and 2017, the Honorable Victoria Pratt, a Black woman, worked as a municipal court judge in New Jersey, spending the last three years as the chief judge.[1] In October 2016, Judge Pratt became internationally known virtually overnight after giving a Ted Talk at TEDNYC about procedural justice and fairness in the U.S. criminal legal system. Her talk titled "How Judges Can Show Respect" has now been viewed millions of times across the TED platforms and YouTube. In the talk, she describes how she engages with litigants in the courtroom, treating everyone with dignity and respect. Her approach to and justification for procedural justice are fully explained in her popular press book *The Power of Dignity: How Transforming Justice Can Heal Our Communities* (Pratt 2022). For Judge Pratt, improving people's experiences with the court system leads to improved outcomes: "When the courts behave differently, naturally people respond differently." The significance of Judge Pratt's approach to courtroom hospitality should not be overlooked.

According to journalist Tina Rosenberg, municipal courts in the U.S. operate in troubling ways.[2]

> The accused stands with his attorney in front of the bench, looking up at the judge on high. The accused is effectively invisible, a bystander to the back-and-forth between judge, prosecutor and defence attorney, who speak in jargon that ordinary people do not understand. The judge may wish the accused good morning when he is first brought in, but he will not be addressed again until the end, when the judge announces his decision and what happens next. Do you understand? Yes, the accused says, although he might well not. Do you agree? Yes.

This general description of court proceedings highlights the alienating and impersonal nature of the courts, and how the accused can be marginalized within the judicial process. In the scene, the accused becomes a passive observer of a process about their fate; the legal professionals use inaccessible technical jargon; and the accused's interaction with the judge is minimal and superficial. This scene lacks procedural justice, which emphasizes transparency and fairness with regard to how decisions are reached and whether all legal parties feel respected, heard, and treated equitably throughout the process (Tyler 2006). Procedural justice is crucial in U.S. courts because people's perceptions of legal processes impact their trust in the system, compliance with decisions, respect and perceptions of legal authorities, and willingness to engage with the system and its actors (Tyler 2006).

A system that prioritizes efficiency over fairness and symbolic participation over meaningful engagement raises concerns about equity and the accessibility of justice for individuals facing criminal charges, especially Black Americans who interact with the criminal legal system at disproportionate rates partly due to systemic biases (Baumgartner, Epp, and Shoub 2018). Black Americans' negative experiences within the courts have led to negative feelings toward the judicial system and viewing it as inherently biased. A recent survey revealed 70 percent of Black American respondents feel the courts and judicial processes are designed to hold Black people back a great deal or a fair amount.[3] Eighty-six percent of Black respondents in an earlier survey said that the courts and judicial process would have to be overhauled or completely rebuilt for Black people to be treated fairly.[4] If Black Americans experience anything similar to the municipal court scene described in Rosenberg's article, then their contempt for and negative views about the court system is understandable.

In her TedTalk, Judge Pratt suggests procedural justice is one solution to these types of court issues and the negative perceptions that they cause (Rottman et al. 2003). If this is true, which evidence suggests it is (Martinez et al. 2023), then procedural justice is a critical Black legal issue and interest. When Judge Pratt is in the Newark Municipal Court adhering to the tenets of procedural justice within her courtroom by upholding fairness, transparency, and respect in court proceedings, she is engaging in advocative representation of Black interests. Judge Pratt's advocacy for and self-reported adherence to procedural justice raises the question of whether other Black judges are similarly engaged in this form of advocative representation, or if Judge Pratt's advocacy and approach are anomalies.

The primary questions I explore in this chapter are whether and how Black judges might be representing Black interests in the courtroom. I address this overarching question by asking two secondary questions. First, do Black judges perceive themselves as representatives of Black interests within the legal system? This question helps us understand how Black judges see their work. Second, connected to Judge Pratt's work in the courtroom, are Black judges adhering to the principles of procedural justice? This question provides important information about how Black judges engage with litigants and the impact of their courtroom hospitality. I draw on the same surveys and interviews with Black judges used in prior chapters to answer these questions. In doing so, this chapter contributes to the large body of literature on judicial behavior. Note that this chapter complements the subsequent chapter because it also focuses on whether and how Black judges might represent Black interests in the courtroom, except chapter 6 focuses more on Black judges' decisions in legal cases.

JUDICIAL DECISION-MAKING

A lot of what judges do and what judges are known to do is sit on the bench and make decisions in individual cases. Popular culture, especially films and television shows, regularly depict judges performing this function, which makes sense because, arguably, the most important role for a judge is adjudication and, quite frankly, they do a lot of it. In 2018, roughly 84 million caseloads were reported by state trial courts. This number is down about 21 percent from the 106 million caseloads reported in 2008 and yet still emphasizes the vast amount of adjudication work judges are expected to handle.[5] Judges' bench-work involves them presiding over proceedings, maintaining order in the courtroom, determining what evidence is proper and legal, instructing the jury about the law, helping to determine facts and decide cases, and sentencing individuals convicted of crimes.

The argument that decision-making is one of, if not *the* most important judicial role is consistent with what Black judges say is one of their primary roles and responsibilities in the judicial system. In the survey I fielded to Black state court judges, I asked what each judge perceived their primary role to be in the judicial system. The overwhelming majority of responses centered on their deciding cases and resolving conflicts. Some descriptors used by the judges include (neutral) arbiter, gatekeeper, finder of fact, public servant, problem solver, dispenser of justice, umpire, and referee.

Because deciding cases is central to what judges do and how judges perceive their role in the legal system, scholars have long been interested in what factors influence judicial decision-making. In fact, this topic is arguably the bread and butter of judicial politics, with countless books and articles published on the topic. This research helps us to understand that judicial decision-making is complex and that what, how, and why judges decide is influenced by numerous factors.

Richardson and Vines (1970) say the varying factors fall into two categories: the democratic subculture and the legal subculture. The former is the determinants of judges' own inclinations, values, perspectives, and attitudes, such as political party affiliation, the traditions of their localities and regions (i.e., localism), and their life experiences as determined by their social identities, especially race and gender. The latter includes the law, the institutional features in which judges operate, and the norms and traditions within the legal system, such as adhering to the process of legal reasoning and established precedent. "The law schools, the bar associations, the judicial councils, and other groups that spring from the institutionalization of the 'bench and the bar'" are responsible for instilling and maintaining the legal subculture (Richardson and Vines 1970, 8–9).

BLACK JUDGES AND JUDICIAL DECISION-MAKING

Although having Black Americans in political offices does not guarantee that those political actors will make decisions that align with Black interests, an extensive body of research has shown that many Black officials do in fact represent Black Americans and their interests via their decision-making in political institutions. Black state legislators and members of Congress, for instance, often propose, sponsor, and vote for legislation that concerns topics of particular importance to Black communities (Brown 2014; Haynie 2001; Tate 2004). There is much less consensus among scholars regarding whether and how Black judges represent Black interests.

In law and courts research, scholars have largely undertaken comparative studies, assessing whether Black judges exhibit distinctive behavior as compared to white judges. Scholars typically operationalize this topic in one of two ways: Black judges vote liberally in civil cases and vote in favor of or are more lenient toward Black defendants in criminal cases. Several authors show that Black judges' decisions tend to be favorable to Black interests (Scherer 2004; Steffensmeier and Britt 2001; Welch, Combs, and Gruhl 1988). For example, Black judges are slightly less likely than white judges to send offenders, irrespective of race, to prison (Steffensmeier and Britt 2001; Welch, Combs, and Gruhl 1988). Gottschall (1986) also finds that in the U.S. Courts of Appeals, Black judges tend to vote for the accused and prisoners more than White judges, and Smith (1983) finds that Black judges are more sympathetic to defendants than White jurists are.

Black judges are also shown to behave differently in noncriminal cases. African American judges are more likely to dissent in U.S. court of appeals cases (Hettinger, Lindquist, and Martinek 2004), and they are more likely to raise questions about police misconduct in search and seizure cases (Scherer 2004). Chew and Kelley (2008) find that in racial harassment cases, Black Democratic judges rule differently than white Democratic judges. On average, plaintiffs before Black judges are 3.3 times more likely to win than when they are before white judges (Chew and Kelley 2008, 1156). Scholars also demonstrate that race of judges in U.S. courts of appeals has been found to positively influence employment discrimination claims (Crowe 1999) and sex discrimination claims (Gottschall 1983), with Black judges being more likely than their counterparts to cast a liberal vote in these types of cases. In addition, at the U.S. district court level, across a wide range of subject areas, Segal (2000) and Walker and Barrow (1985) find that a judge's race has a limited effect on decision-making. Finally, Bonneau and Rice (2009), looking at all criminal cases decided by U.S. state supreme court judges from 1995 to 1998, find evidence of differences between white and non-white judges, but only in states lacking an intermediate appellate court.

Building on the research on the effects of race and judicial decision-making, Collins and Moyer (2008) look at the effects of the intersections of race and gender in judicial decision-making in U.S. courts of appeals. According to their study, Black female judges are more likely than their colleagues on the bench to support criminal defendants, even after controlling for important factors such as judicial and educational background. This particular study, which examines the behavior of Black female judges, is rare in that it is one of the first to thoughtfully and empirically assess how race and gender intersect to affect the decision-making behavior of U.S. judges.

Although some scholars find that race affects decision-making in criminal cases and noncriminal cases, a number of other scholars find that Black judges do not exhibit distinctive behavior. In other words, some studies argue and find empirical evidence that Black judges do not provide representation in the judiciary (e.g., Uhlman 1978; Spohn 1991; Walker and Barrow 1985; Sisk, Heise, and Moriss 1998; Segal 2000). Spohn (1991) and Uhlman (1978) compared the sentencing decisions of Black and white state judges and found that both groups of judges sentence Black offenders more severely than white offenders. The race of judges in the U.S. courts of appeals has been found to have little effect on race discrimination cases (Gottschall 1983) and unfair-labor cases (Merritt and Brudney 2001). In studying the effect of race on U.S. district court judges, Sisk, Heise, and Morriss (1998) find that race did not affect decisions about whether the U.S. Sentencing Guidelines were unconstitutional when they were initially adopted in 1988. Finally, Ashenfelter, Eisenberg, and

Schwab (1995) did not find any differences with respect to a judge's race in federal district court civil rights case.

When considered collectively, the large body of scholarship on the behavior of Black judges is inconclusive as to whether Black judges behave from the bench in ways that align with Black interests. While some studies show that Black judges represent Black interests from the bench, other studies find no evidence of representational behaviors. This incongruity appears to be driven by what particular issues are being focused on and the level of court that is making the decision.

In this chapter and the subsequent one, I seek to contribute to the extant research on judicial behavior. My approach to examining whether Black judges represent Black interests differs from the existing research on the topic in a number of notable ways. First, many existing studies that are aimed at understanding the behavior of Black state court judges examine the jurists' votes in cases or the sentences they hand down. In other words, the previous literature focuses disproportionately on final case decisions. This chapter and the subsequent one, however, rely on judges' own reflections, words, and explanations to assess the degree to which Black judges can be viewed as representing Black Americans. In so doing, I offer an additional means for how scholars might consider representation in the context of judicial decision-making and behavior from the bench.

Interviews with and surveys of Black state court judges allow me to capture broader and more nuanced manifestations of representation as compared to the outcomes that are typically used to address this topic. By allowing judges to share the details of their behavior on the bench, as well as what they perceive are the benefits of having them and other Black judges in state judicial systems, we can see that beyond final case votes, Black judges are representing and can represent Black interests in various ways from the bench. The surveys and interviews discussed in detail below and in the subsequent chapter highlight how Black judges represent Black Americans through their interactions with individuals involved in the legal system and treatment and understanding of Black litigants and their cases.

This study also differs from existing studies because most of the previous scholarship on the topic of Black state court judges' behavior takes a purely quantitative analytical approach. This approach allows scholars to quantify the behavior of judges and to make broad generalizations and predictions based on a sample. Here, I use a mixed-method approach that reveals patterns in the thoughts and behaviors of Black judges, who, as a group, have for the most part been understudied or overlooked by court scholars.

Finally, scholars have rarely, if ever, asked Black judges to self-report whether they represent Black interests. This study asks Black judges explicitly about their self-perceptions of their judicial behavior. Their responses will provide valuable insight into how Black judges view their own behavior and whether they see themselves as representing Black interests. Black judges often serve in systems historically shaped by structural inequities, and their perspectives can shed light on whether they believe their approach to justice represents Black interests. This inquiry will also help to contextualize their judicial behavior and inform broader discussions about Black judges' work in the courtroom.

In the following section, I briefly discuss procedural justice in U.S. courts before turning to the expectations I have for whether Black judges are likely to perceive their behavior as representative of Black interests, and whether Black jurists are likely to adhere to the principles of procedural justice.

PROCEDURAL JUSTICE IN U.S. COURTS

Procedural justice or fairness, or the process by which actors in positions of authority arrive at outcomes and make decisions, is fundamental to the legal system (Thibaut and Walker 1975). Perceptions of procedural justice shape how members of the public behave and how they view the legitimacy of the courts (Tyler 2006). Some existing scholarship notes that people are equally or, in some cases, *more* concerned about how they are treated than they are about receiving an outcome favorable to their position (Tyler 2007). "The procedural justice argument is that, on the general level, the key concerns that people have about the police and the courts center around whether these authorities treat people fairly, recognize citizen rights, treat people with dignity, and care about people's concerns" (Tyler 2001, 216).

In the court system, procedural fairness refers to whether litigants, especially criminal defendants, have an opportunity to express their point of view and voice their questions, concerns, and perspectives in court, and whether litigants are treated with deserved respect and dignity in the courtroom by all legal actors that litigants interact with, including attorneys and judges. Other components of procedural justice include helping litigants understand their rights and expectations, court procedures, and judicial decisions and whether judges are behaving professionally. When individuals evaluate the court, they are particularly attentive to procedural justice concerns, especially individuals with court experience (Rottman et al. 2003, 16).

For Black Americans, procedural justice is a significant concern, with many Black Americans expressing their perception of widespread interpersonal disrespect by legal actors such as lawyers and judges (Rottman et al. 2003). There is evidence that Black Americans are particularly concerned with issues of respect and trust and treatment of individuals within the courtroom and legal system generally (Tyler 2001, 232). In their survey, Rottman, Hansen, Mott, and Grimes (2003) find that "the lack of trust in the courts among African-American respondents is striking. The majority of recent African American litigants disagreed with the two statements that relate to trustworthiness (courts take needs into account and courts are sensitive to concern)" (39–40). And not only do they find that Black American respondents were less likely to agree with statements concerning respect (i.e., that people are treated with respect and that courts treat people politely), they also learned that Black Americans, "particularly those with recent court experience, are less positive in their rating of whether courts do or do not allow meaningful participation" (Rottman et al. 2003, 37–39). Thus, Black Americans are interested in procedural justice. However, it is unclear whether Black judges (beyond Judge Pratt) adhere to the principles of procedural justice in their courtrooms.

EXPECTATIONS ABOUT BLACK JUDGES' SELF-PERCEPTIONS OF REPRESENTATION AND ADHERENCE TO THE PRINCIPLES OF PROCEDURAL JUSTICE

Advocative representation, the theoretical framework I articulated and fully delineated in chapter 2, indicates that we can and should expect Black judges to represent Black interests despite not being charged with or accountable for performing a representative function in the courts for Black people and interests. This expectation is grounded in the belief that Black judges' behavior on the bench may be a function of their racial group membership (i.e., the extent to which they identify as belonging to the racial group and have similar experiences and socialization as Black Americans), racial group identity (i.e., the extent to which they feel connected with other African Americans and the Black community), and racial group consciousness (i.e., whether they are politicized by beliefs about Black Americans' social standing, as well as a view that they, in their role as judges, can help realize Black Americans' interests even or perhaps especially from the bench). The theory maintains that Black judges possessing an identity-to-politics link, such as the link found among Black Americans in the general population, would mean that we can and should anticipate some representative behavior. Thus, an identity-to-politics link becomes an identity-to-representation link among Black state court judges, whereby their socialization, experiences, individual and group identities, and politics influence their judicial work.

Part I of this book demonstrated that many Black judges do indeed possess an identity-to-politics link. Chapter 3 revealed that Black judges' experienced a great deal of anti-Black discrimination as children and adults and have often been racially and politically socialized by their families and communities. Black judges, therefore, have salient life experiences and socialization that resonate among the group and with other Black people. These are the exact preconditions needed for the development of strong Black individual and group identities and a strong Black consciousness.

Chapter 4, picked up where chapter 3 left off by highlighting the implication of their socialization and life experiences. Black judges noted very openly that they possess a race-related identity and group consciousness. The chapter stressed the awareness Black judges had of being Black and their possession of a deep connection and psychological attachment to other Black people. Black jurists reported being fully aware of the social status of the racial group, the many challenges faced by the group within and beyond the legal system, and the significant role Black people, especially Black officials like Black jurists, can and should play to improve the group's status. Taken together, chapters 3 and 4 help illuminate the fact that many Black state court judges possess an identity-to-politics link, which I argue and reason is likely to influence their perspectives and behavior and lead them to engage in decision-making that aligns with and addresses Black interests and legal concerns.

As I have mentioned in this chapter, scholars have largely focused their attention almost myopically on modeling judges' final decisions in cases using quantitative data. While case outcomes represent one critical way to assess whether and how Black judges represent Black interests, being in communication with judges reveals the value of broadening our scholarly thinking and imagination about what representation might look like in the courtroom. I reason that two steps need to be taken in order to achieve this fundamental broadening.

DATA AND METHODS USED IN CHAPTERS 5 AND 6

Responses presented in this chapter and chapter 6 are the judges' replies to the following open-ended questions that were asked verbatim to each interviewee or printed in the survey: Can the presence of Black judges do anything for the justice system? Can the presence of Black judges do anything for the Black community? What do you see as the role of judges in the overall justice system? What factors do you think affect your judicial decision-making? Do you feel that the race and gender of a judge matters for the types of decisions that are made? If not addressed, do you feel your race and gender affect your behavior on the bench? If so, how? To what extent should a judge (you) consider political, economic, and social consequences of decisions?

The decision to analyze responses to open-ended questions does not come without challenges. On the one hand, these questions yield responses that are exciting and dynamic. The format enabled judges to speak to whatever they wanted to share and in whatever way they wanted to share that information. This freedom meant that I was exposed to several topics that I would not have asked judges about. But on the other hand, the open-ended nature of the questions means the responses, while detailed and animated, were not always consistent among the judges with regard to what they specifically disclosed or divulged. I do not read anything into judges not responding in ways that I envisioned they would because I recognize that one reason they may not mention something is that it essentially does not apply to them. But I also know that they may not mention a particular topic or express a particular viewpoint because they do not feel comfortable admitting it.

To this latter point, I am acutely aware that judges are hesitant to participate in studies about politics and judicial behavior. They have been intentionally socialized to avoid responding to certain types of questions and engaging in certain conversations, especially about political topics, in order to maintain the perception that judicial decision-making is not a political endeavor. My understanding about the ways judges would likely interact with me and this project and what they might share and how they might respond to questions compelled me to take a very cautious and deferential approach in the surveys and interviews, especially when it came to asking them about their judicial behavior. For many judges, there was a strong desire to participate in the study, and this is evidenced by the number of emails that I received thanking me for doing this work. Still, many of the judicial respondents also conveyed having a strong commitment to maintaining the appearance of propriety. Accordingly, I asked open-ended questions that allowed them to dictate what and how much they shared about their judicial work. This approach facilitates my centering their perspectives, voices, and self-reports about their judicial work and decentering my expectations about how they might behave based on the existing research in the field on Black judges and judicial behavior.

Despite the idiosyncrasies of the data, a careful analysis of the qualitative survey and interview responses facilitated the identification of several patterns and threads. These findings are presented in the sections below and chapter 6. I present only patterns and threads that are mentioned by at least 10 percent of the survey or interview respondents. The data highlight judicial work that is conventional (i.e., final decisions in cases) and in line with what scholars already focus on in their work on the topic. At the same time, the data reveal judicial activities and behaviors that are less frequently discussed and studied by court scholars (such as decisions in pretrial processes and procedural justice) and yet are significant for understanding how Black judges might represent Black interests.

Black judges' responses, testimonies, and narratives reveal ways their presence on the bench matters for how Black litigants are treated and understood in the legal system. Through their decision-making in pretrial proceedings and procedural and distributive justice–related behaviors and activities, many Black jurists demonstrate that Black judges' behaviors can align with Black legal and judicial interests. Irrespective of whether they perceive themselves as representatives of Black interests, a topic I take up in the ensuing section, their self-reported actions highlight the myriad ways that many of them do in fact represent Black interests.

SELF-PERCEPTIONS OF REPRESENTATION AND
COURTROOM DECISION-MAKING

Prior to discussing Black judges' adherence to procedural justice, I want to shed some light on how Black judges perceive themselves and their behavior. Six of the thirty-two judges interviewed noted that they did not feel race informed or influenced their decision-making. For instance, Judge King, a Black female judge from the South, was quite adamant that her race is not a significant factor influencing her behavior, and she connected that directly with her understanding of impartiality: "We take an oath to be impartial and surely I am." Four judges interviewed emphasized that they did not behave any differently than their white counterparts and that the importance of racial diversity lies only in the perception of increased fairness and justice for Black Americans and not actual increased fairness and justice with Black judges on the bench. These four judges were clear that they feel white judges and Black judges provide the same level of fairness and justice in the judiciary by making the same decisions generally and that there is a misperception that Black judges are somehow distinct or different from their white counterparts. One judge, for instance, said he "knew" race does not play a role in decision-making, and the only factors that matter are the law, the facts, and the eventual decision (Judge Jones, a Black male judge from the Midwest). Although they represent only one-fifth of the judges surveyed and interviewed for this project, a considerable number of Black judges do not see themselves as representatives, do not feel responsible for representing Black interests, and do not see their race as influencing their decision-making.

Yet, most judges surveyed and interviewed reported feeling a sense of responsibility for protecting and representing Black interests (see chapter 4). They also indicated that they felt their behaviors complemented and corresponded with their feelings of responsibility. In the surveys, I asked, "To what extent do you exercise your judicial powers in ways that protect and represent the interests of Black people?" Respondents answered using a five-point scale: 0 never, 1 rarely, 2 some of the time, 3 most of the time, and 4 all of the time. The majority of respondents (69 percent) said they exercise their judicial powers at least some of the time in ways that protect and represent Black interests, with 24 percent saying "most of the time" and 11 percent saying "all of the time." When asked how responsible they feel toward representing Black interests, the majority of respondents (68 percent) said they feel at least moderately responsible, with 29 percent saying "very responsible" and 12 percent saying "extremely responsible." Their perception of their behavior, thus, reflects the perception they have about their personal responsibility for protecting and representing Black interests as a judge.

I also asked, "To what extent do you think your race informs your decision-making?" Respondents answered using a five-point scale: 0 not at all, 1 slightly, 2 moderately, 3 very, and 4 extremely. Among survey respondents, 28 percent reported that race slightly informed their decision-making, 30 percent said race moderately informed it, 16 percent said race very much informed it, and 5 percent reported that race extremely informed their decisions on the bench. Therefore, although 22 percent said race did not affect their decision-making at all, 78 percent indicated race, to some degree, informed their decision-making in judicial cases. These trends found among the judges surveyed reflect the pattern that emerged in the interview data. Twenty-four of the thirty-two judges interviewed indicated either explicitly or implicitly that race matters in judging and that Black judges represent Black interests. That is, three-quarters (75 percent) of the judges interviewed in this study said their race plays a role in how they behave on the bench.

Twenty-four of the thirty-two Black judges described race as generally influencing their behavior on the bench. They made blanket statements and spoke in the abstract about how being Black was important to who they were as judges. Some of these judges acknowledged that a certain level of discretion goes along with judging and that race is one factor that is pertinent in those moments when judges have a choice on how to proceed in a particular case. Other judges discussed race as an important factor in determining the relevant facts and aspects of a case. What is clear from these judges is that, when all things are considered, race is central to who they are and what they do on the bench. And yet other judges simply said that they, as Black Americans with the experiences they have had in their lives, are different from their white counterparts simply because of who they are. For example, Judge Thompson, a Black male judge from the West, described being able to see things that are "gray" and not just Black and white due to his experiences as a Black man in America. In his statement, he insinuates that white judges' backgrounds are too conventional or, as he puts it, too "squeaky clean," and this hinders them from recognizing the level of complexity that exists in the world around them, especially the complexity intrinsic in the lives and experiences of the individuals who are disproportionately present in court as criminal defendants, Black Americans. Judge Hall, a Black female judge from the South, also spoke casually about her race, among other things, influencing her behavior: "Yeah, race, the law, bias [*laughter*], gender bias and racial bias, I see it all the time and I like to at least be aware of it . . . my personal experiences, my mood, how I feel, is it a happy day or less-good day—that's about all."

Also speaking about race influencing judicial decision-making, Judge Adams said, "Even though we are all working with the same sentencing guidelines, there is a wide range of things you can do even within those guidelines, and I do think that our background, our experiences, our race, our gender, all of that, plays into how we handle those things in the courtroom." Along the same lines, Judge Taylor, a Black male judge from the South, talked about race mattering: "Race? Yes, and other things. People's background. . . . For many years, Blacks and whites in many places have been separate and have had different experiences. You bring those experiences to the court when you come." According to Judge Taylor and others, you do not leave your experiences, regardless of whether you are Black or white, at the courthouse door, steps, or lawn. When judges enter the courthouse and courtroom, they bring with them all the experiences of their life and essentially what makes them who they are, and that includes race, background, and identities.

Judge Johnson, a Black female judge from the Midwest, also shared how she felt race matters generally to her judicial decision-making:

> Well, all of us are affected to some degree about the facts and the circumstances that make up who we are—that is, the way in which we see the world. Now having said that, you know the only thing that's supposed to be involved in the decision-making process is the facts of a particular case and the law that applies to those facts. Now, when you come to determining what the facts are, it is who you are and that is true with respect to any fact finder. I mean, in jury cases, you tell people they are entitled to rely upon their own daily experiences in determining what the facts are, and judges are no different. I take into consideration my whole set of lifelong experiences in terms of how I look at the world.

Finally, Judge Hill, a Black female judge from the South, also implies that her race matters: "Race and gender plays a part in who you are and what you do, but I also think it plays a part in how you interpret things. So, that's our job: to interpret things."

These Black judges' accounts of how their race influences their decision-making underscore the long-held belief that judges are influenced by nonlegal factors such as their identities. More specific to them though, their statements reveal that being Black and their experiences growing up and living as Black Americans in the U.S. play a part in how they interpret and determine what the facts are in a case, how they handle discretion, and the extent to which they are able to understand complex issues.

These judges were candid in describing their behavior and in explaining how their behavior was influenced by their race. These judges are clear that they see the world and cases not simply as judges, but as *Black* judges. For them, you cannot separate being an African American from being a judge. Being Black is fundamental to their life, their perspective, and how they view the world. Consequently, being Black is also fundamental to their work and how they judge.

But what do these general, abstract statements about Black judges' behavior actually mean? More specifically, how does race influence these judges' courtroom hospitality and behaviors in legal cases? To understand the specifics of Black judges' behaviors in the surveys and interviews, I asked participants to share the actions they engage in when on the bench. I asked them to reflect on and share interactions they have had in the courtroom and the factors that influenced their decisions. In their responses, many of the judges identified and described specific behaviors and interactions that, I submit, when considered alongside Black interests, are evidence that Black judges function as representatives of Black group interests. In other words, Black judges provide advocative representation of Black interests from the bench. In the subsequent section, I detail Black judges' courtroom hospitality. In the subsequent chapter, I will focus on Black judges' behaviors and actions in legal cases.

BLACK JUDGES AND PROCEDURAL JUSTICE IN AMERICAN COURTS

Surveys and interviews with Black judges underscore the extent to which Black judges represent Black interests via behaviors related to procedural justice. Responding to a survey question, Black judges reported that they view the ability to listen, compassion, empathy, honesty, humility, and patience as some of the main characteristics and qualities that judges should possess. These qualities seem to be directly related to judges' ability to adhere to the principles of procedural justice. I presume that these are the precise qualities and characteristics that many of them possess or aspire to possess. The interviews and surveys provide evidence that Black judges' behaviors on the bench align with the tenets of procedural justice as well as the legal interests of Black Americans.

Respecting Litigants

Several judges interviewed mentioned the significance of respect for their judicial role. To this point, Judge Adams simply said, "You need to show, to make sure that everyone is treated respectfully—not just fairly, but respectfully. And sometimes that's hard because people will try you." Despite it being difficult sometimes, as this judge suggests, she maintains that everyone should be treated with respect. Four of the thirty-two Black judges interviewed explicitly communicated that they tend to treat all litigants with respect, even those who have been found guilty of committing a crime. For example, they talked about using titles such as "Miss" and "Mister" when they refer to litigants. Some of them also mentioned that they offer elderly litigants the option to sit rather than stand for prolonged periods. Two judges, one from the Midwest and one from the South, shared two specific examples that illustrate the respect Black judges give to the litigants who come before them.

In a major city in the Midwest, where many individuals utilize the train to get around the city, Judge Smith talked about his white colleagues being afraid to ride public transportation, because they, unlike him, rarely showed respect to litigants and were afraid of running into any offended or disgruntled litigants.

> I treat other people the way I'd like to be treated. That is, everybody's the same. We're going to listen to everything and we're going to make a decision. And you see, this is how this really ends up at the end of the day. Some of my colleagues on the court are afraid to ride public transportation. I'm not. Because I respect people when they come into the court. I let them have their day in court and then when we leave, I think they will say, "Well, I got my day in court. He didn't agree with me." But you see, a lot of times those people know they were not supposed to win. So, if you're fair and people will say, "I couldn't ask for anything more."

Similarly, Judge Wilson, a Black male judge from the South, talked about not receiving threats while he was a judge because he, like some of his counterparts, was always respectful. "When I was on the bench, I never had a threat made to me even though I put hundreds of people in jail and I sentenced one man to death." Judge Wilson's quote demonstrates that, regardless of the gravity of a decision, treating everyone with humanity (i.e., respect) can diffuse hostility and avert animosity.

Judge Allen, a Black female judge from the West, shared how she makes a point to be respectful toward all litigants and how that often is surprising to other legal actors in the courtroom, who seem to implicitly think there are some individuals less deserving of respect.

> It probably happens more often in communities where there are not that many of us, and they come into the courtroom, be they Latino, be they African American, be they African, be they whatever, and they see a person of color. The expectation is that you are going to understand. You may not agree with what they do, but that you are going to be more patient, you are going to be more tolerant—and I think it's a well-deserved expectation, quite frankly. I think when you are living in a community like we live in, where there are so few of us that have been given access, we have a greater obligation. And you know, that's just my personal belief. And so no, I'm not, as many have said, I'm not biased in favor of Black people, but I do believe that people of color are going to be treated fairly, and I think that the shock and the awe of that and the response I've gotten from mainstream community—particularly mainstream law community, the DA in particular—has been because they've never seen that before. They don't know what that looks like. So, they have a lot of underexposure themselves, because they've never been around Black folks. . . . And so, they feel very challenged or threatened any time somebody's actually calling these people by their first or last name or giving them the regard of Mr. or Mrs., and I'm, you know, very cognizant of that. Or you know, asking an elderly person, "Are you okay? Would you prefer to sit rather than stand?" Just, you know, common courtesies that they're not accustomed to seeing extended to people of color.

Judge Allen acknowledges the procedural justice principle of respect. For her, this is rooted in common courtesies and accommodations, which are often denied to people in the criminal justice system. The small yet profound gestures of respect disrupt patterns of dehumanization and communicate dignity to litigants.

Judge Wood, a male judge from the South, mentioned during his interview that respect is an essential part of a judge's job:

> I have seen judges make statements like "I hope that you spend the rest of your life in jail and that you never see the light." I don't think a judge needs to do that. I think that you don't need to do that in order to do your job. I have never said anything to anybody that I would not want said to me. Now when I say that, I'll challenge anybody to go back and check any record of any proceeding that I was involved in the twenty years I was on the bench, to find something where I said something derogatory to somebody. If I said it to them, I would not mind someone saying it to me. That to me is how simple the job is.

Here, Judge Wood highlights his philosophy of reciprocal respect and restraint. He challenges the idea that you should or can use derogatory or dehumanizing language to a criminal defendant. There is a commitment to treating others as he wants to be treated, and he demonstrates that justice can be administered firmly yet respectfully.

Similarly, Judge Johnson, a Black female judge from the Midwest, discussed how respect is central to being a good judge:

> Obviously, they have to be knowledgeable about the law. They have to have good people skills. They need to understand what it means to be respectful. We're very powerful people when we put the robe on, and so that power should not be wielded in an arbitrary kind of way or discriminatorily. You can't rule in a fashion that discriminates against people. You cannot be nasty, irritating, or insulting. And there's a lot of people that think Judge Judy is, you know, "Judge Judy is where it's at." She's not. That persona that she plays on TV, that is the antithesis of everything that judges are supposed to be.

This quote underscores that respect is a cornerstone of being a good judge. Judge Johnson rejects the idea that the combative and insulting judges presented in sensationalized court dramas are acceptable. Instead, true respect involves professionalism and the cautious exercise of judicial authority.

Finally, Judge Baker, a Black female judge from the South, discussed respecting individuals who appear in the courthouse and requiring her court staff to respect individuals who appear either in her courtroom or in her chambers: "I have respect for people who appear on my docket. I have both criminal and civil cases and I treat everyone with the utmost respect, even individuals who have been arrested and charged with a crime and have not been found guilty. They are entitled to due process and they should receive the same respect as anyone else who comes before this court." This quote highlights the judge's commitment to treating all individuals with equal respect and dignity, regardless of their legal troubles and circumstances. Treating everyone—whether involved in criminal or civil cases—with respect ensures that the courtroom remains a place of justice rather than judgment.

Black judges reported showing respect to litigants in the courtroom. In fact, Judge Brown says that respect is the basis upon which he does everything: "Everything I try to do is about respect. That's why you see the signage out there."[6] Black judges reported that whether or not someone has been found guilty of a crime, Black judges still show respect to litigants. To some judges showing respect for others is a central part of judging.

To some others, showing respect to defendants and attorneys is consistent with their desire to treat others like they want to be treated. This is highlighted in the following two stories shared by Judge Smith, a Black male judge from the Midwest, who explained that experiencing disrespect in the courtroom from white judges on the bench when he was an attorney motivated him to become a judge and influences how he behaves in his own courtroom now.

> I said to you that one of the reasons I became a judge was because of some experiences that I've had. One experience that I can tell you about is trying a case not in [this] county [A] but in [a different] county [B]. It was a motion to suppress. My client was charged with possessing some marijuana—the problem was he was also a suspect in some robberies that had occurred in [city A] [state], which is 200 miles south of [county B]. The officers in [city A] did not have pictures of my client, so they traveled from [county A] to [county B's] police station and said, "Do you have any pictures of the suspect?" The officer that they talked with said, "No, but we know where he lives." They went out to my client's house and arrested him. Then, got him up at 8 in the morning and told him to come down, searched him, and said they found marijuana, charged him with possession

of marijuana, took him to the police station, and fingerprinted him and photographed him. Well, the [county A] officers then took the fingerprints and the photographs back to [county A] and then they charged my guy with robbery in [county A].

But here was the experience that I had. I went to court. I filed the motion to suppress. I have the police officer from [county B] who went to the house . . . I have the officer on the witness stand. After asking the officer his name and his rank and how long he had been a police officer, I then said, "On whatever the date was, did you have an arrest for Mr. [defendant's name]? Did you have an arrest warrant for Mr. [defendant's name] arrest?"

The officer didn't say anything.

I said, "Judge, would you instruct the witness to answer the question."

The judge didn't say anything.

I said, "Officer, did you have a search warrant for Mr. [defendant's name] residence?"

The officer didn't say anything.

I said, "Judge, would you instruct the witness to answer the question."

The judge didn't say anything.

Well, long and the short of it is, at the end of it, the state's attorney got up and asked some questions, and then I said, "Okay Judge, I'm ready to argue."

The judge said, to his credit, "Mr. [respondent's name], that's unnecessary. Motion to suppress granted."

So, I won, but you see what I disliked was the disrespect and the refusal of the judge to instruct the officer to answer my question. Well, you see he didn't have a warrant, an arrest warrant, or a search warrant. I was troubled. See, that was something that I would never permit to occur. I'm going to treat everybody with courtesy and respect. If you're a witness on the stand whether Black or white, you have to answer the question. He could've said "I don't know" or whatever, but he's got to answer the question, okay? I have never forgotten that.

Another thing that occurred that I never forgot was I was trying a case and it was late in the afternoon and the judge said to me around 4:30, "Mr. [Black judge's name], will you hurry up and conclude your examination of this witness. I have to go someplace."

I said, "Okay, fine." So I continued to question the witness.

And at a quarter to five, he said, "Mr. [Black judge's name], I told you, I gotta go someplace. Will you hurry up."

I said, "Judge, you can't rush justice." I said, "If you are in a hurry, maybe we need to continue this case until tomorrow."

Now, what am I saying? When you're in court, you're not supposed to be rushed. It's supposed to be a deliberative process. There are certain people he would not have rushed, but he didn't have any problems rushing me. Now, how has that forced me to change? . . . I feel that if a litigant is going to get all the process they're due, they can argue as long as they want, as long as they're not repeating themselves. . . . I do not tell people they're taking too much of my time. I mean if you're that busy, you should be doing something else. See, that's the kind of effect those experiences have had on me.

This judge's experiences as a lawyer highlight the type of disrespect he experienced in court at the hands of judges and even witnesses. Respecting everyone in the courtroom, including attorneys, is what many Black judges say is indispensable in a court of law. This also includes giving litigants the amount of time they need to say what they need to say. One Black male judge from the Midwest noted that all judges should aim and work "to be respectful of everybody who comes before you. That includes lawyers, of course, but also litigants. Respect for other people. And listen to them. I mean really listen before you make up your mind in terms of what you're going to do." This abundance of respect is significant for procedural justice and also for Black Americans, who indicate they are attentive to the type of respect afforded to Black Americans, especially Black litigants, in the courtroom.

Listening to Litigants

Meaningful participation is an important topic that relates to the quality of treatment in the legal system. Litigants being able to participate means they have an opportunity to express their views to judges and other legal actors. The judge engages with them. When litigants are not given an opportunity to speak in court, their perspectives are suppressed and therefore overlooked, especially if attorneys are not intentionally voicing the perspectives of their clients.

In Rottman, Hansen, Grimes, and Mott's (2003) study, Black respondents were asked whether they agreed or disagreed that courts listen carefully to what people have to say. The researchers found that "African Americans, and particularly those with recent court experience, are less positive in their rating of whether courts do or do not allow meaningful participation" (39). In their study, almost four in ten Black respondents without court experience as well as 51 percent of Black respondents with court experience said they somewhat or strongly disagreed with the idea that courts listen carefully to what people have to say (39). Based on these findings, it is clear that judges should engage with litigants in the courtroom in addition to attorneys so that courts practice listening to litigants and provide litigants with opportunities to meaningfully engage and participate in the legal process.

Black judges who were interviewed mentioned listening to litigants in the courtroom. Not only did Black judges mention listening as an important role judges are charged with, but they also shared how they engage with litigants in the courtroom and how that engagement is a fundamental part of their behavior on the bench and their ability to reach informed decisions.

According to Judge Smith, a Black male judge from the Midwest, litigants routinely complain that they are unable to fully participate in the legal process when they are not given an opportunity to speak. He addresses this issue in his courtroom by making sure litigants know he will always make time for them to speak.

> I think the outcome matters, but you see it's process. That's the real complaint I always hear: "Well, he didn't hear what I had to say. He didn't give me enough time." They're never going to say that when I'm running the show. "I got a chance to make my argument. I could not convince him." So, if people see me on the street, they'll say, "Well, he didn't agree with me, but he was respectful, and he heard what I had to say." I don't think that you could ask any more of a judge.

Similarly, Judge Taylor, a Black male judge from the South, mentioned that in addition to showing respect to everybody who comes to court, including litigants and lawyers, he and other judges must also prioritize listening: "And listen to them. I mean really listen before you make up your mind in terms of what you're going to do." Here, the judge talks about active listening, but more importantly, maintaining an open mind with listening to avoid impulsive decisions.

Judge Johnson, a Black female judge from the Midwest, mentioned how she perceived Black Americans feel when they appear in Black judges' courtrooms: that they will have an opportunity to speak and be listened to.

When they appear before African Americans? Oh, then they, I believe, they tend to feel like you know at least, at a minimum they're going to get the opportunity to be heard. And I think that sometimes, even when you wind up ruling against people, if they feel they got a fair trial, they got a fair shake, it's easier to accept that the verdict did not go your way.

Another Black female judge, Judge White from the Midwest, who works on a specialized court, discussed how litigants in her courtroom are able to develop a professional relationship with her because she fosters an environment that emphasizes open communication between her (i.e., the judge) and litigants. According to Judge White, the development of a relationship with litigants helps them with accountability and helps them to know they are cared for.

Right, when you're in drug court with me, it's an intensive program, and so when you first get in, you see me every two weeks. I get an update. I talk to you. I learn your name. I come down off the bench. I do nontraditional things. I hug. I clap. We give them gift cards. We sanction them also. If they test positive, I might give them a verbal warning, or if they do it again, they might have to be reassessed or they have to drop down a phase. They might have to do community work service. I've had people write their own obituaries, and so you have to be creative with them. But they see me regularly, and I talk to them and I know them by name. And now I see some of them in the streets and I call their name and they go, "[*Gasp.*] Oh, Judge!" And so, making it more personable to them, they do so much better.

This one young lady, she went [missing]. and I knew where she hung out and I went down the street looking for her. So when she finally got caught, I told her, "I know you hang out on [street name] and [street name]. I saw you standing outside that store one day. I came looking for you."

And she was like, "[*Gasp.*] You came looking for me? [*Gasp.*] You was looking for me?"

She's been clean ever since, and she told me yesterday, "Because you had faith in me, more faith than I had in myself, I want to stay clean."

So, you have to do some untraditional things when you're working with this population—a lot of heroin, marijuana, PCP, but they know I care.

This quote emphasizes the value of active listening in court proceedings, particularly in a drug court setting. Judge White's approach goes beyond formal judicial interactions and superficial engagement. Instead, she opts for direct communication. All of this helps her establish a nice rapport with litigants. The personal connection between judge and litigant reinforces participants' sense of value and agency. But this would not be possible without deep, empathetic, active listening, which extends beyond words to understanding and addressing the deeper challenges faced by justice-impacted individuals.

Judge Hall, a Black female judge from the South, shared that she, too, gives litigants an opportunity to speak in her courtroom and that reflects how much she cares about the community.

I have conversations with people who come before me, and I think they realize I'm not in there to be their friend and I'm not in there to give them a break, to give them a free pass, but I am in there because I care about the community. And I think when people see that, when people see that they're respected and that they're being heard, and especially if they know that they've done wrong, which I think a high percentage of the folks who come before me—they know they did wrong, they know they're there for a reason. I think it's a little bit breath of fresh air for them. You've got some who come "fuck the system" and that is what it is, but I think for the most part, they are relieved to see a member of their community who actually cares about what's going on and who is willing to listen.

Like this Black female judge who believes that allowing litigants to speak reflects the kind of care she has for the community and her work, Judge Ingram, a Black female judge from the North, remarked that she allows people to speak because it allows her to center litigants' perspectives instead of her own and show that she is interested in and cares about what they have to say.

A lot of judges like to hear themselves talk, if that makes sense. They want to sound important or feel important and it's like, you're missing there's a reason that the people are in front of you. And a lot of times, at least here it's a little different 'cause you get a lot of litigants who are not represented, whereas in Supreme Court, you're dealing with attorneys mostly. So, it's a little different. But even in there, the judges can be annoying. That's just based on my experience as a lawyer. But just the ability to listen. Some people just have a story they want, or it doesn't even have to be a story, it's just whatever it is that they want to get out. They need to get it out and then you can go from there. I think that's one of the biggest things: to just be able to listen, even if you don't understand. Just let the person have a minute to get it out, because if not, they're more frustrated, they're more angry, they're less cooperative.

Yet another example related to respect is from Judge Wilson, a Black male judge from the South, who discussed how the respect he showed to others paid off. For him and some other judges, there was a clear belief in the idea of respect begets respect.

The ideal judge is one . . . who is respectful to people no matter who they are because respect begets respect. You know if you respect other people, they'll respect you. When I was on the bench, I never had a threat made to me. Even though I put hundreds of people in jail and I sentenced one man to death, but he never got—he's still living, this is almost twenty years ago.

By engaging directly with litigants, Black judges can demonstrate that the courts can listen to their concerns. Engagement and communication between judges and litigants are significant for procedural justice, and based on Rottman, Hansen, Grimes, and Mott's (2003) research, they are also significant for Black Americans, who indicate they are attentive to whether litigants have opportunities to meaningfully participate in the legal process as it plays out in the courtroom.

Understanding Black Litigants' Speech and Rhetoric

Black middle-class and working-class Americans regularly use African American Vernacular English (AAVE) or African American English (AAE).[7] AAVE/AAE has unique vocabulary, grammar, and accent features, and the phonological characteristics of AAVE/AAE are deeply influenced by historical and persisting social segregation (Fasold 1972; Labov 1972, 118).[8] Sociolinguists who study the speech patterns of individuals in the legal system highlight how understanding individuals who speak using AAVE/AAE is challenging for people who did not grow up hearing the vernacular (Jones et al. 2019). Misunderstanding is not necessarily deliberate and is instead a predictable consequence of poor translation and language resonance.

Literal interpretation problems, even the ability to understand references as sensical, create challenges for the administration of justice. In other words, an inability to understand the rhetoric and speech of individuals in the courtroom speaking AAVE/AAE, especially litigants and witnesses, can have considerable legal repercussions and be detrimental to justice ultimately being served (Baugh 2018; Jones et al. 2019). Witnesses and litigants using AAVE/AAE while testifying, for instance, are often deemed not credible by non-AAVE/AAE speakers. Thus, one concern is whether individuals can participate meaningfully in the process, and another concern is whether their participation will be interpreted and understood in the way it was intended to be.

Transcription errors due to court reporters misunderstanding AAVE/AAE when it is spoken are significant for accuracy of court records and fairness within the legal system (Kurinec and Weaver 2019). Temple University law professor Jules Epstein raises an important question concerning other legal actors: "Are the judges and the jurors and the lawyers misapprehending what people are saying?"[9] For Epstein, being understood is fundamentally connected to litigants' right to have meaningful access to the courts.

Black judges note that the use of AAVE/AAE is not a significant challenge in their courtrooms. Many Black judges who were interviewed communicated that, unlike many of their courthouse colleagues, they are able to understand the language patterns among many Black courtroom actors, including litigants and witnesses. Black judges indicate their understanding of AAVE/AAE is an asset and helps them to understand Black litigants, which ultimately helps them render better, more-informed decisions and provide meaningful access to the courts for individuals using AAVE/AAE.

Judge Martin, a Black male judge from the South, talked about being able to relate to Black litigants in ways that he perceived his white colleagues could not.

Same [white male] judge, where there I was again seeking enforcement of the obligation and the person hadn't done what he was supposed to do, but before the judge, he talked to the judge. He talked in a manner that I understand, even identifying the offense. He talked to me in a regular African American manner, and the judge took offense to it and couldn't understand it. I think as a result, the outcome of the case was not what it should have been just because we had a judge who could not relate, who could not understand the kind of person that he was dealing with.

Judge Ingram, a Black female judge from the North, made a similar comment by sharing that she is able to understand the literal words coming out of litigants' mouths and the significance of this exclusive understanding.

> I may understand what you're saying because we may or may not have had similar experiences. I've never been a drug dealer, so I'm not going to sit here and go, "I know what you're talking about, X, Y, Z." But there could be things that people are saying or expressing, I'm understand exactly what he's trying to say or what she's trying to say right now. And I'm not going to hold it against them if they can't—you should conduct yourself. I tell people you need to conduct yourself accordingly. But I'm not expecting them to come in here with a suit and start speaking the king's proper English. But I do expect that you're not cursing, that you're not yelling, that you're not talking over me or talking over the other person. You're going to treat each other with respect. So, when you say represent and when I say people that look like us, you just want somebody to kind of understand, kind of sometimes read between the lines, because we all sometimes have difficulty expressing what we're trying to say. So, you don't want, you definitely don't want to be in front of a judge and you're saying, "You know what I'm saying? You know what I'm saying?"
>
> "Are you trying to say X, Y, Z?" or you just like, "No, I don't know what you're saying."

According to this judge, seeking confirmation that you are being understood is unnecessary in her courtroom because she can understand a lot of what you are saying or trying to say. This might lead to Black litigants feeling more comfortable sharing their perspectives in the courts.

Similarly, Judge Terry, a Black male judge from the South, noted that Black defendants appear to feel more comfortable being in conversation with Black judges because they expect they are being understood.

> When I say Blacks are more relaxed—just the way they talk to you as the judge, because in district court, all the trials and criminal court is to the judge. So, when they're giving testimony, they're in the witness stand,

they're basically talking to you as a judge, and I know that many Blacks are a lot less formal [with me] than they are with my white counterpart because they believe [I] understand their experience. In fact, some of the guys will say, "You know what I'm talking about, judge. You know what I'm talking about." Or, as one woman told me in trying to describe her fights with her husband, "We were fighting like two niggas in the street." Now, I don't think she would have said this to one of my white colleagues. But that's how she described it to me. This is something that I've heard from another judge here, saying a similar thing. They were an attorney, and the litigant was just trying to tell her story, and the judge took offense to it, and really it was just miscommunication because really, this is how this person talks and expresses themselves. The judge just didn't understand. We all want to be heard.

Judge Terry's remarks highlight the importance of Black judges being in the courtroom to understand culturally specific expressions. His understanding of what Black litigants are saying in the courtroom reduces the likelihood of misinterpretation or judgment based on their speech patterns. Having a Black judge like Judge Terry seems to make Black litigants more comfortable, allowing them to be more authentic in their use of linguistic expressions when addressing the court.

All these judges' comments reveal a general sense among Black judges that a type of communication occurs, or at least can occur, between many Black judges and litigants. The ability to communicate and be understood is significant for the legal system because so much of what is decided in the courts relies on effective communication and litigants being understood, or "heard." Black judges such as Judges Martin (Black male judge from the South) and Miller (Black female judge from the Midwest) are clear that one of the primary benefits to having them in the judiciary is that they can sufficiently understand Black litigants. Black litigants can be listened to without judgment about how they are expressing themselves. This approach avoids unwarranted offense or misunderstandings, as seen Judge Miller's example of a white colleague who misunderstood a litigant's intent due to a lack of cultural awareness.

CONCLUSION

This chapter and the subsequent one address whether and, if so, how Black judges represent Black interests from the bench. In this chapter, I asked whether Black judges perceive their work as representation of Black interests, whether they believe their race informs their decision-making, and whether they engage with litigants in the courtroom. Because of their identity-to-politics link, I suspected that Black judges would provide *advocative representation* from the bench by adhering to the principles of procedural justice and self-identifying the influence of race on their decision-making and their work as representation. Evidence from the surveys of and interviews with Black judges reveals Black judges indeed provide advocative representation from the bench in these ways. Black judges self-report representing Black interests through their decision-making and acknowledge race and background as important factors influencing their lives and therefore their work. Moreover, Black judges report adhering to the principles of procedural justice. From their perspectives, we get to see how Black judges see their work and how they interact with others in their courtrooms.

This chapter adds to the rich body of literature on judicial decision-making and the political behavior of Black officials by presenting information about Black judges' own understandings about their behavior and the factors that influence it. Furthermore, this chapter contributes to scholarly understandings of how Black judges behave in the courtroom when it comes to engaging and interacting with litigants, especially criminal defendants.

The self-identification of Black judges as representatives and their acknowledgment of race as influencing their judicial behavior carry profound implications for the justice system. Underscoring the importance of diversity on the bench, these judges bring unique perspectives shaped by their lived experiences in a society marked by racial inequality. This self-awareness may foster a more empathetic and inclusive approach to decision-making, ensuring that marginalized voices are considered in judicial outcomes. By embracing the role of race in their perspective, Black judges contribute to a more nuanced understanding of justice that reflects the complex realities of a diverse society. Furthermore, their openness to describing the influences on their decision-making and the extent to which they exercise their judicial power in representational ways helps to normalize judicial behavior as a human process that cannot be divorced from the personal.

Black judges' adherence to procedural justice indicates that they function as representatives of Black interests via their courtroom hospitality. When Black judges adhere to the principles of procedural justice, their interactions carry significant implications for the legitimacy and trustworthiness of the judicial system. Procedural justice fosters public confidence, particularly among Black Americans historically marginalized by the legal system, by demonstrating that the courtroom can be a respectful space. For Black judges, upholding these principles is especially meaningful, as their presence and conduct challenge stereotypes about the courts and affirm the judiciary's commitment to fairness. By ensuring that all parties feel heard and respected, Black judges not only reinforce the foundational ideals of justice but also bridge gaps of trust between the court and Black Americans who have experience with systemic inequities. Their leadership in embodying procedural justice serves as a model for how the judiciary can be more inclusive.

Based on the patterns that emerged from the data presented in this chapter, it is evident that there is a definite and substantial benefit to having Black judges in the judiciary. But what about Black judges' judicial decision-making? What are some of the kinds of decisions that Black judges make from the bench in legal cases and proceedings, and do those decisions indicate Black judges provide advocative representation of Black interests? This is the focus of the subsequent chapter. Together, this chapter and chapter 6 facilitate a more comprehensive understanding about Black judges' representation in the courtroom. See chapter 6 for a fuller conclusion and discussion about Black judges providing advocative representation from the bench.

SIX

BLACK JUDGES' JUDICIAL DECISIONS IN CASES

We each bring our life experiences to work every day. It's very difficult, but you have to. We're supposed to look at the law and take the self out of it. But unfortunately, your filter, the glasses you use, are your own personal background and experience . . . So, you bring that with you and you bring the experiences of being told you either directly or indirectly. You can't come in. You can't go there or here at the end of the table. And there's a conversation. You're not part of it. You understand this. You can't let it overpower totally what you're there to do. But you look at it as you kind of go through the numbers of making your decisions. . . . But, yeah, your background makes a difference. So, I look at others, and their background is so, I'll call it squeaky clean and main line, they don't see the texture in the layers. It's, using an analogy, it's Black or white. They don't see the fact that depends on what you came from or the other folks out there because they are white.

JUDGE THOMPSON, a Black male judge from the West

Having gone through not all of them, but to know that they [issues related to racism and poverty] exist and how it is that can impact what's going on in your courtroom. It means you don't make allowances for, but you understand that it happens. . . . You don't excuse it, but you recognize that there's an existence. So when it comes time for sentencing, if you sell drugs, it's wrong, it's illegal, but I understand that people are not going to starve to death. People are going to eat, and if you don't leave them one avenue, then, duh, crime is going to take place. My job is to see if the person is convicted, what kind of services we can try to put in place . . . to see if we can steer them to a new course.

JUDGE JOHNSON, a Black female judge from the Midwest

In October 2015, Judge Olu A. Stevens, a Black circuit court judge in Jefferson County, Kentucky, was in the news for his willingness to condemn and delegitimize all-white juries from deciding Black defendants' fates in criminal cases. In one instance, he halted a drug trial by dismissing the entire jury panel at the request of defense attorneys because all the jurors were white. In an earlier case, Judge Stevens also dismissed a jury panel when the thirteen-member jury chosen had no Black jurors. The defense attorneys in that case filed a motion claiming that, for justice to be served, their Black client deserved a pool of jurors more representative of the Louisville, Kentucky, community.[1] Judge Stevens has been clear about his reason for sustaining the defense attorneys' motions to dismiss the juries.

To one jury, he said, "I cannot in good conscience go forward with this jury. . . . There is not a single African American on this jury, and [the defendant] is an African-American man."[2] For Judge Stevens, the fact that the two jury panels were not adequately representative of the community at large necessitated drastic measures to be taken by him to ensure that Black defendants were afforded due process and justice. For Judge Stevens, that meant being judged by a jury of those defendants' peers. In response to individuals who scolded and condemned him for his actions and called him a racist, Judge Stevens noted: "Going to the Kentucky Supreme Court to protect the right to impanel all-white juries is not where we need to be in 2015. Do not sit silently. Stand up. Speak up."[3]

Judge Stevens's response highlights that the absence of Black jurors signaled to him and the court that racial bias persists in the jury selection process and raises questions about a majority- or all-white jury's integrity and legitimacy to judge Black defendants fairly.[4] By feeling compelled not to sit and watch injustice occur in his courtroom, but to instead, in his own words, "not sit silently," "stand up," and "speak up" is significant for helping the courts, in those specific cases, become less unjust and helping ensure due process (or the appearance of it) and equal protection of the law for Black defendants. Judge Stevens's rhetoric and actions are both fascinating and of scholarly interest, as they raise questions about the potential for Black judges' presence on the bench to yield representational results. Judge Stevens purposefully and overtly called attention to the potential for disparate treatment and unequal detrimental outcomes because of race and acted in his decision-making from the bench (i.e., dismissing the jury) to remedy the wrongs and address issues that have long been concerning to Black Americans and civil rights attorneys and scholars (Butler 1995). Judge Stevens's actions in this regard have not gone unnoticed.

The implicit conclusion in various newspaper articles is that he behaved in ways that aligned with what we might expect from Black judges, and differed from what we might see and expect from non-Black judges. The assistant commonwealth attorney Dorislee Gilbert said Judge Stevens acted "based on nothing more than unsupported fear or impression that the jury might not be fair because of its racial makeup."[5] Given the precedent Judge Stevens established with his actions, Gilbert feels that other judges, who may not under normal circumstances question the legitimacy of an all-white jury, "may feel societal, political, and other pressures" to dismiss juries that lack sufficient racial diversity. Gilbert also suggested Judge Stevens lacked careful thought and good judgment when he dismissed the all-white jury: "There was no consideration of whether the commonwealth or the citizens who had sacrificed of their own lives to make themselves available for jury service had any rights or interests in continuing to trial with the jury as selected." Gilbert's critique of Judge Stevens raises multiple concerns: first, that judges should adhere to procedural norms of legitimizing juries unless there is concrete evidence of bias, and second, that there is now a precedent for dismissing all-white juries, which may impact how other judges handle juries when or if a similar situation arises in their courtroom.

However, I would argue that Judge Stevens's actions are not based on unfounded emotions and irrational thinking, as Gilbert suggests. Judge Stevens's dismissal activities are grounded in Black Americans' perceptions about and lived experiences in the courts, as well as in existing academic scholarship. Gilbert's sentiments reveal her astonishing lack of awareness and understanding that racial discrimination and bias have been perpetuated by predominantly white or all-white juries, and prosecutors have been biased toward the presence of Black jurors, especially in cases involving Black defendants (Butler 1995). These are both historical and contemporary legal system issues. Ultimately,

Judge Stevens, a Black judge sitting on the bench in the twenty-first century, seems to have exhibited distinctive behaviors in response to what he perceived and understood as an equity and justice issue. In doing so, Judge Stevens simultaneously highlights his understanding of race and the law and that he is engaging in actions on the bench that align with Black judicial interests. The question is whether Judge Stevens is the only Black state court judge engaging in this type of advocative representational behavior on the bench.

Like chapter 5, this chapter also examines whether and how Black judges represent Black interests from the bench. It explores these primary questions: What are some of the kinds of decisions that Black judges make from the bench? And do those decisions indicate Black judges represent Black interests in the courtroom? In this chapter, I add to the large body of literature on judicial decision-making and the literature on Black political officials' behavior more broadly by taking a mixed-methods approach to exploring the following questions: To what extent do Black judges represent Black interests from the bench in legal cases and court proceedings? Do Black jurists behave in ways that make them representatives of Black group interests, akin to other Black officials (e.g., Brown 2014)?

The preceding chapter included a detailed discussion of the relevant literature on judicial behavior and my data for and methodological approach to the study of judicial behavior. To avoid repetition, I turn immediately to the expectations I have for Black judges' judicial decisions in cases. Then, I present my analysis of Black judges' decisions in pretrial court proceedings and case outcomes. The analysis of interview data highlights how many Black judges engage in representing Black interests within legal contexts.

EXPECTATIONS ABOUT BLACK JUDGES' JUDICIAL DECISION-MAKING

Two primary reasons are often given by scholars to support the argument that Black judges' decision-making will align with Black Americans' interests and reflect that they are concerned about and responsive to them. First, scholars reason that Black judges, like other Black Americans, have likely personally encountered and experienced inequality and racial discrimination and, therefore, they would be responsive to this issue if it ever came up in a case they were presiding over (e.g., Beiner 1999; Farhang and Wawro 2004, 301; Steffensmeier and Britt 2001, 752). Second, some researchers assert that Black judges generally support disadvantaged, marginalized, and oppressed populations because they are likely to be ideologically liberal and see themselves as liberal (e.g., Welch, Combs, and Gruhl 1988, 127; Segal 2000, 140). I concur with scholars who say experiencing racial discrimination and being politically liberal help explain why Black judges might engage in decision-making behavior favored by African Americans. However, I also maintain that scholars do not fully understand and appreciate how and why Black judges' identities might influence their behavior. Literature in the legislative context suggests that Black legislators advance Black Americans' interests in Congress and state legislatures because they possess a high level of group identity and group consciousness (e.g., Broockman 2013; Whitby 1997). The extent to which Black judges possess strong Black individual and group identities and a racial consciousness has largely been unknown to scholars, until now. And the extent to which Black judges represent Black interests is unclear because the empirical research has been inconsistent.

An examination of Black judges' backgrounds, life experiences, identities, and consciousness established that Black judges have an identity-to-politics link. Chapter 5 highlighted how and why that link is significant for Black judges' judicial work in the courtroom. Black judges (1) self-identify exercising their judicial power in a way that represents Black interests and (2) adhere to the principles of procedural justice in their treatment of litigants in the courtroom. This chapter pivots to focus on Black judges' decisions in legal cases and proceedings. I expect Black judges' decisions to reflect their identity-to-politics link and to highlight the ways Black judges represent Black interests from the bench. As in the prior empirical chapters, I draw on the surveys and interviews with Black judges. I turn to Black judges' pretrial decisions before proceeding to case outcome decisions.

PRETRIAL DECISIONS AND THE REPRESENTATION OF BLACK INTERESTS

The period after an individual is arrested for a crime and until they are put on trial for that allegation is a phase informally known as "pretrial." Several significant decisions are made during this period' two of the most important are whether to remand or release defendants—typically on bail—and whether to approve of the jurors selected for trial. Black judges revealed that these two monumental decisions in criminal cases are ways Black judges can and do represent Black interests with their pretrial decisions.

The bail system and the jury selection process represent two aspects of the criminal legal system that have been raised as concerns about inequality among Black Americans. The former is disturbing because defendants' experiences within the legal system seems to be better if they are wealthy (and guilty) than if they are poor (and innocent) (Stevenson 2014). This ends up cutting along racial lines, with a disproportionate number of Black Americans and Latino/a/x Americans experiencing pretrial detention, especially for misdemeanor offenses, or being assigned bails that they are unable to afford without the service of a bail bonds corporation (Demuth 2003). According to the Prison Policy Initiative, about 450,000 individuals are detained in jail waiting for their criminal cases to be resolved, and Black Americans disproportionately make up 35 percent of the pretrial detention population.[6] The majority of detainees are held because they cannot post bail. The latter issue (i.e., jury selection) is troubling because racism continues to be an enduring feature of the jury selection process and often leads to the formation of unrepresentative juries that are charged with determining the guilt of Black defendants in criminal cases.

Black judges' considerations and decisions during arraignment and bail hearings are ways that they can and do represent Black interests from the bench. The decision to either remand a defendant to state custody or release them until their trial begins is an important one. Being detained before and during trial impacts the presumption of innocence. Scholars show that pretrial detention is associated with increased prison sentences (Leslie and Pope 2017; Olesonet al. 2016).

Whether an individual is remanded or can be released depends largely on the type of crime, the safety and health of the community, and an assessment of whether the defendant is "dangerous" or likely to flee or not return for the trial. In the United States, once a determination has been made that an individual does not need to remain detained by the state or can be released under supervision, the conversation turns to whether the judge can release the defendant on their own recognizance or whether the defendant needs an incentive to appear for all proceedings related to their case. Recognizance is usually granted when defendants have roots and a connection to the community and are stable with a steady lifestyle, including employment. For defendants whom the court deems unsuitable for recognizance, the judge or magistrate proceeds to discuss setting bail—some amount of money or property provided to the court with a promise that the defendant will return for their trial.

In some states, bail amounts are standardized based on the defendant's charges and are determined by a bail schedule. In many places, however, a judge or magistrate determines the bail amount by considering the severity of the charges and potential sentence, the defendant's prior criminal record and appearance at past court hearings, the likelihood of the defendant reappearing in court, the safety of the public and any victims, ties to the community, the defendant's wealth and resources, and the recommendation of law enforcement and/or the prosecutor. Upon payment to the court by either the defendant or a bail bonds company, the defendant is released from state custody and can return to their community. If cash is paid directly to the court, the deposit is returned to the defendant at the conclusion of the trial, although sometimes a required processing fee is deducted. For bail bonds companies, the defendant or their friends and/or family typically pay a nonrefundable fee of 10 percent of the bail or $100, whichever is greater, and an administrative fee.

While bail is lauded as one of the least restrictive approaches to assuring public safety and a defendant's appearance during all court proceedings, the bail system is riddled with major issues. One of the notable concerns is that because it relies almost exclusively on cash, a bond, or other capital (such as property), wealthy individuals are able to avoid pretrial detention, whereas poorer individuals either stay in jail until the conclusion of their trial or they have to work with bail bonds companies. This has led to movements across the U.S. to eliminate cash bail for most misdemeanors and nonviolent felonies, to reduce the amount of unnecessary incarceration, to prevent people being jailed simply because they cannot afford to pay bail, and to let people awaiting trial remain in the community for work and/or school and support.

Another concern is that relying on bail bonds companies to help defendants get released from state custody creates support for what some have referred to as a "debtor's prison," especially among people charged with petty charges or misdemeanor offenses.[7] Bail bonds companies profit immensely, especially off defendants charged with misdemeanor crimes. Ultimately, the entire bail system, including cash bail and reliance on bail bonds companies, are problematic because wealth and financial resources, not culpability or measured risk, determine who is afforded the right to experience the long-standing justice tenet: "innocent until proven guilty." Or as Bryan Stevenson, renowned activist, attorney, law professor, and founder/ executive director of the Equal Justice Initiative, puts it, "the opposite of poverty is justice."

Determining Bail

Due to the way class and race work in this country, Black Americans are disproportionately represented among the individuals remanded to jail while awaiting trial. Decisions about remand or release and setting a non-excessive bail represent some of the significant sites where judges exercise a considerable amount of discretion and can represent Black interests. For this reason, in the survey, I asked Black judges to identify "up to 3 factors [they] consider important for making pretrial release decisions." The Black judges surveyed routinely noted that they consider the following factors when determining setting bail: the severity of the crime(s) allegedly committed by the defendant, the defendant's history with the courts, whether the defendant poses a flight risk, and public safety.

Black judges also mentioned other factors indicate they think about the defendants' rights and individual situations as well. One surveyed judge considers "structuring factors related to past." This attention to structural issues suggests that this Black judge attempts to understand some of the circumstances that have significantly impacted defendants' lives and livelihoods. Similarly, judges reported considering defendants' current circumstances. Fifteen judges specifically mentioned that defendants having ties to the community was significant for their pretrial decisions, and ten judges mentioned defendants' resources and support. Eight judges explicitly noted the importance of familial support for the defendant, and eight judges noted that they consider defendants' financial resources and their ability to post bail. While they do not make up the majority of judges who participated in my study, these judges reveal how Black judges are bringing critical defendant-centered perspectives to the criminal legal system, especially when making pretrial decisions such as determining remand or release and setting bail. Though they are thinking about the crime allegedly committed and public safety, they are also considering the needs of defendants. Their calculations appear to consider the economic inequality that permeates the pretrial detention/release system.

Judge Brown's response during an interview underscores how Black judges bring a critical perspective to pretrial detention processes, especially the consultation phase with prosecutors about remand or release. Starting off the conversation, the judge described his general perception about defendants, remand, and the bail/bond system:

> You know, I see no value in locking them up. I'm not going to lock them up simply because they don't have a job. Other than simple inequities, people remain in jail because they can't post the bond money. The bond money, the fact that you can't post the bond money, to me, does not translate to you staying in jail. The argument is somebody's not invested enough in putting their money in to keep up with you, so therefore you won't be kept up with. I mean there's some argument with that . . . there might be something to that, but that's not what the statute says. . . . You have to look at it this way: If you have $10,000 dollars discretionary money, which is not a lot, but if you have that, probably 80 percent of people in jail now wouldn't be in jail. So, is that what it takes? Does it really get down to that? It shouldn't; it just shouldn't.

Judge Brown, a Black male judge from the Midwest, describes the underlying truth of the bail system as he sees it—it is a system that unfairly and unjustly punishes the poor and rewards the wealthy. For him, money determines the type of "justice" and "process" afforded to individuals charged with criminal offenses.

This judge goes on to share a very specific interaction and conversation he had with a prosecutor who he felt did not fully understand the bail system nor the experience of a Black defendant who could not afford bail. This tale highlights how this judge has responded in situations where he felt defendants were being denying justice and a fair process.

> So a bond court judge quickly, because they get hundreds of cases and only certain information, might set a bond. . . . Even if the guy is still in custody, the bond has been set. So, you hear from prosecutors who argue (and which I never accepted), "Judge, there's no need to review the bond. Nothing has changed since the preliminary hearing."
>
> So, here goes [my] questions . . . "Okay, the defendant's been in jail now for two months. Well, first of all, changed conditions. You said nothing changed between the bond court hearing and today. Were you at the bond court hearing?"

"No."

"Do you have a transcript?"

"No."

"Did you talk to the prosecutor before the bond court?"

"No."

"Okay, so that's a problem right now. As the officer of the court, you tell me nothing changed. You weren't there. So, now here's another issue," I said. "He's been in custody for two months. Do you think that's a change? In other words, a bond was set. Nobody in his family can raise money to get him out of the hell hole known as a jail. Do you think that that's a changed condition that he's still in jail?"

"Well, I didn't have a look at that."

I say, "Well, now, one way I can get you to look at it is to put you in jail for two months and then you could see whether or not there's a changed condition. And then I would go through this whole thing again. Should we do that?"

"Oh no, Judge!"

I said, "That's what I'm talking about. You have got to look at what you say in front of me because I'm going to take you literally."

In engaging with the prosecutor in this manner, this judge holds the attorney accountable for understanding how this system works and how the system influences defendants' lives. His reasoning for engaging with the attorney with some sarcasm is made clear in his statements as he concluded his comments on the bail system.

"You have one bond hearing, and your family couldn't raise it. We have to put you in the cell. You have to shower in the face bowl or whatever they do, you know. Get processed the way they do the process[ing], and eat what they eat, and channeled underground in the tunnel, similar to getting on the slave ship. Have you [the prosecutor] ever done time or toured a jail?" . . . "You've never even represented anybody that visited anybody in jail, so you don't even know what the jail is. You think the jail is going to give you ice cream and cookies and pat you on the head, right?"

This judge's interaction with a prosecutor and perspective on issues related to the system reflect some of the ways judges can represent Black interests.

Black judges can specifically help prosecutors recognize the humanity among those they are charging with crimes and prosecuting. Additionally, by asking these types of critical questions and not simply accepting everything prosecutors say, this judge and other judges can ensure pretrial decisions are made in mindful and thoughtful spaces and in ways that do not ignore the life and experiences of criminal defendants. Ideally, this prosecutor will be more considerate moving forward when it comes to reflecting on bail.

Black judges' decisions about bail are consistent with the court reforms they support. At the end of the survey, I asked: "Generally speaking, which of these court reforms, if any, do you support?" Fifty-nine survey respondents, or 34 percent, said they supported abolishing cash bail. Eighty-three percent of respondents (144 judges) indicated that they supported the pretrial release of accused low-risk offenders. These reforms that are supported by Black judges indicate issues that they perceive within the system, at least in terms of pretrial proceedings. Consequently, it is not necessarily unanticipated that they would make decisions about pretrial release and bail that indicate mindfulness about the way the system is structured and how it differentially and unfairly impacts marginalized communities.

Jury Selection

The second way Black judges can represent Black interests in their pretrial decisions is during voir dire, the jury selection process. During this pretrial proceeding, judges, prosecutors, and defense attorneys interview and evaluate potential jurors. The judges assess jurors for their ability to be fair, and attorneys try to keep individuals who they believe will be sympathetic to their case and dismiss individuals who they believe to be unsympathetic to their case.

There is a long history of racial discrimination in jury selection in the United States, with prosecutors disproportionately striking potential Black jurors from jury pools when there is a Black defendant in a criminal case (Butler 1995; Wilkenfeld 2004). Racial discrimination persists in jury selection despite the fact that the United States Supreme Court expressly prohibits attorneys from relying on racially discriminatory justifications (i.e., a juror's race) when exercising their peremptory challenges during voir dire (e.g., *Batson v. Kentucky*; *Strauder v. West Virginia*).[8] Because prosecutors often ground the justifications for striking Black jurors in seemingly race-neutral language, many Black defendants today, like many Black defendants in the past, are judged by juries that are not racially diverse and do not reflect the community.

The tendency among prosecutors to disqualify capable Black jurors has meant that Black defendants have rarely been judged by a jury trial of their peers, a constitutional right, because Black defendants' peer group in the community is likely to be more racially diverse than most juries. And there are significant implications of unrepresentative juries. Gau (2016) says that there is a tendency in all- or majority-white juries to convict Black defendants despite a lack of evidence, and that racially mixed juries "deliberate better and are viewed by the public as more legitimate than all-white and mostly white juries" (75). Thus, diverse juries are not only important for symbolic reasons (i.e., making the defendant feel they are being judged by their community peers), but these panels are also known to arrive at more-reasonable decisions and conclusions.

Although striking Black jurors because of their race is explicitly prohibited by the court, this pattern of exclusion still occurs (Wilkenfeld 2004). Because prosecutors employ race-neutral justifications when striking Black jurors, judges have often not intervened. Prosecutors' actions and judges' inaction have meant that at least some Black defendants in criminal cases end up being judged by all-white or mostly white juries, thereby denying them due process and equal protection of the laws. Consider the outrage Judge Stevens faced after calling attention to the racial composition of the two all-white juries. If what Judge Stevens did was common, there would have been no outrage about it.

The two steps in the jury selection process that often produce "jury 'whitening'" and are detrimental to ensuring proper representation of racial minorities on criminal juries are (1) the "procedures by which venires are pulled from the population" and (2) peremptory strikes and for-cause removals of racial minorities from venires (Gau 2016, 84; Wilkenfeld 2004). The former source of whitening "appears to be lingering deficiencies with the process for selecting potential jurors, delivering summons to them, and ensuring their appearance in court for jury service" (Gau 2016, 84), while Butler (1995) and Wilkenfeld (2004) consider the latter source of whitening as stemming from a presumption that racial minority voters are overly sympathetic to racial minority defendants. The first issue can be addressed by passing a policy that prioritizes the creation of diverse pools from which to draw potential jurors. The latter issue about striking minorities from venires can be addressed from within the courtroom. Not only can defense attorneys air their concerns about the lack of diversity within a jury via submitting a motion, but judges can also play a role.

In the same way that Judge Stevens did (see the introduction to this chapter), Black judges can monitor and address this issue in their courtrooms. Black jurists can be mindful of this phenomenon and ensure that jury selection in their courtrooms does not lead to jury panels that are unreflective of the broader community (as per the U.S. Census), especially when it comes to judging Black defendants. Black judges can also play an active role in jury selection by asking questions of potential jurors to uncover any racial bias that may negatively influence jury deliberations and outcomes in cases involving Black defendants.

Surveys and interviews reveal some of the ways Black judges view the nation's jury system. Ten Black jurists see the jury system as a legal system strength. One Black judge (Judge Johnson) shared in her interview her perceptions of the jury system and why she perceives it to be a tremendous benefit:

> Well, the strength of the current judicial system is trial by jury. It's not something that exists everywhere. In this world now, you know, the fact that racism pervades our society means that sometimes the jury trial might be a false hope, but it's there. That I think is the hallmark of our judicial system: the fact that there is a place where you can go hoping to find justice, hoping you can resolve your disputes peaceably and that does not exist everywhere else in the world. The weaknesses of it? Where does one start?

At the same time this judge is lauding the jury system, she is also raising concerns about it. The jurist highlights that racism pervades the work that jurors engage in. This cautionary message about the integrity and fairness of jury trials echoes concerns raised by other judges in the study. For instance, one judge surveyed maintained that the following factors are important for deciding a criminal case: "Seat an impartial jury; make sure jury is properly advised of all applicable jury instructions and law; litigate only pretrial motions and ruling according to law." Another judge identified "jury selection process; juror agendas/untruthful jurors; quality of some legal representation" as system weaknesses. Finally, Judge Martin, a Black male judge from the South, noted, "It's kind of like you don't want to be on trial and the jury be all white. You want to be assessed by a jury of our peers. Well, I don't hang out with any people that look like that. It doesn't really feel like my peers." Although these judges were responding to different questions, they made clear references to issues within and concerns about the jury system, including the fairness and legitimacy of (potential) jurors and juries and the absence of jurors of color.

The dearth of Black jurors is both a jury pool issue and a jury selection issue (Gau 2016). In the thirty-two interviews I conducted for this project, I asked Black judges, "How much of an issue is peremptory jury strikes based on race in your court, if at all?" Black jurists were clear that these strikes were commonplace within the legal system. When asked about the prevalence of race-based peremptory jury strikes in their courtroom, Judge Hall said, "I don't do a lot of jury trials, but I do think, and I see them. You can see 'em a mile away." Judge Adams said, "I think it's come up a few times." Relatedly, Judge Taylor said that peremptory jury strikes based on race were an issue:

> Oh yeah, we had cases where this occurred. And, in this particular state, in both civil and criminal cases, each side had peremptory challenges and they were exercised very freely. And, in many cases, [lawyers] used all of their peremptory challenges. And in criminal cases, especially where you had a Black defendant, they, the prosecutor, used all of his peremptory challenges to get Blacks off the jury.

Some Black judges noted they had been aware of the role race plays in jury selection prior to becoming a judge and from their judicial colleagues. For instance, Judge Wilson, a former government attorney, shared that he and other Black attorneys were aware they should not expect diversity in the jury box.

> Traditionally, when I used to try cases, you knew that very few Blacks were going to be on your jury because race was, across the board, a reason that—my feeling and it was also the feeling of a lot of other people, Black lawyers—you knew you weren't going to have many Black people on your jury, especially if you had a death penalty case because Blacks were not likely to vote for the death penalty because most Black folks, they feel like the death penalty was inappropriately applied to Black defendants. And you know that's the whole racial justice thing.

Black judges also noted conversations about fraught jury selection processes occurring among those working in the legal system. Judge White, a jurist from the Midwest, said although she does not think race-based jury strikes are a major issue in her court "since we handle misdemeanors," it is a topic between attorneys. "I hear them arguing about it upstairs a lot. I've heard a number of prosecutors and defense attorneys saying the prosecutor struck this person because it wasn't a group of his peers because he's African American male and they struck all the Black people." These narratives from Black judges underscore the fact that there is clearly an awareness among some Black jurists that racism in jury selection continues to be an issue in today's criminal legal system in the same way that it was an issue historically.

But what does this awareness actually mean in terms of Black judges' behavior? The narrative about Judge Stevens that opened this chapter emphasizes how one Black jurist addresses his concerns about racial bias in the jury selection process. By dismissing two entire jury panels because they lacked what he considered sufficient diversity, Judge Stevens helped to restore the appearance of fairness in the courts. Although no Black judge mentioned they had dismissed entire juries because they were inadequately diverse, some judges indicated they had dismissed individual jurors when they perceived them to be prejudiced. One Black female judge from the Midwest (Judge White) mentioned exercising her judicial power to keep bias out of the jury box:

> The parties have their jury strikes, and then I've done some for racial bias. I've had a juror in a domestic violence case say that for minority women, they're a little tougher or sassier. That if their man hit them in the mouth for being sassy, that should be okay, because they're known for running their mouth and talking back. And this was a white lady, and she said that about Latino and Black women. Saying, you know, they're known for talking back and everything, so you just have to shut her up. . . . She was in her fifties probably. I couldn't believe it, and this was a domestic violence case. . . . So, what happens is they have the voir dire question and everything. I'll call the lawyers to the side. and then I may strike people based on what I thought was bias. and I talk to the lawyers about it, and of course, the defense attorney was like, "I wanted her," but I said, "No, she cannot be fair." So, I remove people, not a lot of people, and I have removed people for being ill and cannot sit real long or and really just being biased.

The interviews and surveys indicate that Black judges are aware of diversity issues on juries and they notice all-white or mostly white juries and perceive them to be potentially unjust. While some judges will dismiss potential jurors, there was also the sense that Black jurists feel constrained in what they can do to address the issue. Take, for example, Judge Taylor, who talks about noticing racism in jury selection but feeling constrained as a result of gaslighting by attorneys who cunningly hide what he imagines to be their true reasons for striking Black jurors:

> In this particular state, both criminal and civil, each side had peremptory challenges. They were exercised very freely. And in many cases, [they] used all of their peremptory challenges. In criminal cases, especially where you had a Black defendant, the prosecutor used all of his peremptory challenges to get Blacks off the jury. And we've begun to change that a little bit. But the problem is, do people have a reason for removing all the Blacks on the jury? Lawyers are pretty smart folks, now. I think in many cases, it was whether a person realized the tendency of people to do certain things. . . . Well, that matter [racism in jury selection] went all the way to the U.S. Supreme Court, and the essence of the rulings was that race cannot be the factor. You can't remove a person because of race. And the problem of course is, did you have another reason? And people came up with some creative reasons for removing all Blacks from the jury. . . . Lawyers are pretty smart folks, now, you understand? . . .
>
> Let me give you this little quick story. There was a guy who lived out in the country, and there were dirt roads. And people would come by after there'd been rain, and they'd get in the ditch. They would take his mule and go out and help him get back home. Then one night the guy came and said, "I'm in the ditch. Would you mind helping me get out?"
>
> They said, "I can't do it. My daughter is getting married tomorrow."
>
> And after the person left, his wife asked him, "What's that got to do with, you know, whether you help the man get out of the ditch?"
>
> He said, "Well, when you don't want to do something, one excuse is as good as another, okay."
>
> So, when you want to do something, one reason is about as good as another.

This particular judge is communicating his understanding and awareness of the issue of racial bias in jury selection, particularly through the racialized misuse of peremptory challenges. He notes prosecutors' strategic use of peremptory challenges in order to manipulate the racial composition of juries for the purpose of disadvantaging Black defendants despite legal decisions aimed to mitigate discriminatory jury selection practices. The judge also notes pre-textual justifications in legal contexts and how prosecutors are exploiting a loophole in the system. Still, he articulates a bind he finds himself in, which is simultaneously being aware of the reason behind removing many Black jurors from a venire and being unable to do much because lawyers try to obscure and conceal the fact that they are systematically striking Black jurors due to their perception of how the jurors might behave. Nonetheless, his remarks highlight the need for judges to be aware and vigilant about subtle forms of discrimination.

For some Black judges, racism during jury selection is not a major issue. Judge Moore, a female jurist from the Midwest, remarked during the interview, "I don't think it's an issue. I'm trying to remember if I ever had someone raise the Batson challenge, where they're eliminating people because of race. So, I don't see that as an issue." This is particularly true for Black judges living in areas with large Black populations. Judge Clark, a Black male judge from the Midwest, said that striking Black jurors is not a major issue in his court-room because the jury pool is such that "you couldn't exercise enough peremptory jury strikes to get rid of all the Blacks on my juries." But for some of the judges in this study, the use of peremptory strikes to systematically remove Black jurors from venires remains an issue, especially in criminal cases. More-over, there is general concern about racial bias among jurors. Black judges not only identified being aware of these jury-related issues, but they reported ways that they can and have responded to these issues.

Disqualifying qualified Black jurors and implicit racial bias among poten-tial jurors are two jury-related issues that significantly impact Black litigants' constitutional rights. Thus, these issues continue to be Black legal interests. The fact that Black judges are aware of these issues and can respond to these concerns about jury composition indicates that they can wield their power in ways that align with Black interests. Interviews and surveys revealed that, at times, some Black judges indeed function in this capacity via their decisions during jury selection.

DISTRIBUTIVE JUSTICE AND THE REPRESENTATION
OF BLACK INTERESTS

There is consensus that procedural justice or fairness is the primary criterion most people use to evaluate the courts in their communities, though for Black Americans this is a bit different (Rottman et al. 2003, 5). Although Black Americans, like others, use perceptions of procedural justice to judge their courts, because they are disproportionately involved in the legal system due to the racial bias in criminal justice, Black Americans also judge the courts on how Black Americans fare in the system in terms of outcome. That is, among Black Americans, both the treatment of individuals within the courtroom (i.e., procedural justice) and the fairness of outcomes (i.e., distributive or distributional justice) for litigants are concerning. According to Tyler (2001), Black Americans' perspectives about procedural justice are influenced by their beliefs about how Black Americans fare in court as compared to other groups. Tyler's work shows that Latinx and white Americans focus primarily on the quality of treatment litigants receive in courts, whereas Black Americans are attentive to and care about quality of treatment throughout the legal process and the outcomes of the legal process. In the same way that Black judges' behavior in the courtroom signals that many of them are deeply committed to the tenets of procedural justice and making sure that the quality of treatment in the courtroom is satisfactory to litigants and therefore represents Black interests (see chapter 5), Black judges' self-reported descriptions of their decision-making stress the ways they can and sometimes do represent Black interests via case outcomes, or distributive justice, as well.

The times we are living in have been described by many as a period of mass incarceration because the United States has become the world's largest jailer despite the country housing only about 4 percent of the world's population (Alexander 2010). "Today, the U.S. incarceration rate is nine times higher than Germany, eight times higher than Italy, five times higher than the U.K., and 15 times higher than Japan" (Cullen 2018). In 1950, the United States incarcerated fewer than 200,000 people, and as of 2016, the country incarcerated almost 1.5 million people, many of whom were "in prison without any public safety reason and could have been punished in a less costly and damaging way" (Cullen 2018).

A critical aspect of mass incarceration is that it is racialized. Black people represent roughly 13 percent of the United States population and yet are over-represented among the nation's confined and detained population. Drawing on statistics from the Bureau of Justice and numerous scholarly studies, Sawyer (2020) concludes that racial inequality and disparities are evident in every stage of the criminal justice system, from policing to sentencing. Black Americans are more likely to be stopped by the police, experience use of force by law enforcement officers, experience arrest and booking in jail irrespective of age, experience pretrial detention and posttrial incarceration in local jails and prisons, serve sentences of life and life without parole, be given the death penalty, and be placed in solitary confinement.

Numerous reasons explain how and why Black Americans have come to be disproportionately represented in the criminal legal system, including racialized policing especially profiling, legislation, and prosecution (Alexander 2010; Baumgartner, Epp, and Shoub 2018; Pfaff 2017). Still, another reason for the overrepresentation of Black people among imprisoned individuals relates to the outcomes of criminal cases involving Black defendants. Judges, like police officers and prosecutors, also play a role in maintaining mass incarceration. As mentioned previously, Black Americans disproportionately receive longer sentences and more extreme sentences.[9]

As race disparities have been revealed in the legal system, scholars have raised questions about the extent to which race influences case outcomes, and they have been concerned with both the race of the defendant and also the race of the judge. The effects of the race of defendant are clear (e.g., Alexander 2010; Berdejo 2018; Mustard 2001). The effects of the race of judge, however, are much less straightforward. Some scholars find judges' race influences their handling of cases, whereas other scholars find no race affects (e.g., Boyd 2016; Chew and Kelley 2008; Collins and Moyer 2008; Harris 2024; Kastellec 2013; Scherer 2004; Segal 2000; Spohn 1991; Steffensmeier and Britt 2001; Uhlman 1978; Welch, Combs, and Gruhl 1988).[10] Nonetheless, distributional justice (i.e., fairness of case outcomes) and influences on judges' decision-making remain significant topics among criminologists, political scientists, and other scholars of law and courts.

Irrespective of whether Black judges view race as influencing their decision-making or their judicial work as representation (see chapter 5), I was interested in knowing what activities and work they engaged in and did on the bench. I encouraged Black jurists in this study to share how they envisioned and understood the significance of being a Black judge in a legal system that historically excluded Black people from its judicial ranks.

Understanding Black People

Not only are Black judges listening to Black litigants and relating to those litigants via their speech and rhetoric (see chapter 5), but Black judges also said, on a fundamental level, that they understand Black litigants with regard to their stories and experiences. They were outspoken about being able to understand Black litigants and other litigants from underprivileged groups in ways that many white judges are not. Judge Brown, a Black male judge from the Midwest, noted this during his interview:

> I know that a lot of these [white] judges have no relationships with African Americans except in the courtroom. They didn't go to high school or go to grade school with them, have some contact with them. It's always when they were former prosecutors and it was in their courtroom, and they didn't even know Black lawyers, except for the few that float through, but they never really took the time to know anything about them. So, when they're looking at this like, "Man, I'm getting ready to sentence him to like fifteen or twenty years," I mean they didn't even look at him sometimes. Or if they looked at him, they basically looked at the prosecutor, like, "This side fifteen years." [They just] nip the issue [and say] bye.

This judge is articulating a type of disconnect and lack of cultural empathy that he understands exists between many Black litigants and white judges. Instead of relying on the prosecutors' narrative, this just pushes for critical engagement with defendants' humanity or individual circumstances. Black defendants become cases to dispose of efficiently instead of complex human beings. What results is impersonal, mechanical decision-making instead of personal, nuanced deliberation. This Black judge suggests these are systemic issues in judicial decision-making.

Being able to relate to the individuals who appear in Black judges' courtrooms helps Black jurists to understand litigants' concerns and needs and see them as human, which are both necessary components for being able to engage with empathy and administer justice. But more than understanding litigants, Black judges also highlight that they decide cases with a great deal of care and compassion. Their discretion provides them with opportunities to be responsive to litigants and, when possible, show grace and mercy in a system that has often been merciless and dehumanizing to Black litigants, especially Black defendants.

Black judges were adamant that it has been their experience that their white counterparts struggle to understand what it means to be Black in America. This inability to understand the lives and experiences of Black Americans have, at times, resulted in judgments against Black litigants. Black judges shared that they did not have this issue. They were able to identify with and understand many of the litigants, and Black judges deemed this understanding to be important for their decision-making and their ability to reach proper and conscientious decisions. Twenty-six of the thirty-two (81 percent) Black judges reported or implied being able to relate to and understand the individuals that come before them.

Judge Adams, for example, said her life experiences as a Black woman from the South help her complete her job on the bench.

> Well, as a Black female, I've certainly been subjected to racial discrimination and gender discrimination. I've had a wide range of experiences, and they have been helpful sitting on the bench because I can relate to folk who come before me. . . . When I used to be a district court judge and I would hear shoplifting cases, and if you hear people come in and talk about things that happened to them in the store, you can kind of see their side of it instead of always assuming the store is right. You can empathize and sympathize with the Black defendants and in some cases even find them not guilty.

This jurist directly traces her life experiences with marginalization and how those experiences inform her judicial approach to cases. Her relatability fosters an empathetic approach to cases, whereby she challenges the presumption that institutions are always right and defendants are always wrong. To be clear, this judge is not indicating that she is biased or partial. Instead, she suggests that her nuanced understandings of the scenarios brought before her help her make fairer decisions in cases where she might otherwise have been biased against defendants.

Judge Allen, a Black female judge in the West, shared her perspective about the importance of understanding diverse experiences on the part of judges in local-level courts and how that relates to the "well-deserved" expectations that litigants from underprivileged communities have as they enter the courtrooms of Black judges and other judges of color. She also highlights the value of understanding not only circumstances but also understanding diversity within groups of people.

When you work in a limited jurisdiction court like I do, municipal courts, county courts, courts where most of the people come in are not represented by counsel, typically are not very well educated, typically have some financial barriers to access to justice that makes them rely on a public defender and on the system and that's both on the criminal side and the civil side, where they may not be represented by counsel, they may be in debt up to their eyeballs on payday loans, they know something's wrong, but they just don't know what they signed, don't have a lot of time, so they can't take time off from work, if they do, they lose their jobs if they don't show up—all of those kinds of barriers that really impact people of color, poor people, people who in most instances have never had to deal with the court system. When you have a judge that presides over that kind of court, my honest opinion is that not only do you need someone who is learned in the law, but you also need someone who's had some real-life experience . . . who doesn't have a disconnection with people of color, people who are in poverty, people who are undereducated and underexposed. You need somebody who has an ongoing relationship with the county or the community to make certain that they remain connected with the kinds of issues that impact the population that you serve. Because quite often, those kinds of issues are very straightforward, contractual or otherwise, but being able to communicate so that they understand, being able to access services so that they actually get the kind of help that they need, being able to be learned enough not to allow folks to take advantage of them, because that's what happens. You see that a lot on the civil side, small claims and small civil cases, where people just didn't read what they signed. . . . They were just so anxious to get into whatever kind of situation they got into, be it an apartment, . . . TV, be it a payday loan, they didn't read the fine print. And a lot of those people are taken advantage of, and they're paying interest rates, 24 percent, crazy. You know, buying a car, paying someone every week for interest on a car and they're paying. They could have bought a limousine by the time it was all said and done. . . . So, understanding that

that's not necessarily the most appropriate way to do [it]. You are also faced with having to be culturally competent, which I think is something that all judges should be. But, particularly in the lower-level courts because we are now a melting pot of communities. It is no longer just Black-white; it's Latino, and it's not just Mexican, it's not El Salvadorian, it's all of that. You need to understand all of that. It's not Asian, it's, you know, it's Chinese, it's Korean, it's Filipino, . . . you need to be interested enough and engaged enough to understand that you're not the only one that exists. Your way is not the only one that exists. We have a number of immigrants from Ethiopia, and it's always very interesting to me, you know, and they say, well, they understand English, but, you know, they may not understand the process because this is a process that is different from what happens where they live. So, you know, cultural competency is, like, key. Absolutely, without a doubt.

Judge Allen's reflection underscores that importance of her being on the bench because she insinuates that she, unlike some of her colleagues, is both knowledgeable about the law and empathetic to the lived realities of the people she serves. This ensures justice is not just procedurally correct but also equitable and accessible.

Judge Martin, a Black male judge from the South, also illustrated that Black judges are uniquely capable of understanding Black defendants. Judge Martin discussed witnessing white judges' struggle to understand Black defendants and how their inability to relate to Black defendants often resulted in judgments against them. He shared the following story:

I worked as an attorney for Child Support Enforcement. I had two cases with the judge where I was seeking to enforce child support obligations. Two people in the court at that time had not done what they were supposed to do—one was Black and one was white. These are the two that I remember, two cases equally egregious in terms of the person not having provided support for their child and could have because they had the ability to. And so I was asking for incarceration in both cases. And the gist was that the Black man went to jail and the white man didn't. And it was a white male judge and I'm the Black attorney for Child Support Enforcement asking for enforcement. And so, at that point, at least before that particular judge,

I was not going to let the judge be the decider anymore because the judge wasn't fair. The judge wasn't right in my mind. And, uh, that did heavily influence me.

Judge Martin's story suggests the white judge did not understand and connect to the Black and white fathers' justifications for nonpayment of child support the same. His account highlights the critical importance of fairness and equitable decision-making, particularly in cases involving racial dynamics. The white judge's implicit bias in the two cases influenced Judge Martin, helping him understand how the absence of diverse perspectives in the judiciary can perpetuate systemic inequalities.

In her interview, Judge Lee, a Black female judge from the South, also talked about Black judges being able to uniquely understand the Black experience and that some judges might struggle to relate and understand the experiences of others because of their privileged identities:

We want judiciary systems to truly appreciate the persons in front of them, and to that extent race and gender are important because I don't think— and I don't mean no disrespect, but I don't think white males understand what either Black or white females' or Black males' experience. And so, I think that you do have to, as a backdrop, to have a truly representative and appreciative and diverse system. You do have to have some element that takes into consideration not only did I make an A or a B, but also my experiences and what do I bring to the table. That needs to be considered.

Judge Wilson, a Black male judge from the South, shared that he witnessed white judges reach improper decisions because they simply could not understand the experiences of the individuals before them:

By appearing in courts, I saw sometimes minorities weren't getting a fair shake. Sometimes discretionary calls, discretionary decisions, and if the judge doesn't understand the life conditions that bring people into that courtroom, in my opinion, they aren't really able to ascertain a proper judgment. They don't know what you've been through. They don't know why you've done what you did. Not knowing where you've been, they can't adequately address your decision-making process.

Because Judge Wilson understands the circumstances and life experiences of some of the people who come before his court, he feels he is able to reach proper decisions in the cases he presides over.

Similarly, Judge Hunter, a Black male judge from the South, shared the following, which sheds light on how he felt he could understand litigants:

> Having someone there [in the courtroom] who has had diverse experiences allows the courts . . . to understand what it is that the community is feeling on the base level. I think coming up poor, you have a different perspective than someone who's affluent, who had an easier road to hoe. I'd like to believe we are more compassionate if you come from humble backgrounds. I think that we are generally more desirous of working hard and maintaining the positions we have, and we are probably a little more understanding of the perspective of people who come from similar backgrounds.

Judge Hunter's narrative highlights how his upbringing facilitates a deep awareness of the challenges faced by those with similar backgrounds. In doing so, his decisions can be more grounded, compassionate, and reflective of his understanding the realities of the communities he serves.

To be clear, Black judges articulate that having an opportunity to speak in court is significant, but it is the first step to meaningful participation of litigants. The second step is to have the legal actors in courtroom, especially the judge, process and understand what litigants are offering via their spoken statements. This particular viewpoint is captured by Judge Lee, a Black female judge from the South, who shares that understanding can lead to appreciation: "It's very important in any aspect to feel like there's an ability to have your message heard and understood—not just heard, but heard and understood, and I think diversity in both race and gender allows for that understanding to take place." This judge's narrative reflects the narratives of numerous other judges who demonstrated that many Black judges have a unique perspective because they can understand the issues facing many of the litigants who come before them in court, even the "stuff that [they] can't see or [they] can't hear" (Judge Ingram, a Black female judge from the North).

Many Black judges felt this understanding was unique to them and directly related to their own background and life experiences. Some of them even expressed the unlikelihood that white Americans/judges can understand the experiences of racial minorities and white women. Black judges, on the other hand, report possessing a deep understanding of litigants, especially Black litigants. This understanding does not necessarily mean that Black judges agree with litigants' actions, which is something a number of them mentioned in their interviews, but many of them understand the lives and experiences of many Black litigants, as well as many of the challenges. Black judges and I perceive understanding to be, arguably, the foundation for empathy, and both understanding and empathy are important factors that can inform and exert some influence on the decisions made by Black judges in legal cases.

Just Mercy

In 2018, the Sentencing Project submitted a report on disparities in the United States' criminal legal system to a United Nations special rapporteur (The Sentencing Project 2018). In the report, the Sentencing Project highlighted the work of the Kerner Commission (1968), which noted community and social factors that undergird and influence our legal system. The Sentencing Project's report said that the factors the Kerner Commission had noted five decades earlier remain influential:

> In 1968, the Kerner Commission called on the country to make "massive and sustained" investments in jobs and education to reverse the "segregation and poverty [that] have created in the racial ghetto a destructive environment totally unknown to most white Americans." Fifty years later, the Commission's lone surviving member concluded that "in many ways, things have gotten no better—or have gotten worse."

Understanding these factors that influence the work of the courts may influence decision-making by legal actors.

This is what I observed in the interviews with Black judges. Interviewees communicated that they tend to show mercy to African American criminal defendants. Seven of the thirty-two judges (22 percent) interviewed described showing mercy to Black defendants because as Black Americans, they feel they understand some of the factors that have led other Black Americans to the court, including discrimination, lack of education, and underemployment. The decisions of these judges are informed by understanding the structural systems and environments that many defendants come from, especially those from marginalized groups.

Judge Brown, a Black male judge from the Midwest, discussed race-based barriers to educational and employment opportunities for Black Americans and how understanding these barriers made him more understanding and merciful when it came to a Black defendant violating his probation because he could not find employment:

> The best-case scenario is education opportunities and entering into the trades. The trade unions have historically not been easy for African Americans to get into, and it is important for you to get in and be certified by the union. So, if you have the skills to compete to be in a trade union, or they keep you out of the trade union, or you don't have the education, I don't buy that you have to go commit the crime because there are too many poor people that historically were Black that did not do that. But when you don't have the home training to say that even when you don't have something, you don't go steal it, it becomes self-help after that. . . . All of us have blame. Law enforcement has blame. In certain communities, people are not being arrested; they are being adjusted. They are being corrected, they are being admonished, taken home to family when there is a family to take them home to—other options are given. In our community now, we don't see that. The easiest thing to do is process a young or not-so-young person and not to do anything else, process them and get that person off the street for a while, and then you can count that and check off that you did that. I think in the back of some law enforcement officers' minds that if we lock them all up, even though they're going to come back, at least on our watch, we got these off. It becomes their simple-minded analysis of how to deal with immediate issues that they see as easiest as possible. We have no community adjudication centers. There is no place for people to work when I put them on probation. You know, I see no value in locking them up. I'm not going to lock them up because they don't have a job.

Here, you have a judge who understands the underemployment issue and its connection to race and maintaining a racial hierarchy that has ensured Black Americans are on the bottom and have to live with perpetual economic impoverishment. This understanding of the structural and institutional systems operating in the background of defendants' lives helps him to not punish individuals for things that are primarily outside their control. Instead, he can approach these cases with more empathy and understanding.

Another judge, Judge Jackson, a Black female judge from the South, described how being Black helps her relate to litigants' circumstances and helps her show mercy. She described finding a Black female defendant guilty of a misdemeanor offense, petty theft. The defendant asked that if the judge was going to give her jail time, that she be permitted to serve her jail time on the weekends because she was concerned about her children being cared for. The judge shared during the interview that she, too, was concerned about the woman's children and therefore, allowed the woman to complete her jail time on the weekends when family could care for her children. After explaining this case, Judge Jackson said, "Most of the mothers who come here are Black single mothers, and that's primarily what you saw in my community growing up. I think that that has helped me to have more compassion just for the entire situation."

Judge Jackson also shared a case she had involving another Black female defendant. In that case, the defendant was on probation and responsible for paying fines. The individual did not pay her fines and ended up in court again. When the judge asked the defendant why she had not paid her fines, the defendant replied, "I cannot pay my fine because I had to pay my light bill." The judge said that she apologized for not being considerate and insinuating during her questioning that the defendant was simply ignoring a court order. She said she also did not penalize the defendant more because she did not pay her fines and did not have her arrested, although she says she imagines her white colleagues would not have been as merciful with this Black defendant.

According to Judge Thompson, a Black male judge from the West, "We each bring our life experiences to work every day. It's very difficult, but you have to. We're supposed to look at the law and take the self out of it. But unfortunately, your filter, the glasses you use, are your own personal background and experience." One example that highlights how his experiences help him to be more compassionate is around termination of parental rights. He reports understanding that there are disparities between parents who are brought before the court to fight to retain their parental rights and parents who never have to, despite there clearly being parental issues. He considers this fact, among others, as he makes decisions about the best interests of the family.

> I look at families as not being either from this generation, the Cosby family, or my three sons from a generation back before the families are perfect and people are perfect. There are people that have never been brought before

legal agencies or child services who drank and who popped pills and do other things, and they managed to raise their kids okay, and never get reported. And there are others who seem to get reported. And then you get the concept of what is the best interests of the child, who should have their children taken away and who shouldn't? . . . I'm more prone to not want to see a family broken up, because I've seen the families and I understand that they love each other and love their children. You know, sometimes they shouldn't have them, but there are other times you shouldn't take them. They should be given the opportunity.

Other examples that came up in the interviews that revealed how Black judges can show mercy is through the types of penalties, especially fines, that they levy against poor litigants, thinking beyond punishment as a consequence for some infraction and understanding pretext. One Black female judge from the South, Judge Hall, shared the following story that highlights these issues and how her experiences influence her work as a judge in a large cosmopolitan city.

Coming from a middle-class family, I think that helped me appreciate, you know, people who are trying to struggle. You know, I get it. I get that struggle. I worked two to three jobs when I was in college. So, I'm not as quick, and we talked about this, I'm not as quick to levy fines on people. Some of the other judges, you know, we have one of the other newer judges who comes from a very affluent family levying like $800 worth of court fines on people, and we're [Black judges in her jurisdiction] like, "Dude, don't you realize that's never going to get paid?" It's not a big number to him . . . even in domestic violence cases, you know. It's something I feel very passionate about and I think my experiences [influence my work]. Or, even better, like drugs, you know—I got family members, and everybody, most people do.

But I try to be keenly aware of what we need to do to address the problem as opposed to just punishment, punishment, punishment. That is definitely a part of what I do, but it's not my primary focus at all . . . One more thing. But also, you know, having a Black husband and having Black men in my family who have dealt with so much, that's probably the biggest, one of the bigger things when I'm listening to those trials and I hear pretext, pretext, pretext. Or when I'm doing those bond hearings, that's a bias I also have to kind of keep under control. You know there is not, it's recognizing that while it's not all contextual, a lot of it is, and you know I can't throw everything out, so maintaining some balance there from those experiences that I know personally, people in my family have experienced, and just, you know, sometimes you just want to balance it out by saying, "They're not guilty, they're not guilty, they're not guilty." [*Laughter.*] And you can't, and you know that you can't but [you want to].

This lengthy quote highlights how personal experiences lead to empathy, and empathy informs the Black judges' approach toward sentencing. She critiques the punitive tendencies of some affluent judges who seem to struggle to grasp the devastating impact of fines or harsh sentences on already marginalized individuals. Instead of punishment, she considers restorative justice. Importantly, she acknowledges the tension that exists between personal bias and professional duty, balancing compassion with farness. She suggests that her decisions reflect both grace and justice.

Judge Brown, a Black male judge from the Midwest, also shared how mercy plays out in his courtroom. For him, mercy means understanding the types of individuals that you have before you and how, instead of punishment, you can provide help and support.

Poverty is the uneven distribution of economic opportunity and resources [and] is one of the foundations that causes a lot of issues. Lack of education causes a lot of issues. Family, or the breakdown of the Black family, is maybe even more serious than all of that. And that has nothing to do with Black people except that indirectly, say, we're not getting the education, jobs, etc. . . . Out of all the folks I see out here—and I have the rapes, I have the murders, I have everything—I would say less than 5 percent [of the people] I have in front of me are bad people. Maybe 3 percent are bad people. The rest of them are people that have not fared well with respect to economically, judgment-wise, educational-wise, family-wise. I only have 3 percent that are really, really bad. So, the really, really bad, I have to punish. The [other ones], I try to correct or repair, challenge, and change.

But it's problematic that when you have to sentence somebody—and some of the cases the person's convicted and you can't give them probation, [but] there's a small percentage of the cases where you can—and the legislature keeps getting tougher and tougher and they're trying to figure out ways to take discretion away from judges so that people all have to go to jail. What they don't realize is that even though they go to jail, they're going to be coming back out. So, what you're doing is creating a much more ruthless return than you had before. . . . So, you know, that's frustrating because a lot of these folks—we're paying for it [prisons], but it's not going to change the situation.

In this quote, the Black judge distinguishes between truly dangerous offenders and the majority of offenders who can benefit from corrective and rehabilitative measures. This compassionate approach to justice is difficult when judges are losing discretion.

Another example of Black judges; mercy comes from their being flexible. In her interview, a Black female judge from the Midwest, Judge Moore, shared how she had experienced mercy in a Black judge's courtroom when she was a prosecutor:

I remember when I was a prosecutor and I had a case. I was a prosecutor, the defense attorney was Black, and the judge was Black. So, [the defense attorney] had an older client. His client had the opportunity to participate in a first-offenders program, but he rolled the dice and wanted to have a trial. And the judge found this client guilty.

So, then [the defense attorney] goes, "Well your honor, I'd like my client to participate in the first-offenders program." Of course, he's not eligible [because the trial had concluded and the judge had made his ruling].

So, the judge looked at me, and I go, "I don't have an objection, if you don't have an objection."

And [the judge] just said, "This was a Black thing that happened right here!" [*Laughter.*] Because we all had to be in agreement and he probably would not have thought about [that if the actors in that case were not who they were].

In this case, the judge was okay with not sending the defendant to jail. A Black male judge from the Midwest, Judge Brown, expressed the reason for such a choice: "Further incarceration, extending incarceration is not advancing the improvement of our community. It just means we're spending more and more money warehousing people." Many Black judges understand punishment and incarceration are not always justice and just, or the best way to respond to an infraction. Moreover, the judge showed incredible patience and mercy with even the Black attorneys in the room who technically missed the window to negotiate a plea.

Part of the mercy, it seems, comes from being able to understand the circumstances affecting the lives of individuals who find themselves in criminal courtrooms. Judge Thompson, a Black male judge from the West, articulated this perspective while sharing how he takes a nuanced approach when encountering cases dealing with drugs and makes significant distinctions that he presumes include some consideration of the broader community.

> I look at criminal law a little different. . . . As much as I want to make sure that these people have a fair trial and everything else, I'm also sensitive to the community they came out of. Do I necessarily want this individual back in the community because they are a problem in the community? So, it's an interesting thing as a trial judge and having to sentence people and you look at, say, two different units of people who are into substance abuse: the ones that are sellers for profit and the ones who are just users. And so, understanding what that does to a community. Some of it's correctible, because the person is a user. The other, if they are a high-volume trafficker or seller, it's a business proposition. They don't give a damn—and I'll tell you that. That's a wild thing if somebody's telling you it's sentencing. "I have an honest job, I do this [high-volume trafficking or selling of narcotics]. I take care of my family and me." Yeah, but you're dealing death to these other folks. So, you hear all kinds of wild things. But your background makes a difference.

This judge's quote demonstrates the complex interplay of mercy and accountability in judicial decision-making, particularly for a Black judge who is deeply aware of the societal and communal impacts of crime. The judge reflects on the need to balance fairness to the individual defendant with the broader implications for the community from which they come. By distinguishing between individuals struggling with substance abuse and those profiting from the sale of narcotics, the judge reveals a nuanced understanding of criminal behavior. Users are viewed as potentially redeemable through corrective measures, while high-volume traffickers, seen as prioritizing profit over community well-being, are met with a firmer hand. This perspective illustrates how grace and mercy in sentencing are not about excusing behavior but rather about tailoring responses to the context and underlying motivations of the offense. The Black

judge's acknowledgment that his personal background influences those decisions highlights the importance of lived experiences in shaping a nuanced and
empathetic approach to justice, one that seeks individual rehabilitation but not
at the expense of community protection.

Judge Thompson also remarked that sometimes grace and mercy are found
in the number of chances a Black judge gave a litigant:

> But there are other times you go against the grain of what parole and pro-
> bation recommended and you give people a second or it might be third or
> fifth opportunity, and they take advantage of it. And that's a good thing.
> I ran into people that, because we were able to get into a drug diversion
> program or we put strict conditions, they met them and they made it. It
> worked. They're now doing what they're supposed to.

This judge reported that these judgment calls are scary because there is a
chance that giving someone a chance is the wrong decision to make. "And you
have the folks in the middle, the gut calls. And they're the scariest because at
the end of the day, and not what the newspapers have to say, but if somebody's
on your watch, goes out and hurts somebody else that you didn't put in jail,
it becomes a real personal." Despite the obvious potential uncertainties that
come with the decisions Judge Thompson has to make regarding whether to
give individuals a second chance, he noted that he does choose to take a chance
sometimes and he has personally witnessed his chances pay off.

Judge Thompson also described the compassion he has for minority litigants: "You want minorities coming to the bench who care, who remember
what they're part of. They may not have had bad things happen to them personally, but they saw family and friends, and they are aware of that." Whereas
some judges might turn to incarceration as the simple solution, for Judge
Thompson, it means that he exercises that power more judiciously: "It doesn't
mean everybody gets a get-out-of-jail card free, but everybody doesn't go to
jail."

Judge White, a Black female judge from the Midwest, noted that she shows
grace and mercy when sentencing. By understanding the purpose of laws, she
is able to render decisions that prevent miscarriages of justice. Judge White sees
this as simply making a "fair, justice decision." She also identifies this part of
her job as "level[ing] the playing field, because [Black judges] can see through
it and [they] can tell when something is a driving-while-Black case, and I think

we can make it a little equal, because we have that final say even though an individual probably was mistreated on the street, and we can find him not guilty and do different things. I've done it many a time." She gave one example with open container citations:

> You have to look at legislative intent sometimes. People want to be strictly by the law, or what it says now, but when the law was written, you have to see what was the purpose of it. Just like for open containers. The law was written because they don't want people standing on the street drinking and everything, or actually having open containers while they're driving or in a vehicle drinking. I've had officers pull people over and they've come from a cabaret party and they have opened liquor bottles in their car—not open, the top is on, but the seal's been broken because the cabaret. They want to give them a ticket because they're transporting it and it's open. . . . Well, that's not the law, what the law was written for. I always say to them, "What do you want them to do? Drink the whole bottle and then be driving under the influence of alcohol?" So, you have to have that common sense and say what the legislative intent was for: they're able to transport the liquor even if it's been opened, as long as they're not drinking, it's not in a cup. I've found "not guilty" on those. Some judges will still find them guilty, which I think is crazy.

Another example that demonstrated how Judge White shows mercy and grace is with decisions that involve individuals struggling financially. She talked about finding ways to render decisions that might help them in the long run. In ways discussed by other judges, Judge White noted that she does not turn solely to incarceration but considers the needs of the litigants and how she can exercise her power in ways that are helpful.

> If someone says "I did this 'cause I'm poor," I don't consider all that because, you know, it's right or it's wrong. It might be a mitigating factor in my sentencing if someone says, "I was stealing cause I had to feed my children." I've had that before. Then I would put that person on probation. What I do with that person was put them on probation and got them job-training skills, helped them with their education, make sure they got their GED, and I put them on probation long enough. Because we can put someone on probation up to five years, so I put them on probation long

enough to make sure that they got all of the requirements or the necessary skills to be competitive out there and then sent them to a job fair. And that person still comes back to see me now because they're working and doing well and feeding their children.

The significance of this type of grace and decision-making is that litigants' lives can be improved. Judge White shared that former litigants come back and still "check in" despite not being required to: "They're not on probation anymore but every year they'll stop in: 'I just wanted to let you know that you changed my life and thanks.' Yeah, so you can use that as a mitigating factor, but I'm not going to find them not guilty because of that."

In sum, some Black judges acknowledged that when it makes sense, they show mercy to Black defendants. This does not mean that there are Black judges who do not show compassion, mercy, and grace with Black litigants. In fact, Judge Allen, a Black female judge from the West, described Black judges that she encounters who are harsh toward Blacks litigants due to respectability politics and show non-Black litigants compassion.[11]

> What I've seen at conferences and from talking with other Black jurists. I remember when I first joined the [organization], I was so excited because I saw all these Black folks that were judges. I was like, "Yes!" And they came from different parts of the country. But what happens is you see the same dynamic that you see when you're dealing with just folks in the community generally [i.e., white judges]. A lot of us don't like each other—you know what I mean? We don't like it because you make us look bad. They think we're all like you. And that can work against you, sometimes, if you are standing before a Black judge. You think they understand, but they're mad because you're standing there, making them, in their minds, look bad. A lot of people, they're much harder on each other than they are on the other races. And more compassion for them.

Despite Black judges who may render decisions that lack mercy, care, compassion, and grace, numerous Black judges interviewed in this study report judging with these sensibilities. Oftentimes, this mercy comes from understanding Black defendants' life experiences and the circumstances they find themselves in. These judges describe how they show compassion and empathize with Black defendants by not sending some of those who violate court orders to jail and by being thoughtful and considerate when they have to hand down their sentences. In other words, this is not about Black judges showing preferential treatment or excessive leniency toward Black litigants, especially defendants. The important point Black judges are making and communicating is that they show mercy in a system that they believe is supposed to be merciful and compassionate, and not ruthless and overly punitive. For them, showing mercy and compassion is tied to justice, and they seem to be more than familiar with the fact that the legal system has often been excessively ruthless and punitive to marginalized groups, especially Black people.

Equal Justice Under Law

Section 1 of the 14th Amendment is the Equal Protection Clause. This clause, which declares "nor deny to any person within its jurisdiction the equal protection of the laws," articulates the ideal that is equal justice under law. This ideal is supposedly the bedrock of the United States legal system. It is a commitment and a promise that laws in this country are going to be just and that everyone, irrespective of their race, gender, and wealth, for example, will equally be held accountable if they break those laws. Still, despite the ideal, racial disparities are evident from policing to judicial decisions.

Equal justice is one of the primary concerns of Black Americans. They are interested in and attuned to the fact that Black people regularly experience unequal justice under law. As previously discussed in this chapter, Black Americans feel that they are treated not only unfairly in court, but they also feel that they are treated unequally in court. Rottman, Hansen, Mott, and Grimes (2003, 41) find Black Americans, especially those with court experience, perceive the courts as treating Black people worse than other groups. Fifty-two percent of the Black respondents in their study with court experience, as compared to 45 percent of Black Americans without court experience, said that Black people are treated worse in the courts than other groups always or often. Both numbers reveal that a large proportion of Black Americans perceive unequal treatment and justice under law.

One of the important threads from my interviews was that Black judges are committed to equal justice under law. For some of them, that meant administering justice for white Americans, who have historically and contemporarily been less penalized for crimes that they commit than Black Americans are. Some Black judges reported that when a white American appears in their courtroom, they are committed to justice and that often means handing down the sentence that a Black American would likely have received. For them, that is equal justice. No one gets treated worse or better.

One narrative that highlights this is by a Black female judge from the South, Judge Hall. She talked about listening intently when litigants speak and also being able to make decisions regarding where and how she exercises empathy in the courtroom and for whom.

> I wasn't raised by my parents, and so how I see a lot of those juvenile cases is pretty critical, and especially when I have abandoned children or foster children. I will have to be careful not to fight extra hard for them, not to be an advocate when I'm there to make a decision. I learned that I don't have as much empathy for white females. I think they have benefitted the most from everything that's happened in the United States, ranging from just being on a pedestal for the white male to gaining more of the benefits from affirmative action than [Black people] did. So, when they're in my court and they start crying, I'm like, "Oh my god, cry me a river," number one. Number two, this is not going to impact her nearly as much as it's going to impact the next person before me. I have to really rewind and make sure that I don't let that bias go too far on the other side. You know, if there's a trial on least level of suspicion and they're questioning whether or not there was a pretext for the stop, I don't think there's pretext if it was a white woman who's a defendant. I'm like, "No, it's probably pretty legitimate," and it may not be fair. So, I try to be careful about that.

This quote highlights the self-awareness of this judge who actively works to counterbalance or keep in check potential biases. More importantly, the judge reveals how she tries to treat litigants before her similarly to avoid biased decision-making.

Another Black female judge, Judge Allen, albeit from the West, shared that she is concerned with equal justice for white Americans and that they should experience justice under law in the way Black Americans have experienced it. Her story about her decision in a case involving a troubled white teen and the tremendous efforts his family went to in order to get her to show him grace and mercy highlights this equal justice way of judging.

A kid whose mother works here in the building and she works for a white judge and she's white, and this boy has been in and out of some kind of trouble since I've been on the bench, I think. And usually nothing major— like traffic tickets, that sort of stuff. Now, he's in jail. Oh lord, you would have thought the Lord himself was over there in the detention center. They ran over here and they wanted me to release him. I said, "No, I'm not."

And they just, you know. Ha!

"No, I'm not."

"Well."

"No, I'm not. This has been coming for a long time, and he's very troubled." I said, "Okay, let's be real. He's a crackhead. He's been at a crackhouse, he got raided, and he got picked up. He stood out because he was the only one in there that was white, but you know, nevertheless, he got picked up just like everyone else. Nobody's running in here for Joaquin. Nobody's running in here for Pookie." You know what I mean? But this boy is all "Oh, "what's gonna happen?" He can go to the crackhouse, but he can't go there [jail]? So, you see what I mean?

This judge shares that despite tremendous pressure to show the white youth special attention and leniency, simply due to his race and connections, she said could not because it would not be fair. What about the Black and Latino boys who were facing similar or more severe circumstances but were not privileged enough to receive the special advocacy that the white youth received. If she had not been vigilant, she could have made a decision that would have been implicitly biased in favor of the white youth, which would have undermined the principle of equal justice for all.

White and Black Americans should be afforded equal justice in the courts and should be treated the same in the courts. This is not to say that adjusting the sentencing baseline for everyone to reflect where Black Americans are is not at all problematic, because it is. Black Americans continue to be treated punitively in the courts. Nonetheless, Black judges point to the idea that, in their courtroom, when they are faced with white litigants, especially criminal defendants, who want mercy and grace, they consider equal justice under law and how Black Americans are typically treated within the courtroom. They refuse to coddle and overprotect white defendants in the face of Black defendants being historically and contemporarily over-punished and unprotected in the courts. Black judges seem to be on board for less punitive approaches universally, but never at the expense of racial minority or poorer defendants.

DISCUSSION AND CONCLUSION

Assessing Black judges' on-the-bench work in cases underscores precisely how we can and should be considering Black judges as functioning as representatives of Black interests. Notwithstanding their view of themselves, when sharing their activities on the bench, Black judges report behaviors that, when Black subjective and objective judicial interests are taken into account, reveal that Black judges do represent Black interests in myriad ways from the bench. That is, by assessing and analyzing their self-reported behaviors, it becomes clear that Black judges' actions show that they function as representatives of Black interests. This chapter, therefore, adds to the rich body of literature on judicial decision-making and the political behavior of Black officials by addressing whether and how Black judges can be viewed as representing Black interests in the judiciary. Evidence from interviews with thirty-two Black judges reveals Black judges indeed provide *advocative representation* in the judiciary and that there is a definite and substantial benefit to having Black judges in the judiciary.

Because of their backgrounds, Black judges understand and respect diversity and the complexity inherent in the lives of Americans, especially Americans who belong to marginalized communities. Additionally, they report being able to relate to and understand African Americans who come into their courtrooms. Because they can understand the circumstances in Black communities and the experiences of Black Americans, they are also able to reach more informed conclusions and make more attentive decisions. When they are capable of exercising discretion in their decision-making, they tend to be merciful with Black defendants. Additionally, their approach to dealing with Black litigants is markedly conscious of and responsive to their perceived needs and reflective of the respect and regard they have for the individuals who find themselves in the courthouse.

There is one main conclusion in this chapter and chapter 5: Black judges represent Black interests in the courtroom. The personal experiences and perspectives of Black judges in this study inform their judicial decision-making.

Who Black judges are matters for what they do. Judges did not hold back from sharing the personal, painful experiences that they had with racial discrimination or their secondary connections with discrimination. The judges were also not silent or discreet about their behavior and the influence of their experiences as people of color on that behavior. Furthermore, and perhaps most interesting, is the fact that Black judges consciously and unconsciously behave in ways that represent Black interests and Black Americans. That is, irrespective of their intentions, many Black judges behave as representatives. Some judges were explicit about behaving in ways with Black Americans and Black interests in mind; other judges, however, simply described their behavior. Nevertheless, it is the behavior, not the intention behind the behavior, that signifies many Black judges are on the bench representing Black interests.

Race also matters in the judiciary because Black political officials in the judicial context—that is, Black judges—behave in ways that indicate they advocate for and represent Black interests and Black Americans. They, like their Black counterparts in other branches of government and other political offices, are confirming with their behavior that the push for more descriptive representation and the fight for increased diversity in the judiciary was not futile and in vain. They are living up to both the expectations of those who championed increased diversity in the judiciary and the need of Black Americans to be respected, heard, understood, and treated fairly within the courtroom.

Black judges also engage in actions and behaviors that might highlight that they serve a representational function in other contexts and spaces. One important aspect of Black judges' work is their interactions with other legal actors. How do Black judges interact with, for instance, their judicial colleagues? In addition, Black judges are active beyond their courtrooms. Within their courthouses and in their communities, they are often active in organizations and doing community outreach. What type of initiatives and programs do they choose to align themselves with and support? What is the significance of their decisions around community outreach? These are the questions that I take up in the remaining two empirical chapters of this book, which focus on whether and how Black judges may represent Black interests beyond their courtroom decisions.

SEVEN

ADVOCATIVE REPRESENTATION
IN THE COURTHOUSE

Hopefully when we talk to our white colleagues, we express some of
our beliefs to them and they hear us.

JUDGE ADAMS, a Black female judge from the South

This chapter pivots from the last two chapters by exploring how Black judges
represent Black interests beyond their decision-making in the courtroom.[1] Specifically, chapter 7 examines how Black judges can represent Black interests in
the legal system by engaging in meaningful and impactful conversations with
their judicial peers. The chapter addresses two questions: How do Black judges
engage with their judicial counterparts, and what are the implications of those
interactions for their colleagues, Black Americans, and the court system? Like
previous chapters in this book, this chapter draws on interviews and surveys
with Black state court judges. I present these judges' self-reflections on and
recollections about conversations and interactions they have had with their
judicial colleagues. By drawing on interviews and surveys to highlight how
Black judges engage, work with, and support other judicial actors, this chapter
demonstrates that Black judges' dialogue with their judicial peers can help to
educate their colleagues and facilitate those colleagues' development of cultural competency, humanize Black Americans, and increase diversity in the

judiciary, legal profession, and court system more broadly. By focusing on Black judges' engagement with their colleagues, this chapter reveals additional instances in which Black judges function as representatives by providing advocative representation of Black legal interests in the courthouse.

DIVERSITY AND JUDICIAL BEHAVIOR ON COLLEGIAL COURTS

Collegial courts are tribunals with several members that operate as a collective and decide cases jointly. There are collegial courts at the state level (e.g., state courts of last resort) and the federal level (e.g., United States courts of appeals and the United States Supreme Court), and most collegial courts are appellate courts. Regardless of the level, state and federal collegial courts have substantial power, control, and influence over legal doctrine in our common law society. Consequently, these courts with several members are seen as preferable to courts with judges who operate in isolation, such as many of the nation's trial court judges.

Law and court scholars writing about the significance of judicial diversity have often focused their attention on collegial courts because all the judges on these courts hear the same cases and facts. These courts, therefore, offer a unique opportunity for researchers to examine whether judges from marginalized backgrounds behave differently than their counterparts when adjudicating cases. Additionally, scholars can assess whether judges from marginalized backgrounds influence and impact their judicial colleagues' decision-making and understanding.

Generally, scholars maintain that racial diversity among judicial officers matters on collegial courts. Not only do judges from marginalized backgrounds frequently render individual decisions in cases that differ from their colleagues' decisions, but these judges, who are underrepresented in the judiciary, have also been shown to impact the decision-making of their judicial peers (e.g., Allen and Wall 1987; Boyd 2016; Collins and Moyer 2008; Farhang and Wawro 2004; Gill, Kagan, and Marouf 2019; Gruhl, Spohn, and Welch 1981; Kastellec 2013; Peresie 2004; Songer, Davis, and Haire 1994; Songer and Crews-Meyer 2000). These scholars demonstrate that racial and gender diversity on collegial courts increases the likelihood of decisions by white and male judges that support the side of the gender or racial minorities.

DIVERSITY AND JUDICIAL BEHAVIOR
ON NON-COLLEGIAL COURTS

How does judicial diversity matter on non-collegial courts such as trial courts, which is the court type for most of the judges in this study? Scholars highlight how judges' individual racial and gender identities influence their decision, leading them to make decisions that differ from those made by their colleagues (Boyd 2016; Collins and Moyer 2008). Most researchers have generally over-looked the potential ways that judges on non-collegial courts can and perhaps do impact their colleagues via their communication and the significance of such engagement. Although they operate as the sole judicial officer in their courtroom and their collegiality does not extend to the adjudication and de-ciding of cases, trial court judges may also have a broad impact on the legal system through collegiality and their interactions with other legal actors that they regularly engage with in their official capacity as judges. They are es-sentially monarchs in their individually assigned courtrooms, but trial court judges' work on and off the bench requires that they interact with other legal actors. Analyzing the engagement and interactions affords us with an oppor-tunity to better understand the broader impact Black judges are having within the court system, beyond just the individual cases that they preside over.

Judges on non-collegial courts frequently interact with their judicial col-leagues. They work collaboratively to discuss and fashion court rules. They also gather to discuss and consult with one another about issues occurring within their court system. Drawing from their experience on the bench, they also advise one another about common trends they are seeing with their cases and ways to understand what they are seeing. And when possible, drawing from their life experiences, judges may share their insights and perspectives. As a result of the close contact and interactions among judges, jurists can pro-foundly affect other judicial officers' understanding and, therefore, work and behavior.

RACIAL DIVERSITY WITHIN THE COURT SYSTEM

Judges regularly interact with two legal actors: other judicial officers and at-torneys. Eighty percent of judges and 86 percent of lawyers are white (George and Yoon 2017, 1903).[2] This, of course, varies by state and local area, but for the most part, Black people and other people of color are underrepresented nationally among legal professionals. This overwhelming lack of diversity and the persisting overrepresentation of White Americans throughout the legal system means many Black judges are working in environments in which some, if not most of their peers do not share their racial background. While interactions among judges are commonplace and necessary, *how* Black jurists interact with white legal actors may be important for understanding the impact that Black judges can and are having throughout the legal system.

Racial minorities are underrepresented as judges and attorneys in the legal system despite the fact that the individuals interacting with the criminal legal system are often racial minorities (Alexander 2010; Van Cleve 2016). Research on the backgrounds of state and federal judges indicate that they are an elite bunch in society, having attended college, received an advanced college degree, and being at least middle class. Because of race and class disparities with regard to who ends up justice impacted, many judicial officers are unlikely to have had lives or life experiences similar to those who appear before them. This lack of common life experience between judges and litigants, especially criminal defendants, may make it challenging for these jurists to understand litigants' perspectives. Moreover, extreme racial and income/class segregation in the United States makes it unlikely that white legal professionals have been proximate enough to Black people to adequately understand their concerns and unique circumstances (Rothstein 2017). Consequently, if Black judges share their insights via judicial communication with judicial officers who lack understanding of Black life, concerns, and perspectives, Black jurists can positively impact the social awareness and understanding other judges have, and perhaps their decision-making.

At the same time that Black judges might interact in ways that can create a more racially informed and sensitive court system, these judges may also go along to get along. That is, they might self-censor during interactions with white legal actors and conform to the (perceived) norms within the legal system in order to be accepted and have job security. They may try to downplay or "transcend" race in ways similar to other Black officials who are not often vocal about race and racism as they have try to be widely acceptable and not unsettling (Clayton 2010). Similarly, Black judges might also downplay their own racial identity for a professional one, focusing on their legal identity as a law school graduate and legal professional versus a Black American who is working in the legal field. Finally, Black judges might just focus on the technical work of the courts and not engage in conversations concerning identity.

COLLEGIALITY AND COLLEGIAL LEARNING BETWEEN
BLACK JUDGES AND THEIR JUDICIAL COLLEAGUES

The social science concepts collegiality and collegial learning help us to understand how Black judges might interact with their judicial peers. *Collegiality* can refer to the collective decision-making of a group of people (Cohen 2009; Edwards 2003). It refers to collaboration and deliberation that must occur between people charged with making decisions jointly. In this chapter, however, the concept is employed in reference to *how* judges interact with and engage one another (see Cohen 2009, 21). *Collegiality* refers to the relationship that exists among people in similar positions of power. It removes the hierarchical nature of power from the equation by focusing on how colleagues similarly situated in terms of authority interact and engage with each other. For the most part, *collegiality* carries a positive connotation, with the term being synonymous with cooperation, understanding, and support among colleagues.

In research, the concept of judicial collegiality has mainly referred to the interactions, positive or negative, between judges on collegial courts or multimember courts (Edwards 2003). Cohen (2009) says *collegiality* "refers to the continuous, open, and intimate relationship judges share with one another. A collegial court is marked by a lack of competition, pettiness, and enmity, and is measured by cohesiveness, friendliness, and mutual respect" (22). The existing scholarship maintains that healthy relationships among judges are important for a positive court system because, despite judges not always directly working with one another, to a certain extent their work is collaborative as it maintains the functioning of the court system.

Collegiality is important because it helps ensure collective-mindedness among colleagues, respect, and a healthy work environment. But I am less concerned about whether judges cooperate with and are "nice" to other judges; instead, I am most concerned with and interested in understanding how Black judges communicate and interact with other judges, what the substance of those interactions is, and what the implications of those interactions are for the operations and functioning of the courts and the administration of justice.

Because judges occupy the same positions in the legal system as other judges, and judges have an opportunity to discuss judging and legal issues with their colleagues, judges may interact with one another in ways that the education field calls collegial learning. Collegial learning is learning that happens horizontally among a group of professionals who do the same or similar work. In the education field, collegial learning typically involves teachers educating other teachers to help them develop better and deeper understandings of their work and practices. Similarly, in the judiciary, collegial learning would be judges educating and teaching other judges to help them develop better and deeper understandings of their work and practices so they can be better, more-informed decision-makers.

Scholarship on the impact Black judges have on their colleagues has not often included judges sitting on non-collegial courts like trial courts, where there is only one judge making the decisions. Most existing research focuses on the impact judges from marginalized racial and gender backgrounds have on their colleagues when they sit en banc or on panels with them on collegial courts like appellate level courts. This work theorizes and finds empirical support showing that the presence of racial minority and women judges impacts their colleagues because mixed-gender or mixed-race panels of judges decide cases differently than more racially or gender homogenous judicial panels (Kastellec 2013; Peresie 2004).

Although research about collegial learning usually overlooks judges on non-collegial courts, advocative representation leads me to suspect that these judges, despite not making decisions with other judges, will still have a positive impact on other judges via their communication with them off the bench. In fact, this type of collegial engagement might be considered collegial teaching and learning, as well as advocative representation, if Black judges are imparting wisdom and knowledge about topics unfamiliar to their white colleagues, knowledge that Black judges have obtained and developed based on their lived experiences and proximity to people who are disproportionately represented among litigants, especially defendants.

In sum, drawing on previous research on judicial diversity's impact on judicial decision-making via judicial communication, an understanding of the lack of racial diversity among legal actors, and the backgrounds of Black judges, my primary expectation is that Black judges will communicate with their judicial peers, but most importantly, that at least some of that communication is collegial education about topics related to race, racism, and the experiences of Black Americans. I argue that, if Black judges engage in racial collegial education with their judicial peers, these jurists might be inadvertently helping their judicial colleagues develop culture competency, which can make for more racially sensitive and informed judging in American courts. Finding that Black judges are helping their colleagues develop cultural competency would signal that Black judges are representing Black interests in their interpersonal communications and relationships with their colleagues. I discuss the topic of cultural competency in more detail after the presentation of the findings to highlight why it is significant for a study on Black representation in the courts.

DATA AND METHODS

To understand Black judges' communication with their colleagues, I analyzed the same in-depth, semi-structured interviews with Black state judges used in prior chapters. Again, elite interviewing is an appropriate methodology for this study because Black judges are treated as experts about the topics discussed (Leech 2002). Who better to shed light on judicial communication between them and their colleagues than Black judges themselves?

Although judge participants were asked almost one dozen questions, they were not asked about judicial communication. Yet, in the interviews, Black judges routinely made statements about how they communicated and engaged with their judicial colleagues. Because I did not ask a specific question about judicial communication during the interviews, the topic of judicial communication emerged from the data. From judges' responses to the interview questions came the clear message that Black judges were sharing information on a topic that I had not thought to ask questions about. The analysis of the interview data led to the identification of several patterns in the judges' statements related to judicial communication, which I discuss and present examples from in the following sections.

BLACK JUDGES' COMMUNICATION AND
INTERACTIONS WITH THEIR JUDICIAL PEERS

Sixteen out of the thirty-two judges interviewed implicitly or explicitly referred to the ways Black judges interact with their judicial colleagues. These judges shared that they were imparting knowledge and their beliefs to their judicial counterparts. Their remarks reveal the ongoing practice of collegial education and teaching in American courts that occur between Black judges and their peers. The interviews also underscore the importance and nature of collegial education in the courts, highlighting how Black judges help white judges develop an understanding of Black life and experiences.

Collegial education is necessary because racially marginalized communities, like the Black community, have distinctive and unique experiences as a result of their salient social identities and living in a racialized social system (Bonilla-Silva 1997). Sadly, people with criminal justice experience are rarely represented within the judiciary. Moreover, many of the people charged with handling legal matters involving people from marginalized communities have not come from those communities. Due to racial and class/income segregation, legal actors, who are disproportionately white, have not often lived or spent significant time near or in those marginalized communities. Moreover, the education system in this country has not often adequately exposed K–12 and college students to the experiences of marginalized communities, and this is not formally part of most legal curriculum. Judge Hall makes this point when she says that "the experience of a white man in America today is a lot different from the experience of a white woman, very different from the experience of an African American male or female." As Judge Hall suggests, in a judiciary dominated by white men, litigants come from different backgrounds, and it is important that judges understand these differences and acknowledge them, when making judicial decisions. Because people's experiences can impact why and how they end up in court, it is necessary for judges and other legal decision-makers to possess an understanding of those experiences. Gaining this understanding can happen a number of ways, including by collegial or peer-to-peer (i.e., judge-to-judge) education.

Many of the judges interviewed mentioned why a rich and deep understanding of the experiences of people from marginalized communities was important. Judge Thompson, for instance, notes that people's background can make a difference in how they understand facts and cases: "So, I look at others and . . . their background is so, I'll call it squeaky clean and main line, they don't see the texture in the layers. It's, using an analogy, it's Black or white. They don't see the fact that depends on what you came from or the other folks out there, because they are white." The way judges hear, interpret, and understand facts can be affected by their own background and experiences. Being able to more deeply understand a situation based on their own upbringing or their familiarity with a situation helps judges to accurately understand how a situation may have transpired the way it did and how a litigant may have felt in that moment, leading to a clearer understanding of the facts.

Judge Johnson makes a similar statement about perspectives and understandings influencing how judges interpret facts of cases. For this reason, Judge Johnson says it is important to have diversity throughout the judiciary to equalize things: "You have a different perspective when you are listening to the evidence sometimes, and that's why you need to have diversity. It should not always be seen through the eyes—facts and circumstances should not always be seen through the eyes of white males. There needs to be another take on it." Diversity matters because diversity affects how facts are interpreted, which bear significance on the outcomes of cases. If facts are interpreted only through a white male lens, then the judicial system will discriminately favor the white male perspective compared to all others. Another take on it can stem from one's own experiences but, without those experiences, it can also stem from a broadened horizon made possible by collegial education.

Another judge, Judge Wilson, a Black male judge from the South, put it slightly differently, suggesting that cultural competency could be considered a specialized understanding necessary for judging. He suggests that broad and diverse understandings enhance the judiciary because they equip jurists with knowledge about communities that can help them make better judgments about litigants who come from those communities.

> You got individuals who are making judgment decisions, even from the police officer on the street on up to the highest—in this county, to the district attorney and the judges who are making discretionary calls, and it's important that these people be equipped to do that. . . . You know judges make a lot of discretionary calls, discretionary decisions, and if they don't understand the life condition that bring people into that courtroom, they are not really able to ascertain a proper judgment in the court. They don't know what [litigants] have been through. They don't know why [litigants] did what [they] did. By not knowing where [they] have been, [judges] can't adequately address [litigants'] decision-making process.

Judge Wilson raises the importance of understanding litigants' lived experiences and life conditions to make better informed judicial decisions. This judge also highlights the importance of judicial education around the issues and experiences of people who frequently come before the court. It helps judges understand *all* the facts of the case, including why litigants make certain decisions.

In order to help white judges build and develop a broad perspective and understanding of Black life and experiences, Black judges report engaging in collegial education. Judge Lewis, a Black male judge from the South, suggests that Black judges' presence and engagement with their colleagues could help facilitate the development of racial awareness in white judges. He said, "Well, I think there are great judges out there that are fair and impartial. But there are some judges who may not be so fair and impartial. Having Black judges out there will make them [white judges] more aware of somewhat leveling the playing field versus just ruling at will. They [white judges] may become more conscious of minorities and African Americans." Similarly, Judge Martin shares that judges meet and interact with each other and do not withhold their different backgrounds, unique perspectives, and understandings.

> I can't say how other counties operate, but the judges, we meet once a month, and we discuss issues. You get to hear and understand different perspectives, because we have judges who are Republican, we have judges who are Democrat. we have judges that are white, we have judges that are Black. we have judges that are male and judges who are female. Everybody comes from different walks of life, so it adds a lot of different perspectives that you can learn from, and that's good because in court, you got all kinds of people in front of you.

Both Judge Lewis and Judge Martin demonstrate that communication between jurists from different backgrounds can expand judicial consciousness of minority experiences. This kind of communication/education can lead to a more diverse judiciary and more equitable outcomes. This is consistent with research in other contexts, such as K–12 and college classrooms, that underscores the effect of communicating with diverse people (Hurtado 2001). Studies indicate that diversity within teams help individual team members develop racial awareness, primarily as a result of close interactions and communication.

In addition to meetings, Judge Hunter notes how, in his area, judges interact informally and formally, and cross-pollination of ideas, experiences, and perspectives occurs in all these settings. "Judges do tend to talk with each

other. You learn from each other. You get educated together at judicial conferences. Having diverse people in that room allows those of us who don't
have the other perspective to learn about it. It's almost like getting cultural
competency by being associated with people from different backgrounds." This
communication and sharing of experiences is particularly important because
it allows judges to gain a broader perspective and better understand different
viewpoints. This exposure to different perspectives can help judges develop
cultural competency and make better decisions.

Similarly, Judge Hall supports having jurists, with their respective experiential understandings, collaborate and engage in collegial learning by sharing
their experiences and knowledge. This type of collaboration between judges
across racial or gender lines, for instance, leads to a stronger court system and
benefits everyone impacted by that system. "Together though, I think we comprise a strong bench because there are things that they see that I might not see
and vice versa. I think when we have discussions and collaborations, I think
that's what benefits the community as a whole." It is impossible for a single
judge to be able to understand every litigant based solely on their own life
experience. That is why it is crucial for judges to interact with one another as
they are more likely to gain that understanding from a trusted colleague who
has lived that or a similar experience.

Beyond the meetings and informal conversations, judicial conferences and
seminars are yet another site for collegial education. Judge Adams remarked:
"We bring our experiences to the work that we do, and as we're coming up
in the system, we have our conference, so we talk about these things in conference. Hopefully, when we talk to our white colleagues, we express some
of our beliefs to them and they hear us, maybe it impacts them. . . . So, in
that way, you can have an impact sometimes in the way things are handled
in courtrooms." Judicial conferences are an important site for collegial education because they are a space where beliefs are exchanged, and Black judges
have the opportunity to convey their life experiences to their white colleagues.
Judge Washington shares some details about the education received at annual
seminars for new judges in his area. In addition to discussing the difficulty of
the job and affirming the new judges as they embark on a new professional endeavor, the judge shares how new judges receive some collegial education about
their treatment of litigants because it will affect their long-term reputation:
"You will make your reputation in those first three to six months that you're on

the bench and you will make that reputation based upon how you treat people. You have to be careful how you treat people." The significance of Judge Washington's advice is that, without being overly prescriptive, he signals that the litigants the judges will encounter are people and should be treated as such. In doing so, he issues a warning that ultimately will benefit both the judges and the litigants. If judges treat people appropriately, judges will be able to develop positive reputations and the people will benefit from being viewed and treated positively. On the other hand, if judges fail to treat people appropriately, judges will develop negative reputations and the people will suffer from being treated negatively. And to treat people appropriately and with dignity and respect, it is crucial that judges have some understanding of their circumstances, an understanding that can be bolstered by the perspectives of their colleagues.

All these collegial learning opportunities are possible because these judges are similarly situated in terms of power. Judge White underscores her openness to engaging in frank and honest and perhaps difficult conversations with her colleagues when necessary. "You have a certain relationship, and you know that you can say something to a judge [of a] different color. And so, with the two of the judges on our bench that are Caucasian, I know that I can say something, and they know that they can come to me with that." In order for collegial learning to be possible, Black and white judges need to be open to hearing each other's perspectives like Judge White is. Judge White suggests that once this relationship is established, each judge knows that they can rely on each other to learn from each other when faced with a difficult decision. Judge White's comment supports my argument about collegial learning being made possible because of the professional relationships between judges who work in the same area. It is not important that these judges do not make decisions together on cases. What is important is that these judges are interacting with each other both formally and informally and have, over time, developed a rapport that can lead to comfort with vulnerability. At the end of her comment, the judge noted that some of her colleagues were not going to ask her for information ("I know with a lot of them, they would not [come to me] "). While sobering, the fact that some judges are engaging in conversations makes me hopeful that at the very least, some collegial education is occurring.

Black judges' functioning as collegial educators may lead their colleagues to decide cases differently than they normally would have. However, Black judges' colleagues' newfound understandings may not lead to different verdicts (i.e., guilty/not guilty), but they may impact how Black judges' peers decide and address post-verdict issues. Judge White mentions this in her remarks about the impact that a deep understanding about someone's environment or experiences is having on justice administration. This information may not just impact their colleagues' understandings, but possibly those judges' decisions, broadly conceived. Judge Clark shares a remark that reflects this idea perfectly: "The only thing that may be different when it comes time to decide [is] on remedies. . . . It's not about discernment on the adjudication side, but it may be that there be some differentiation with regard to the remedial side."

Judge Hall shares how she and other Black judges had to respectfully pull a newer white judge to the side to let him know that he had to understand the financial constraints of the litigants before him in order to be effective. She shares that she understands financial constraints because of her own upbringing: "Coming from a middle class family, I think that helped me appreciate, you know, people who are . . . struggl[ing]. You know, I get it. I get that struggle. I worked two to three jobs when I was in college, so I'm not as quick, and we talked about this, I'm not as quick to levy fines on people. Some of the other judges, you know . . . we have one of the other newer judges who comes from a very affluent family saying that, levying like $800 worth of court fines on people, and we're like, 'Dude, don't you realize that's never going to get paid?' It's not a big number to him." Judge Hall's statement sheds light on how she and other Black judges educated their newer colleague on the absurdity of fining people who come from a community that is economically marginalized and are unlikely to be able to cover the cost of fines. In doing so, these judges are sending a signal to their colleague to think beyond restitution as the best way to respond to an infraction. As Judge Hall suggests, there are many affluent judges who are unaware of the financial burden that they impose on low-income defendants when they make these kinds of decisions. Collegial education can prevent this from happening by bringing judges from different socioeconomic backgrounds together and raising awareness about the vulnerabilities of being a low-income individual.

Judge Thompson also calls attention his white colleagues' decision-making that he thinks reflects the lack of a broad understanding of the Black community. "I have one judge who's critical, liberal Jewish judge on our court . . . he says I'm too conservative. And I said, 'Well, I'm sorry [name of the white judge].' I said, 'I look at criminal law a little different than [you].' He was a defense attorney. As much as I want to make sure that [defendants] have a fair trial and everything else, I'm also sensitive to the community they came out of." Judge Thompson suggests that the white judge is focusing too narrowly on Black defendants in criminal cases and not enough on the Black communities they are from and that have possibly been harmed by the Black defendant's actions. Although it might be easy for the white judge to side with the Black defendant, given his career background, the Black judge is urging the liberal white judge to think more carefully and critically about who and what the white judge is siding with and whose interests are being overlooked.

Judge Baker sheds light on the interaction between white judges and the Black legal professionals they work with that educate them. Judge Baker says that before reaching the bench, he worked as a public defender and educated the white judge because the judge lacked an understanding, which was a detriment to his ability to make sound and fair decisions. "A lot of times I had to explain to the judge that 'you know I know what the criminal code says and the definition of a crime, but I don't think this is considered criminal because there are good people who may engage in a certain type of behavior, which may not necessarily be criminal.'" Here, Judge Baker was able to educate one of his colleagues about the issue of judging strictly based upon the law and the criminal code without carefully considering the underlying conditions that go into a criminal act. This judge is saying that committing a criminal act does not necessarily make someone a criminal; it might just mean that they are a good person who happened to commit a criminal act one time.

One Black judge, Judge Clark, highlights two other ways that Black judges are impacting their colleagues: "Keep it honest. Because there are things that people won't say in a roomful if I'm in that room that they'd say if I wasn't there. And my job really is not necessarily to be the universal Negro, but it is when I see things that are inconsistent with what I know to be true—to speak on it. I feel an obligation to do that." On one hand, this judge indicates that some Black judges are reacting and responding to things that they deem problematic or wrong. They are explicitly addressing issues when they arise and educating. On the other hand, this judge also indicates that sometimes just being in the room can be impactful. That is, that Black judges' presence in a space can deter others from doing or saying things that are inappropriate and that they would not feel comfortable doing or saying in the presence of a Black person. In sum, Black judges' impact on their colleagues may not always be what Black judges are saying or sharing with their peers. Instead, the interviews also suggest that Black judges' presence alone, without any commentary, is enough to impact their colleagues' thoughts and behaviors and lead to the creation of a system that is more authentic. Whether it is their presence alone or their being vocal upstanders when something is wrong, Black judges are both passively and actively helping to ensure that the legal system is transparent.

One theoretical argument for diversity has always been that Black judges will decide differently than their counterparts who are not Black. There was an understanding that they may see things differently, which would impact their decision-making. Judge Wilson, for example, said a Black judge "is going to take into account what the case is and what precedent is and what the law says, but [they] also may see things a little bit differently." His understanding is that the consequence of looking at things differently is "if a white male looks at a case and [a Black judge] looks at the same case, that they'll get a different conclusion." Collegial education functions as an equalizer of sorts, so that an informed and culturally competent white judge can potentially look at the same or a similar case as a Black judge and arrive at the same conclusion because both judges possess an understanding of the issues present in the case or cases. But also beyond supporting understanding of specific issues in cases, collegial education and cultural competency can help judges understand the broader implications of their decisions and these issues within the communities litigants are coming from and how their backgrounds influence the issues.

Measuring or assessing exactly how collegial learning impacts white judges is unclear because, as Judge Adams aptly reminds us, "We don't sit in each other's courtrooms." In other words, Black judges are not necessarily witnessing or observing their white colleagues making decisions. They are unable to observe the impact or consequences of their collegial education. But because the communities of legal professionals working in courthouses are small and they talk, Black judges do get some information through what others observe of white judges' behavior. "We hear lawyers talk, and lawyers talk to us about other judges. We may hear what other judges are doing," says Judge Adams.

Judges' lack of understanding and life experience threatens the possibility of just and fair decision-making. Consider, for example, Judge Martin's story about a judge who could not understand the litigant: "The litigant was just trying to tell her story and the judge took offense to it. Really, it was just miscommunication because, really, this is how this person talks and expresses themselves. The judge just didn't understand." Judge Martin is referring to a Black litigant who was exercising her constitutional right to testify and share her story. However, because of the litigant's use of African American Vernacular English (AAVE), the judge did not seem to understand and took offense to something she said. As mentioned in chapter 5, sociolinguists have written about the impact of the use of AAVE in legal proceedings, and how if misunderstood, it can result in outcomes unfavorable to the individuals who speak the dialect simply as a result of language barrier between the speaker of AAVE and the decision-makers in the courtroom (Dworin 2021; Jones et al. 2019; Rickford and King 2016). While we do not know the outcome of the case the judge is referring to, the judge clearly remembers it and was impacted by it, signaling how much miscommunication between judges and litigants is an issue, especially if a litigants is using AAVE and the judge presiding over the cases does not understand it.

Judge Moore shared a similar story related to miscommunication in the courtroom. The judge shared that she is always trying to get her colleagues to think less about what is said to them that might lead them to hold someone in contempt of court and more about litigants' positionality and how their life and even being in court can be a source of stress that leads them to say things that they normally would not say. "I think you have to have an ability to look beyond how a person says what they say to have an understanding of what they are saying. . . . If a person says [something] with an attitude . . . that [might be] just the way they talk, or they are on the edge—you know, [the] circumstances of their life causes them to be on the edge" (Judge Moore). She goes on to say that some judges might put a litigant in jail for getting smart or cursing at the judge, but she asks herself, "Am I going to trip?" This pause for reflection and this question about whether she is going to respond by "tripping," or losing her composure, is important because it may lead the judge to decide not to punish someone for losing control of their own composure. In other words, Black judges are not only recommending an assessment of the intention behind a litigant's words and behavior, but they are engaging in this practice as well.

Collegial education can also improve white judges' ability to understand not just what litigants are saying, but why they do the things they do. For instance, Judge Wilson contrasts how a white judge and Black judge might look at a case involving "a Black male who was running from the police at 3 o'clock in the morning." He says the white judge might perceive the Black defendant's action as "fleeing the police" and therefore, the defendant "should go to jail."

Judge Wilson says that the Black judge, on the other hand, might say " 'Wait a minute! There is a history of white police officers abusing Blacks late at night," insinuating that the Black judge may not necessarily consider the action fleeing law enforcement, which is against many state penal codes.

Another example of Black judges' distinctive understandings about what happens in marginalized communities involves rental cars. Judge Johnson says,

> When a kid says he rented a car from a crackhead for ten dollars, you need to know that that happens. If you don't know that that happens, then you are very apt to conclude that that young person is lying. Well, I know that it happens. I have a brother who was a crackhead, used all the time. You know that those kinds of things happen, and so it helps give you a different perspective on events and how things actually happened in life. Sometimes when police tell me things that happened, my experience suggests to me that no, it probably did not happen exactly like that.

This judge explains how sometimes, when the lived experience of a judge and a defendant are very different, the judge will be dismissive of the defendant's story simply because it does not conform to their idea of what is normal. Misinterpreting the facts of a defendant's experience can lead to wrongful convictions. Thus, it is crucial that white judges are educated about minority experiences to properly administer justice.

Black judges also help white judges develop critical thinking through collegial education. Judge Smith gives an example of white judges not thinking critically when they were presented with numerous cases that were too alike to overlook. Judge Smith says his colleagues "should have recognized that the defendants were right. When you have ten men during ten different periods in time who do not know each other but who tell essentially the same story about what went on, they are probably telling the truth. . . . It's just the little things that you put together." Their city had recently settled a lawsuit with numerous defendants after evidence showed that police officers had repeatedly engaged in misconduct that Black and Brown defendants had long shared with the courts. Had the judges thought critically about the issue and seen the humanity of the defendants and treated them accordingly, the judges would have responded differently all along and protected the defendants and community from police misconduct. The defendants were not treated as humans because the judges were thinking in terms of the roles and labels that govern the justice system. In the justice system, defendants are stripped of their humanity and reduced to the role of perpetrator/criminal, and thus the judge views them in that way. On the other hand, police officers are always viewed in a positive light, as the morally upright protectors of the community. Part of collegial education is about humanizing the Black experience and uprooting the systemic thinking that categorizes it as criminal behavior.

Black judges are also educating their colleagues about history. Judge Smith says he wants to "remind the people that I work with that we have to keep the scales balanced. . . . I'm convinced as I study history that they have not always been balanced, and as a consequence of that, I want to remind my colleagues because it's very easy for the scales to become unbalanced." An important part of collegial education is historical education about the Black-versus-white lived experience in this country and how it is still affecting the judicial system today. This judge shows that it is very easy for the scales to become "unbalanced" and for Black defendants to be treated unfairly, as the judicial system has been doing for decades.

This appellate judge, one of the only ones in the study, went on to discuss how he calls or decides things differently than his colleagues because of his understanding of the Constitution: "I disagree with my colleagues who say we have to interpret [the Constitution] like the founding fathers. I cannot give any credibility to a constitution that treated me as three-fifths of a person [and] that did not give women or Blacks the right to vote." Judge Smith says he willingly challenges "disparate treatment":

Some of my colleagues on [the] court can take the position that we do not need to effectuate the Constitution because in fact the defendant is guilty. That is not the way I come to a case. I look at the case based on the issues being presented by the defendant. . . . Often, the position is taken by my colleagues that "Well, the drugs were there . . . I don't see a violation." Well, see, I am a strict constructionist, If the Constitution provides that you can only arrest upon the finding of probable cause, if I don't see any probable cause, I am going to effectuate the Constitution and say that is a bad arrest. I do not care what they find. I do not care how bad the person is, because that is not my job.

Yet another example of collegial education is from Judge Johnson, who shares a story involving court testimony from someone who says they casually interacted with someone else without getting a lot of personal details. The judge said her white colleagues struggle to make sense of such testimony, but it makes perfect sense to her, given her understanding of interactions in marginalized communities.

> When I'm sitting as the fact finder and somebody says they were sitting at a bar drinking beer with somebody but they can't tell you what the person's name is and what they did for a living and all that, I don't find that unusual, like folks from middle-class backgrounds do. As a matter of fact, [folks from middle-class backgrounds] find it sort of incredulous: "You mean you talked to them all evening long and you didn't find out what his last name was? You don't know where he lives? You don't know what kind of work he does?" No, because . . . sitting in bars in African American neighborhoods, you start asking them kind of questions and they want to know, "What the eff is it to you? We [are] just having a beer. You don't need to know all of that about me." But I know when [folks from middle-class backgrounds] go out, . . . right after [they are] introduced to somebody, five minutes later they are asking, . . . "So, what kind of work do you do?"

Her view is that judges need to have a broader understanding than the one their limited experiences have given them. She says, "There needs to be another take on it" (Judge Johnson). In the case of this judge, a socioeconomic barrier is preventing middle-class judges from understanding the experiences of lower-class defendants. This is just one of many barriers that separate the lived experiences of judges from defendants and the lived experiences of white Americans from Blacks Americans. Judges, like all people, have preconceived notions about certain situations, which may not be applicable to people of all backgrounds. Hearing other perspectives is crucial for overcoming these preconceived notions and understanding how and why situations may have transpired as they did.

Although Judge Johnson was not referring to miscommunication between judges and litigants, her comment suggests that there are judges in the court system who are not familiar with different communication patterns. Judge Allen noted this as her own experience interacting with people in the courthouse who she felt did not quite understand her or speak the same language that she did: "The way that I deal with coming to work every morning is I'm going to a foreign land because, you know, I'm the only one in here and I speak a strange-language tongue." (Judge Allen). Beyond differences in the lived experiences of judges and litigants, linguistic differences, as this judge exemplifies, further prevent these actors from understanding each other. One way to address this issue, especially between judges and litigants, is by having judges develop understanding of how different communities communicate and how all communication styles are a product of the environments in which they are developed.

Collegial education around racialization and racialized experiences may be controversial, but it need not be because it seems to happen about other topics as well. Judge Baker suggested that education about age and generation is important for judges' ability to understand the nature and facts of cases they preside over involving youth and elderly people. "Whenever there's something that young people start talking about, and I don't understand it, [I] look at my young employees, and say: 'What are they talking about? Explain it to me.' And, of course, looking at the other end of the spectrum, like somebody's older—when an older person comes through, I can try and relate to that person, too." This judge is highlighting the need for age and generational diversity among those working in the court system, which is similar to what Judge Taylor indicated when he discussed needing broad diversity among jurists. Not just race and age but also other identities and experiences are important to have represented among those charged with justice administration. He said, "You don't want all your judges from the same schools. You don't want all your judges from the same race. You don't want all your judges from the same background in the sense of whether they're rich or poor, or whether they grew up on the farm or the city, or what type of experiences that they've had. So, when it comes to the court, I think you need definitely some variety of background and experiences." Judicial diversity is important when it comes to judges' individual decisions, but because judges communicate with one another, they can share their diverse experiences and understandings to help other judges develop competency about things they have no direct or even vicarious experience with.

Diversity among those wearing judicial robes, therefore, leads to a diversity of understanding of experiences. Similarly, Judge Hall notes that the system functions best when those working within the system reflect those who are impacted by the system because understanding the experiences of those who come before the courts leads to better decisions: "We need as many Black faces [in the judiciary] as there are Black faces out in the community. . . . It's just necessary [that] there are opportunities and experiences that I have that enhance my behavior or my decisions in here, just like there are opportunities and experiences that someone who is polar opposite from me can have." Judicial outcomes can be truly equitable and unbiased only when the representation of Black judges in the judiciary reflects the diversity of the community.

BLACK JUDGES' COLLEGIAL TEACHING AND THE DEVELOPMENT OF CULTURAL COMPETENCY AMONG THEIR JUDICIAL PEERS

By engaging in collegial education, I argue that Black judges may help others in the legal profession develop cultural competency, a concept that emerges out of social work. When someone is culturally competent, they have the capacity to recognize, understand, and respect the values, attitudes, beliefs, and behaviors of people from different backgrounds and cultures. Thus, cultural competence is not inconsequential; culturally competent people are often the very people who make decisions in their spheres of influence in ways that reflect their broad understandings of different groups of people, and therefore, they can be said to make decisions that are more informed and empathetic.

Cultural competency can come from growing up in a diverse community where one interacts with people from different backgrounds. This would mean being raised in neighborhoods that are diverse or going to schools that are diverse. Unfortunately, the United States is still a country with high racial segregation (Rothstein 2017). If a person does not develop cultural competency early in life, they can still develop it in their later years via college, self-selected education, and even the people they choose to engage with. This is where collegial learning can be impactful because colleagues have a rapport that can lead to sharing knowledge and thoughts in informal, yet potentially highly impactful ways.

Cultural competence is routinely mentioned in the clinical world, where therapists and other human service providers engage with and support clients from a variety of backgrounds. These providers need to possess sensitivities and understandings that will help them to be more empathetic and responsive to the population with which they work. In the judicial world, cultural competence is not a frequently used concept, but we would argue that the principles still apply. In the courts, judges who are culturally competent have a great potential to be better judges than those without cultural competency because they possess sensitivities and understandings of people from diverse backgrounds.

As mentioned previously, white judges are overrepresented among state court judges. Because of persisting segregation, they are unlikely to have been socialized in communities that were diverse or to have come from marginalized backgrounds, and many of them likely have lacked opportunities to develop a cultural competency that would aid them in their judicial role as decision-makers of law and fate for people from very diverse and marginalized backgrounds. This is precisely how, where, and when judicial diversity might matter in the courthouse, beyond the courtroom.

There are some opportunities for judges to gain cultural competence via collegial learning outside the courthouse. For instance, many judges attend conferences that bring together judges and court administrators to discuss and create policy intended to help courts across the country function.[3] Duke University has a program for distinguished jurists to visit and work with faculty and students.[4] The Bolch Judicial Institute's Distinguished Judge in Residence centered diversity within the judiciary by recently having Black and two other judges of color in residence—a Black woman in 2020 and an Asian woman and Latino man in 2021. While in residence, these jurists had the opportunity to attend conferences and workshops, engage with academic professionals, and work on their own writing projects. The National Judicial College Summit, typically attended by hundreds of appellate judges and legal practitioners, is also a space for gaining cultural competence through panels and courses that are often taught by judges.

But as I showed in this section regarding Black judges and collegial education, when the court system includes judges from diverse backgrounds and with diverse perspectives and they are communicating with their fellow judges and collegial education is happening, because of the content and substance of at least some of that communication, judges are also developing their cultural competence. Because Black judges are sharing their experiences, understandings of marginalization, and knowledge of issues within the Black community, they are helping their judicial peers develop their cultural competency, which can significantly impact proceedings and outcomes of cases involving litigants from marginalized communities.

CONCLUSION

This chapter focused on Black judges' engagement with their judicial peers. Black judges interviewed for this study described how discussions with their colleagues when they are sitting in meetings, walking in the hallway, attending conferences or seminars, or even over lunch are often enlightening to individuals who do not know or understand the lived experiences of people of color. Many of the Black judges interviewed described how having Black judges on the bench matters to justice via the individuals they encountered. To these Black judges, their presence, the discussions that occur, and the information that they provide is virtually equivalent to giving a diversity training or cultural competency session. Many of the Black judges interviewed see these conversations as valuable to their colleagues and crucial to justice in the long run because they help White judges and attorneys understand the individuals and the experiences of the individuals they encounter while working in the judicial system. These judges' belief about the value of diversity is demonstrated by research in judicial politics that shows that race and gender diversity on collegial courts such as state supreme courts results in judges being more likely to rule in favor of racial minorities and women (Kastellec 2013; Peresie 2004; Songer and Crews-Meyer 2000). The premise behind this work is that minority voices on the bench matter to their colleagues, who have an opportunity to understand cases and litigants from a unique perspective. I find that, despite not adjudicating on the same bench and over the same cases, Black judges are educating their colleagues and helping them to develop cultural competency, which may ultimately impact white judges' decision-making.

Black judges' helping their colleagues develop cultural competency represents another example of the unpaid challenging work/labor that many Black professionals, such as Black professors, often engage in (Gordon, Willink, and Hunter 2024). Black judges are not necessarily being altruistic, but I suspect they engage in this work because they know it matters or, at the very least, are optimistic about being able to make a difference. They know that having more culturally competent judges presiding over cases that disproportionately involve people from marginalized communities can lead to better and more informed and equitable decision-making. If Black judges can make white judges more knowledgeable and those white judges decide cases in more informed and culturally sensitive ways, then the system will be a fairer, more just place for everyone, especially for Black Americans, who are disproportionately processed through it.

Scholarship by researchers who study decision-making in state and federal collegial courts generally conclude that judicial diversity matters and significant value is added by the presence of Black judges. This chapter reveals how, besides being jurists, Black judges also appear to behave as teachers. Their interviews reveal that they are frequently involved in conversations with white judges. These conversations often provide an opportunity for Black judges to describe the experiences of African Americans and share their insights about Black life in America. The Black judges in this study described these encounters as friendly and respectful and as teachable moments for the individuals involved. These Black judges are illustrating yet again that they are engaging in advocative representation of Black interests and why it matters that they are present on the bench.

EIGHT

ADVOCATIVE REPRESENTATION
IN THE COMMUNITY

Black judges' work and impact as jurists extend far beyond the courtroom. As the prior chapter illustrates, Black judges often engage in collegial education with their judicial peers, helping them to become more culturally sensitive, informed, and competent. Black judges' courthouse work, therefore, involves helping to diversify the minds of the judges already present in the legal system. In doing this work, Black judges are providing advocative representation in the courthouse because Black Americans desire more cultural awareness in an institution that regularly impacts people and communities of color.

Black judges' representational work extends into various communities as well. Black judges are active in their community court system, their local residential community, and the broader legal professional community via outreach, the development of programs, and establishing organizations. Unfortunately, scholars have largely overlooked these activities and engagements as significant for understanding not only the work that Black judges engage in but also the narrow and broad impacts these judges are having across the United States. By ignoring Black judges' community engagement, scholars are missing an opportunity to appreciate how and where Black judges can and do often represent Black interests.

This chapter examines Black judges' reported community engagement. The following questions guide the analysis: What community outreach efforts do Black judges engage in when they are not on the bench? What programs and initiatives do they sponsor and involve themselves with? Finally, what are the consequences or results of their community, organizational, and institutional engagements, and how does these relate to Black legal interests? Because of the dearth of public and scholarly information on Black judges' non-adjudication work, I did not have any specific expectations for Black judges' community outreach, organizational programs, and institutional initiatives that build on what other scholars have previously shown. Nevertheless, I generally expected Black judges to engage in activities, develop and support programs, and establish organizations that reflect their interests. As a result of their background, socialization, and group identities and consciousness, which I highlighted in chapters 3 and 4, I anticipated that Black judges' community, organizational, and institutional work would often connect to and be in support of marginalized groups and group interests. And if their community work is supportive of marginalized groups and group interests, I argue that this work should be viewed as additional manifestations of advocative representation by Black judges.

This chapter highlights how Black judges' work in their court system, their local community, and the broader legal profession, emphasizing the community- and institution-building Black judges engage in, in their official capacity as judges. Black judges, regardless of judicial selection method, often engage directly with the local residential community, which often is a community disproportionately impacted by the legal system. Black judges are also active and engaged members of their local judicial system, developing programs to improve the administration of justice in their area. Moreover, Black judges see themselves as belonging to more than just the local legal community. As members of a vast network of legal professionals that stretches across the United States, Black judges establish, advance, and support the development of organizations that support legal professionals of color. The community activities, programs, and initiatives that Black judges are involved in improve the relationship between marginalized communities and the local legal system, facilitate the just and equitable functioning of court systems, and support diversity in the legal profession. In other words, Black judges' community work highlights yet more ways that Black judges are providing advocative representation of Black interests since the consequences of their actions align directly with Black Americans' legal interests.

COMMUNITY ENGAGEMENT AND OUTREACH

State and local officials, especially those working in the legislative and executive branches of government, such as state or county legislatures, often conduct outreach into the communities they represent. In legislative studies and executive branch studies, this outreach is viewed as part of constituent services, which encompass various activities, such as being in the community. Such community engagement is generally believed to be a representational responsibility of elected officers.[1] The purpose is tied to these officials' representative role to better understand their community's policy interests and needs, so that these officials may be well-informed when they represent and advocate for their constituents' interests.

Community engagement and outreach on the part of state and local officials are also significant because their presence in the communities they represent also helps them with electability. Representative officials being seen in the community is important for constituents because it helps them feel connected to their representatives and reelect them to office (Fenno 1977). Social scientists have long understood that maintaining one's position in government via successful electoral politics drives much of the actions of representative officials (Mayhew 1974).

Although they are less discussed in the literature on community outreach, state judges also engage in community outreach, or at least they are encouraged to engage in community outreach. "Outreach seeks to provide the public with accurate information about the judiciary and, in turn, receive feedback from the public to inform administrative decision-making. It usually takes the form of a series of discrete events" (Rottman 2015, 1).[2] Rottman (2015) summarizes court experiences with outreach by identifying five outreach approaches/mechanisms that have been deployed by state courts:

Explaining the role of judges and demystifying court processes;

Social science research tools to assess public opinion about the courts;

Active listening to community concerns and feedback;

Reform of court processes that could be developed and implemented with collaboration from the public; and

Local delivery of justice through the creation of community courts that respond to community needs.

The goal of court outreach is to build a relationship between the courts and communities that can lead to intentional deep engagement and partnering. "Engagement is an ongoing forum allowing two-way interaction with the public in which both sides listen to one another, recommend reforms, and take joint steps to address community and court concerns" (Rottman 2015, 1). Meaningful engagement requires trust and a belief among community members that engaging judges and the courts is possible and will result in tangible changes in the legal system and community. For these reasons, judges are generally encouraged and have an incentive to engage the public when possible.

BLACK JUDGES' COMMUNITY ENGAGEMENT AND OUTREACH

Surveys and interviews with Black judges shed light on how Black judges engage with the local communities in which they work. The survey asked judges to identify three professional organizations to which they belong. This open-ended question allowed judges to share which professional organizations they regard as meaningful affiliations. Based on the organizations' missions and values, we get a glimpse of what Black judges deem important to them professionally. The affiliations mentioned can be divided into three main groups: race-related organizations, gender-related organizations, and bar associations. The most common professional membership affiliations were race-related. More than half (54 percent) of the Black judge survey respondents reported belonging to organizations that either assembled racial minorities or focused on race-related issues. Race-related organizations mentioned include Black Barristers and associations of Black (women) attorneys. Almost one in five judges (19 percent) affiliate themselves with a gender-related organization, such as the National Society for Black Women Judges (NSBWJ) and National Association of Women Judges (NAWJ), which makes sense given the large number of Black women judges in this study. And finally, Black judges commonly associate themselves with both local and nationwide bar associations or legal associations, which are groups of attorneys, judges, and other legal actors that collaborate to handle issues arising in and affecting the legal profession and system. Typically, bar associations host workshops and conferences, bringing together members for legal education and conversations concerning the legal system and profession. While 15 percent of Black judges reported belonging to the American Bar Association, the largest association of lawyers and law students in the world, almost double that amount (29 percent) reported belonging to the National Bar Association, the nation's oldest and largest legal association of predominantly Black legal professionals, such as attorneys and judges.[3]

Recognizing that membership does not necessarily indicate where Black judges spend their time when they are in the community in an official or professional-related capacity, I also asked Black judges to share some of the organizations or institutions they volunteer with in their official role as judge. Despite judges working on different issues and in different communities, overlap was considerable between the organizations that they mentioned in their responses. Table 8.1 lists the most common organizations mentioned. Four types of volunteer organizations were common across the survey respondents:

TABLE 8.1: Most common types of professional affiliations, volunteer organizations, and initiatives for Black judges.

Professional membership affiliations	Volunteer organizations	Types of initiatives started or involved in
Race-related organizations 147 (54%)	Bar associations 36 (13%)	Drug court programs 42 (16%)
Local bar associations 75 (28%)	Diversity 33 (12%)	Youth education and court programs 36 (13%)
Gender-related organizations 51 (19%)	Youth 25 (9%)	Diversity programs 25 (9%)
National Bar Association 78 (29%)	Church 11 (4%)	Mental health programs 23 (9%)
American Bar Association 41 (15%)	—	Domestic violence 11 (4%)
—	—	Diversion 8 (3%)

Source: Author.

bar associations, diversity-related organizations, youth-related organizations, and church organizations. It is not clear how much time judges spent volunteering with these various organizations, but from the surveys, judges indicated that when they did volunteer, these types of organizations were most important to them and where they devoted at least some of their time.

It is one thing for a Black judge to be a member of an organization as a judge and to volunteer their time with that organization. It is an entirely different thing to develop or start an initiative, which requires extensive work, energy, planning, and time. Table 8.1 includes the most common types of initiatives or programs that Black judges have started or been involved in as a judge. These are teen court, diversity, youth education, mental health, and drug court. Other program themes mentioned more than once but slightly less common include veterans affairs, domestic violence, law day/law week, accessibility, community, and family and school.

Drug court programs are the most common type of program Black judges started or supported. This makes sense given the racialized nature of drug-related policy and the number of drug-related cases in the criminal legal system that disproportionately impact Black people and other racial and ethnic minorities. Some Black judges who preside over cases where they witness and participate in the criminalization of addiction choose to support treating this community and legal issue differently in their courts. Slightly more than 10 percent of judges also indicated starting or being involved in youth education and court programs (e.g., teen diversion programs and youth education programs), and almost one in ten judges were involved in diversity programs or mental health programs. Finally, 3 percent of respondents shared starting or involving themselves with diversion programs in their communities. People are often redirected from prosecution and incarceration into these programs, where they can be supported and have their record expunged, thus preventing the long-term impact that comes with having a conviction on one's record (Middlemass 2017; Middlemass and Smiley 2020).

Numerous court system programs were mentioned in the surveys and during the interviews that were developed and significantly supported by Black judges. These programs are complex, coordinated, and organized, and they are meant to play a distinctive role in the local court system and how that system addresses or handles certain issues. Considering the programs that Black judges mentioned, they are trying to respond to the distinctive needs and circumstances of the communities in which they live and work. While these programs are unable to resolve some of the underlying societal issues, they do provide alternative ways for judges to have societal impact and address legal matters in the communities they work in. Instead of simply sitting on the bench and sending people young and older to prison, the courts can respond differently. The next sections examine several court-system-specific programs, underscoring how these programs constitute examples of Black judges' functioning as representatives of Black interests in their local community. These sections focus on the three topics around which Black judges have established initiatives/programs: adult court diversion programs and programs that offer alternatives to incarceration, programs that disrupt the youth pipeline to prison, and initiatives that connect and support black legal professionals.[4]

ADULT COURT DIVERSION PROGRAMS AND PROGRAMS THAT OFFER ALTERNATIVES TO INCARCERATION

Large numbers of similar legal cases and recidivism can lead to developments within court systems that better address reoffending and common legal challenges in a comprehensive way. Problem-solving courts are different from traditional courts because their approach is often grounded in the rehabilitative model of justice, and they combine treatment and services inside and outside the courtroom in a plan personalized to each defendant. Unlike a traditional court, whose processes prioritize efficiency and often result in punishment, problem-solving courts emphasize holistic and personalized justice that strives to facilitate and support the behavioral change of offenders by meeting important needs. Offenders revisit problem-solving courts regularly and, as a result, develop a professional relationship with judges and other court officers.

Problem-solving courts often offer specialized diversion programs designed to account for the fact that circumstances surrounding crime in urban areas are distinctive and, therefore, warrant a different form of treatment. Imprisonment is not the only form of redress available to the courts, and Black judges understand how they can think expansively and creatively about the power they have in the legal system to define the consequences for violating certain laws. Specifically, they can enact judge-led interventions into a system that has often offered only punishment and confinement as responses to activities

TABLE 8.2: Some initiatives and programs established by Black judges.

Name	Black judge(s) involved	Year est.	Purpose/Mission*
Judge Larry A. Jones Drug Court**	Larry A. Jones	1998	"Simply put, drug courts are judicially supervised court dockets that provide a sentencing alternative of treatment combined with supervision for people living with serious substance use."
Green Y.A.R.D. Program	Lisa Green	— —	"6 month diversion program for first-time offenders between the ages of 17 to 25. This program's core purpose is to redirect young, first-time offenders out of the criminal justice system."
Pipeline to Possibilities	Amber Givens, Lisa Green, Shequitta Kelly, and Stephanie Huff	2016	"[Is] committed to educating youth on various aspects of the justice system and inspiring youth to become leaders in society."
Scales of Justice	La Tia Martin	2009	"Introduces promising students to the study of law through a pre-college preparatory program conjoining course work in law and leadership with intensive training from judges, law school professors, and legal practitioners."
Ohio Black Judges Association	Emmanuella Groves and Cassandra Collier-Williams	2021	"Resource for Black judges across the state aimed at continuing legal education for judges and giving them a space where their voices and concerns can be heard."
Just the Beginning – A Pipeline Organization	Ann Claire Williams	1992	"Encourage[s] students of color and from other underrepresented groups to pursue career and leadership opportunities in the law."

* Purpose and mission information was pulled from the initiative's website.

** Formerly called the Greater Cleveland Drug Court

Source: Author.

criminalized by the state, such as drug addiction, and behaviors impacted by mitigating factors, such as untreated mental illness or history of trauma.

Numerous Black judges who participated in the study mentioned developing and supporting adult court diversion programs and programs that offer alternatives to incarceration. By creating alternative institutions, Black judges change the court systems in which they operate by advocating for and instituting different processes that can help defendants overcome personal health conditions and yet take accountability for their actions. In creating and supporting diversion programs, Black judges are being responsive to the distinctive needs and circumstances of the community members they serve. These judges can understand and account for, for example, drug use and minor distribution offenses in urban areas and the impact of untreated or mistreated mental health conditions on community members' societal behaviors, as they consider defendants' charges. Individuals struggling with drug use and mental health disorders are vulnerable populations in society who disproportionately end up justice-involved. While judges are not positioned to fully address drug use and mental health needs, some Black judges have acted within their local legal system to respond differently when these individuals end up in court. These alternative programs try to meet the needs of the community and legal system by institution building because of failed health policies. Because these programs are often established in or near urban or metropolitan areas, they disproportionately benefit people of color living in close proximity to inner cities.

Larry A. Jones Drug Court

During interviews with judges from the Midwest, one organizational program was mentioned repeatedly: the Greater Cleveland Drug Court, a problem-solving court established in 1998 by Judge Larry A. Jones.[5] This court has since been renamed the Larry A. Jones Drug Court (LAJDC). Interviews with judges from the South drew repeated mentions of various Black judges working to establish mental health courts. I discuss these programs below and highlight how they respond to the needs of the community.

Judge Jones was a Black Ohio jurist who served on multiple courts over forty years. Prior to becoming a judge, he worked as a prosecutor in Cuyahoga County and then as a Cleveland City Council member. Jones's first judgeship was as a trial court judge on the Cleveland Municipal Court.[6] In 2009, he became an appellate-level judge when he joined Ohio's Eighth District Court of Appeals. Jones served on the appellate bench for twelve years before passing away in October 2021. When he passed, Judge Mary Boyle, the administrative and presiding judge on the Eighth District Court, described Jones as "the quintessential public servant—dedicated to making the judiciary and the community better."[7] I argue that one of the clear ways Jones made both the judiciary and community better was by establishing Cuyahoga County's first drug court, the Greater Cleveland Drug Court.

According to the National Drug Court Resource Center, "drug court programs are for people charged with or convicted of criminal offenses, are likely to re-offend, and who are experiencing serious substance use disorders." Two common processes within drug courts are pretrial and post-adjudication. During the pretrial process, defendants are diverted from traditional court proceedings prior to a guilty plea. During the post-adjudication process, defendants plead guilty, and their sentence is deferred while they participate in the drug court rehabilitation program. To date, more than 3,800 drug courts have been established in the United States.[8]

Like most drug courts established in the late twentieth century, the context for the LAJDC's creation is the devastation created by the crack epidemic and the subsequent war on drugs. During the 1980s and 1990s, Cleveland, like most urban cities, experienced the swell of crack cocaine use and addiction as a result of the drug's affordability, availability, and potency (Watkins and Fullilove 2000). Crack cocaine hit the Black community particularly hard, leading to increased addiction, overdoses, and violence including homicides (Watkins and Fullilove 2000). Instead of treating drug addiction and use as a public health issue as we currently do with the heroin epidemic, crack cocaine use and users were criminalized by the laws in a coordinated campaign, known as the war on drugs, that is now widely understood as having been racially motivated and discriminatory (Alexander 2010).

The war on drugs was both a domestic and international crusade against drug trade and use in the United States. Laws severely penalized drug use, addiction, and distribution, and their enforcement over several decades, along with mandatory sentencing guidelines, contributed to mass incarceration (Alexander 2010). By the late 1990s, Black communities had been devastated during the crack epidemic by the war on drugs on both the supply (distribution) and demand (addiction and usage) sides. As a result of the criminalization of drug use during the war on drugs, the criminal courts, jails, and prisons were inundated with people from primarily impoverished communities who struggled with addiction. The lack of addiction treatment led to an ever-revolving door of individuals in and out of the legal system, thanks to heavy enforcement, especially in Black communities.

For judges working in the late twentieth century like Judge Jones, it is unsurprising that they would seek to establish drug courts as a way to respond to the surge of drug-related cases before their courts and the constant reprocessing of people. In addition to creating drug courts to address some significant community issues (addiction and use), some drug courts were also created out of sheer necessity to alleviate docket pressure (Lurigio 2008, 1–2). For Jones, presiding over countless Cleveland cases involving people struggling with addiction meant that he would need to do something differently on the court side of things to address this issue, which state and federal laws were unconcerned with viewing as a public health crisis.

In 1998, a federal grant to the Cleveland Municipal Court provided the funds necessary to create a drug court that could oversee a specialized docket. With this funding, Jones was able to establish the LAJDC. Before Jones's election to the Eighth District Court of Appeals in 2008, he judicially supervised the drug court's docket for two decades, which provided an alternative to typical jail sentencing for Clevelanders struggling with drug addiction by combining treatment with supervision and regular check-ins in court to ensure steady progress toward sobriety. Like other programs, Cleveland's LAJDC diverted "offenders through deferred prosecution tactics or suspended sentences, supervising offenders and then dismissing their charges after the successful completion of court conditions" (Lurigio 2008, 2).

Reorganizing Cleveland's court system to include a drug court produced significant benefits. One benefit of drug courts, generally speaking, is that they help reduce recidivism, sometimes by up to 35–40 percent (National Treatment Court Resource Center 2025). Similarly, a study involving evaluations of ninety-two drug courts found that "the average effect of participation is analogous to a drop in recidivism from 50% to 38%; and, these effects last up to three years" (Mitchell et al. 2012). Additionally, drug courts reduce city costs. A ten-year study conducted by the National Institute of Justice found a nearly $1,400 difference in the cost of drug court participation compared to traditional justice processes. These and other factors created a $6,700–$12,000 public savings per participant.[9]

Considering the decrease in recidivism and costs, drug courts keep people in their community and help them reach sobriety, and they free up funds that can be diverted to supporting social services. In other words, drug courts benefit not just the individuals using them but the broader community, which benefits financially and socially by keeping families and communities intact, drug addiction and crime low, and taxpayer funds available to address community needs.

According to the Cleveland drug court's website, LAJDC has had more than 1,900 people complete the program. The website reports that the average treatment cost is around $3,000 and the average cost of six months' incarceration is around $14,000. Therefore, just those 1,900 participants have saved the city roughly $20.9 million, which might have gone into incarcerating people, highlighting the cost efficiency of drug courts to handle chemical dependency in the community and the successful completion of a treatment program as an alternative to incarceration.

Another important factor of the Cleveland drug court is that after successful completion of the program and payment of a fee to be supervised by the courts, the participant's guilty plea for the first-degree misdemeanor is vacated and the charge is dismissed, and the case is expunged from the person's criminal record. Expungement is particularly important because possessing a criminal record negatively impacts individuals' social and political life by influencing their access to housing, employment, voting, student loans, and so on (Middlemass 2017; Middlemass and Smiley 2020). Again, considering the fact that 1,900 have successfully completed LAJDC's program, we see the impact that an organizational program like a drug court can have on individuals' ability to live meaningful, socially and politically engaged lives.

Being on the bench for four decades means that Jones became a legend in Cleveland's legal and political community. His important achievements while on the bench, such as helping to establish a problem-solving court to address a major issue in the local legal system, made him a pioneer. Establishing the drug court also highlights how Jones represented Black interests. His work directly addressed concerns around the need for special processing of drug-related cases during the war on drugs, which hit the city of Cleveland hard, especially the predominantly Black areas as a result of the racialized drug laws. The LAJDC has continued to be administered and led by Black judges.[10] After Jones's departure 2008, Judge Anita Laster Mays presided over the docket until 2014, when Judge Lauren C. Moore assumed the position.

Mental Health Courts Across the Country

Unlike drug treatment courts, which have been around since 1989, mental health courts were not established until 1997. Florida judge Ginger Lerner-Wren is credited with establishing and presiding over the first mental health court. These therapeutic treatment courts were created as a response to the increasing number of criminal defendants with serious mental health conditions.[11] Like drug treatment courts, mental health courts facilitate a holistic justice approach compared to the traditional process that prioritizes efficiency over personalization.

Individuals with common diagnoses, such as anxiety disorder, bipolar disorder, and schizophrenia or psychotic disorder, are served by these courts' pre-adjudication model. Unfortunately, not enough mental health courts have been established, despite the prevalence of criminal defendants and incarcerated persons with mental illnesses and the persisting criminalization of mental illness. Still, there are a number of Black judges who have committed to working to establish a mental health court in their area. I discuss some of those judges below and highlight how their initiatives qualify as advocative representation, given that the creation of therapeutic courts aligns with Black legal interests.

According to the Marshall Project, the Honorable E. Faye Peterson is one of "the five most powerful people in Mississippi's Hinds County justice system."[12] Judge Peterson is a Hinds County circuit judge. Her approach to judicial decision-making includes "leading with humanity while balancing the facts of what they did and who had been harmed."[13] She is known to challenge the prosecution on excessive criminal charges and check the prosecution when it tries to "be the moral or parental police." In listing the programs she has implemented during her judicial tenure, she mentioned a "fatherhood initiative . . . in Chancery Court that helped fathers find jobs and pay child support, to live-streaming current court proceedings. She said she is working to implement a mental health treatment court as an alternative to criminal court for people with mental health disorders."[14] Perhaps her desire to establish a mental health court relates to her grace and mercy approach to justice.

Similarly, in Georgia, the Honorable Cynthia C. Adams works as a superior court Judge. She's been on the bench since her appointment in 2017. She is the first woman and first Black person to serve as a judge in the Douglas County state and superior court level judicial system. She presides over the Douglas

County Mental Health Court. Like those of other mental health court judges (such as the Honorable Teresa Johnson, a city and county court judge in New York state[15]), Judge Adams's court oversees the treatment-based program for criminal defendants with a documented mental health diagnosis. Her goal is to "improve mental health, promote self-sufficiency, reduce recidivism, and offer cost effective alternatives to incarceration and hospitalization."[16]

Other Black judges working to establish mental health courts include Judge Gloria Reno, presiding judge of the 21st Circuit in St. Louis County Missouri, and Judge Robin Ransom, the presiding judge of the 22nd Circuit.[17] Judge Reno summarized the general sentiment about the reason to establish these courts: "It costs a lot of money to incarcerate a person. . . . This is a cheaper way of dealing with those who come into the courts for alcohol, for drugs and for mental-health issues."[18] These courts support defendants getting the assistance that they need.

Mental health courts are unmistakably aligned with Black judicial interests. These courts attempt to divert cases from the traditional court process involving prosecution into a process that tries to ensure that individuals dealing with serious mental illness receive the services they need and to help to prevent criminal charges in the future. The ultimate goal for these courts is for the individuals helped by it to have less involvement in and interactions with the legal system by addressing the mental health factors that might lead them to engage in criminalized behaviors and actions.

Establishing mental health courts is beneficial because, whether undiagnosed or (mis)diagnosed and untreated, mental illness often impacts individuals' decision-making, making them more likely to engage in risky behavior and criminalized activities (McGinty et al. 2016). Also, when individuals in mental health crises interact with law enforcement officers, instead of receiving the treatment and community-based services they need, they are often arrested, which leads to their overrepresentation in carceral institutions.[19] According to a recent study, nearly two-thirds of incarcerated individuals in jails and over half of state prison inmates have mental disorders, percentages higher than in the general United States population.[20] This leads to this nation's prisons and jails holding mentally ill individuals who would be better served elsewhere. In forty-four states, carceral institutions hold more mentally ill persons than the state psychiatric hospitals.[21] In fact, "the number of mentally ill persons in prisons and jails was ten times the number remaining in state hospitals."[22]

This was not always the case; in the mid-twentieth century, during the dein-
stitutionalization of public psychiatric hospitals, jails and prisons became the
new "asylums" and de facto mental health care providers and initiated the
persisting criminalization of mental illness. Currently, people with untreated
mental health conditions represent roughly 18 percent of all admissions into
the nation's jails.[23]

Mental health courts intervene at an important stage in the development
of a criminal case, the post-filing stage. In this stage, the court process has
already commenced but the final case disposition or outcome has not been determined. In other words, police decline police-led interventions before arrest
and prosecutors decline to intervene before charges are filed, and instead, the
case evolves to the point where the person is before the courts. Judge-led in-
tervention via the mental health courts permits the completion of the post-
filing diversion program and can lead to the initial charges ultimately being
dismissed without a trial and expunged.

These courts are available to defendants whose criminal charges are related to long-standing mental illness. Instead of typical trial and prosecution,
participants in the mental health court receive treatment services and other
community-based services such as housing and case management. When a
study asked criminal defendants whether they would accept diversion to treatment as part of a deal with the legal system, 78 percent of defendants said yes,
indicating most people would want this restorative justice approach to the
traditional court process.[24]

Because mental health courts facilitate cooperation between the defendant,
the state mental health system, local mental health service providers, and the
court, they can reduce the amount of involvement in and out of the legal
system that exists among people with mental health conditions. Recidivism is
generally high, but this is especially the case for people with mental disorders,
and these courts aim to help reduce recidivism. Examining the effectiveness
of fifteen mental health courts, Jalain, Lucas, and Higgins (2024) found that
these treatment courts significantly reduced recidivism (42.46 percent) for individuals who successfully participated in the treatment programs. By reducing recidivism and improving their clients' ability to function and thrive in
their community, these courts also help ease the workload of the court and
take pressure off the incarceration system.

By working to establish these courts, serving as a judge on them, and helping to develop these newer court programs, these Black women judges are an important part of the response to the issue of mental illness in the local community and criminal legal systems. These judges will preside over *all* related court proceedings, monitoring the success of the program. With these women and other Black judges like them as the sole judge in the courtroom, they will be able to develop strong rapport with the program participants. In chapter 5, I discussed how Black judges regularly engage in and deliver procedural justice in their courtrooms. The same will be true for these Black judges, who will engage with, encourage, and celebrate program participants. Because of the nature of the judging work in these cases, these Black judges will illuminate how the court system and its judges can operate differently than what most people might think about the court, given its typical adherence to traditional processes. Successful completion of these programs would lead to charges being dismissed. As I mentioned previously in the discussion about the LAJDC, not having a criminal record is advantageous in a society that perpetually punishes individuals with criminal convictions. Scholars have discussed the short- and long-term collateral consequences of incarceration, which include lack of access to employment, housing, and community services (Middlemass and Smiley 2020).

Both the LAJDC and the mental health courts will ideally be established in urban areas to respond to the societal need for alternatives to incarceration for criminally-charged people with substance abuse or mental disorders.[25] Black judges' deep involvement in these institutions highlight how they are functioning as representatives of Black interests. Both problem-solving courts facilitate connections to mental health and drug treatment services for individuals involved in early stages in the criminal legal system's processes. Mental illness and drug use are significant issues in inner cities, especially among marginalized communities. While these judges are unable to provide community-based services that might alleviate these conditions, through the establishment and development of these courts, Black judges highlight how they are thinking about ways to help individual defendants who struggle with these issues while also helping the broader community because addiction and untreated mental illnesses are detrimental to healthy communities.

PROGRAMS THAT DISRUPT THE YOUTH PIPELINE TO PRISON

The second group of programs Black judges created are youth-related. Unlike initiatives described in the prior section, which offer alternatives to prison and are available to adults with cases pending before the courts, Black judges mentioned developing programs that would disrupt the youth pipeline to prison. Instead of waiting to address issues once litigants are before them in the courtroom, some Black judges around the country have built and supported programs that aim to keep youth out of the court system. Many of these organizations target youth in urban areas.

Youth living in metropolitan areas face distinctive challenges that often lead to involvement in the criminal legal system (Krivo and Peterson 1996). Poverty remains concentrated in urban areas, with three in ten people living in poverty.[26] Recent disruptions in the economy, including the COVID pandemic, have increased the number of families living in poverty or almost in poverty.[27] Unemployment rates are also higher in urban areas.[28] Despite workforce training programs, cities' unemployment rate hovers around 15 percent, well above the national average of 9 percent.[29] Considering these circumstances, challenges in schooling, housing, homelessness, and crime facing youth and families living in inner cities are also unsurprising. Recent statistics are clear that urban crime and victimization are lower today than thirty to forty years ago (Gramlich 2024). Nonetheless, crime and victimization persist as major social problems in metropolitan cities, especially motor vehicle theft, burglary, robbery, and rape (Gramlich 2024).

Metropolitan areas are becoming more racially diverse as a result of gentrification by primarily white middle-class people moving into inner-city neighborhoods and displacing racial minorities who struggle to keep up with the increasing costs of the newly gentrified neighborhoods. Nevertheless, the racial segregation projects of the twentieth century that led to suburban and rural areas being primarily white and urban areas being primarily Black and other minorities persist. As a result, programs that target youth in urban areas inevitably end up reaching mainly children of color and children from poorer economic backgrounds.

All these statistics are sobering and help explain why Black judges adjudicating cases near urban areas are more likely to develop programs that try to reach and support youth before they become adults. These youth tend to be most at risk for involvement in the criminal legal system because of the economic and social circumstances in urban areas and racialized policing (Brunson and Miller 2006). Urban policing practices mean these young people face interactions with police that are quite different from the interactions their white urban, rural, and suburban counterparts experience (Brunson and Weitzer 2009).

While none of the youth programs that Black judges develop are identical, they share some general aspects. Each program typically has a mentoring component, whereby individuals who have gone to college or who work in a high-profile industry establish professional relationships with the youth. In these relationships, they can offer educational and career advice, as well as serve as role models. Additionally, the programs try to equip and empower the youth to fulfill their dreams. These programs often do this work by granting them access to opportunities for trainings, skill development, and programming. The goal of these programs is to keep these urban youth out of the legal system, giving them the support and development that might inspire them and put them on a track that would avoid involvement in criminal activities. Although diversion programs are typically conceptualized as court programs that divert people from traditional sentencing and punishment in the legal system, the youth programs that Black judges create also function as diversion programs because they try to divert youth from a future of justice involvement and court appearances so that they can realize their full potential and lead a purposeful life. These Black judges are signaling to youth of color that their background or where they grew up does not matter because they can dream big and achieve those dreams. Black judges' programs exist to support that work.

One fairly typical example is Pipeline to Possibilities, based in the Dallas, Texas, area.[30] It is "a program committed to educating youth on various aspects of the justice system and inspiring youth to become leaders in society." It was founded in 2016 and is managed by four Black women judges: Amber Givens, Lisa Green, Shequitta Kelly, and Stephanie Huff.[31] The goal of the empowerment program is to reduce recidivism and keep youth in their communities, especially in school, and out of the local legal system.[32] The program has helped support more than three hundred at-risk youth in Dallas from lower economic backgrounds, guiding them to paths that will keep them from being justice impacted. Most of the individuals participating in the program are in their late teens and early twenties and are first-time offenders. One of the issues the founders recognized in their work as judges was the school-to-prison pipeline playing out in their own court system, with youth being given punishment instead of help and services, thereby pushing them into the criminal legal system. Pipeline to Possibilities tries to disrupt this pervasive pipeline in Dallas by having programming directly in the schools and community. The four-week program includes a comprehensive curriculum that teaches youth about the legal system. Because the program is primarily targeted to at-risk youth in urban Dallas, it engages primarily with young Black adults and therefore directly benefits the Black community by helping these youth avoid incarceration by disrupting the school-to-prison pipeline.

Like Pipeline to Possibilities, the Scales of Justice Academy also supports Black youth and other youth from marginalized backgrounds. This organization was founded in 2009 by Justice La Tia Martin of the New York State Supreme Court.[33] As a legal professional and young Black female judge, she felt that young women, especially women of color, particularly those from underserved school systems, were missing from the legal profession. In response, she created the Scales of Justice Academy as a pre-college preparatory program to train and support young women of color to pursue law degrees. The comprehensive program includes course work in law-related topics and leadership training and mentorship from various legal professionals, including judges, practicing attorneys, and professors. The ultimate goal is keeping these promising young women from being justice impacted and to, instead, help them pursue higher education in law. On the program website, Justice Martin reflects on the program's accomplishments: "The Justice Academy has already motivated students to go on to college. They now credit the Justice Academy with exposing them to the tremendous opportunities of a legal education and giving them the confidence and inspiration to pursue careers in law." This program, like Pipeline to Possibilities, is individually supporting young Black women and other women of color, trying to ensure they are not justice impacted and feel supported to pursue legal careers.

The Green Y.A.R.D. Program is yet another example of a youth-related program. This program was started by Judge Lisa Green, a Dallas County, Texas, criminal court judge.[34] Judge Green's program has three major goals: empower young adults to reach their full potential as productive, responsible, and caring citizens; engage with young adults so they may learn the value of helping others through community service; and provide character and leadership development through mentoring and life-skills training. Her program is intended for first-time offenders between the ages of 17 and 25. Like many of the youth-related programs that Black judges involve themselves in, this program aims to divert young people from the criminal justice system who many Black judges feel make up a disproportionate number of people entering the system. Importantly, the program uses an expanded age range for youth, making it accessible to larger numbers of young people.

Pipeline to Possibilities, the Scales of Justice Academy, and the Green Y.A.R.D. were founded by Black women judges to support youth of color from disadvantaged backgrounds. These programs' close work with youth was intentionally designed to help keep them from being part of the local Dallas and New York school-to-prison pipeline and motivate and support them in pursuing higher education, especially law degrees and careers in the legal profession. The programs' mentorship, curriculum, and leadership and skill development have meant that they help disrupt systems that have historically led Black youth to be disproportionately justice impacted early in life. Thus, these programs align with Black judicial interests and indicate another way in which Black judges are representing Black interests in the community.

INITIATIVES THAT CONNECT AND SUPPORT BLACK LEGAL PROFESSIONALS

Black judges have established organizational programs to support and address local-level issues. These are typically local judges working within a particular court system or community that responds to the particular social context. Where the previously discussed organizational programs are locally focused, institutional initiatives are focused on topics across court systems and even the country. The third and final topic area that Black judges have developed initiatives around tries to connect existing legal professionals and allow them to amplify their voices. Black judges' institutional initiatives bring judges and other parties together to collaborate on widespread and common issues that necessitate statewide or national institution building.

Various institutional initiatives were discussed during interviews with Black judges, with many of these initiatives being only recently founded. Some initiatives exist at the state level, bringing together Black judges across a state, such as the Association of Black Judges of Michigan (ABJM) and the Ohio Black Judges Association (OBJA). Other institutional initiatives are nationwide, connecting Black judges across the country, such as the National Society for Black Women Judges (NSBWJ) and Just the Beginning (JTB). I discuss the OBJA and JTB in more detail below, highlighting how these initiatives reflect Black judges' functioning as representatives in the community.

Since the first Black Ohio judge was seated in 1942, almost eighty years later, the number has increased to only fifty-six judges concentrated in only nine of Ohio's eighty-eight counties, reports the OBJA.[35] These fifty-six judges are only 7.7 percent of all 723 judges in Ohio, despite Black Ohioans representing 14 percent of the state population, according to the Cleveland Metropolitan Bar Association.[36] Additionally, these judges are not distributed evenly across the state; forty-two of the fifty-six work in just three counties: Cuyahoga (Cleveland), Franklin (Columbus), and Hamilton (Cincinnati).

Unlike some Black judicial associations, such as the ABJM, which was founded in 1979, the OBJA was established more recently, in January 2021, to serve as a resource for both current and prospective Black judges. The founders of the association wanted to ensure continuous Black representation within the Ohio state judiciary. Moreover, OBJA aims to intentionally develop a "collective voice" among Black judges to better understand and address social and racial inequality in justice administration by bringing them together regularly to be in conversation with one another about what they are seeing in their respective areas.

OBJA is a space for current Black judges to convene and discuss common issues facing them in their role as judges in Ohio, as well as to strategically complete their required continuing legal education credits. One of the co-chairs said that Black judges in the association are "committed and passionate about [their] responsibilities to have a distinct role" in addressing issues such as the overrepresentation of Black Americans among those involved in the Ohio criminal legal system, and that doing so with a "collective voice will be impactful." Additionally, OBJA works with Black youth as prospective Black legal professionals, and junior Black legal practitioners as they enter and navigate the legal field in Ohio. OBJA is trying to respond to the fact that Black Americans are underrepresented in careers in the legal system (e.g., as police officers, attorneys, and judges), but Black Ohioans are overrepresented among the arrested and incarcerated. This understanding has led them to bring awareness to this under- and over representation issue because they recognize that institutional legitimacy is directly tied to representation.

Some initiatives bring together Black judges across various states, such as the National Society of Black Women Judges (NSBWJ). While women judges as a gender minority in the judicial profession are likely to share some similar experiences, Black women judges' experiences may differ as a result of other socially and politically salient identities such as race (Crenshaw 1989). Intersectionality highlights why Black women would want to have a space unique to their positionality. White women judges' experiences and professional needs may differ from the experiences and professional needs of Black women judges because Black women judges are a racial minority in the judicial profession in addition to being a gender minority and may experience the legal profession and their work differently. Therefore, the National Association of Women Judges (NAWJ) may not be the best organization to fully support Black women judges because they may need support specific to their intersectional identities as a result of marginalization because of their race and gender. This is not to say that NAWJ and its chapters have not worked to better support racial-minority women in the law, because they have, such as through their Color of Justice Program,[37] which endeavors to "advance minority students' interests and pursuit of a career in the law." Nonetheless, grouping women judges together without attention to race when race is such an important and salient identity for Black women judges has necessitated the need for a more specialized initiative. This was the impetus for the creation of the NSBWJ, founded by Judge Lashawn Williams of Houston, Texas, who felt that Black women judges were having similar experiences and would benefit from developing a support system centering them.

NSBWJ is a newer nationwide initiative that is intentionally taking its time to fully develop and grow its membership base and programming. The association aims to support Black women throughout the legal pipeline. Specifically, the initiative works with young Black girls to encourage them to pursue law degrees and careers. It also supports Black women law students and practicing lawyers through mentorship and experiential opportunities, which together support these young legal professionals' education and careers. Finally, the initiative supports current Black women jurists, offering them a space to convene, network, discuss, collaborate, and strengthen ties, therefore supporting their professional careers as judges.

Unlike NSBWJ, which is new, Just the Beginning—A Pipeline Organization (JTB) is an established organization founded in 1992 in Chicago, Illinois.[38] The organization aims to increase representation in the legal profession by encouraging and supporting students of color and other students from underrepresented communities to pursue a legal education, law careers, and law-related leadership opportunities. The organization does so by clarifying the path to law school and a successful legal career.[39] JTB is a nonprofit organization, founded by Judge Ann Claire Williams, formerly of the United States District Court for the Northern District of Illinois (1985–1999) and the United States Court of Appeals for the Seventh Circuit (1999–2017).[40] Although multiracial, JTB's founder and many of its current members (i.e., judges and lawyers) and participants are Black Americans.

It is unsurprising the Judge Williams would help establish an organization focused on increasing representation when she has shared publicly that she sees a lack of diversity in the legal profession as an issue impacting Black people's experience with the legal system. In an interview with David Levi, the director of Duke Law School's Bolch Judicial Institute, Judge Williams said: "Being a Black woman coming out of Detroit and seeing the unfairness, to me, in the criminal justice system particularly in terms of representation, . . . we need . . . representation all up and down the food chain—the criminal justice food chain."[41] Although this quote represents what led Judge Williams to the U.S. Attorney's Office for the Northern District of Illinois, her view that representation matters throughout the legal profession is consistent with her creating JTB, which develops programs for middle school and high school youth and undergraduate and law school students. On September 19, 1992, in Chicago, JTB began as a celebration of the racial integration of the federal judiciary.[42]

JTB has continued to find ways to maintain a racially diverse judiciary and legal profession. The organization articulates its intended outcome and vision as "a legal profession in which lawyers and judges reflect the backgrounds and perspectives of the populations they service."[43] To achieve this outcome, JTB has developed various free in-person and virtual scholar and leadership programs.[44] Two programs are most likely to lead to increased judicial diversity: the Summer Judicial Internship Diversity Project (SJID) and Share the Wealth (STW). SJID is a national program and a collaboration between JTB and the Judicial Resources Committee of the United States Judicial Conference. The program affords undergraduate and law students career-building and leadership-developing opportunities by placing interns in state and federal judges' chambers. STW is a referral program coordinated by federal judges that provides law students and recent law school graduates with an opportunity to interview for highly selective federal judicial clerkships.[45] Since its inception, STW has placed over one hundred students from underrepresented backgrounds in federal judicial clerkships, and these students will ideally go on to become prominent members of the legal profession, including the courts.

Across its programs, JTB takes a three-pronged approach. First, its programs expose participants to legal professionals and careers. Second, they help educate participants by supporting the development of important professional skills. Finally, they broaden participants' networks by helping them connect with the organization's members, who are leaders in the legal profession and include lawyers, judges, and alumni. The connections are meant to provide the program participants with the "inspiration, encouragement, and support" necessary to continue legal educational and career paths. JTB has served the legal community for more than thirty years and has played a significant role in increasing the representation of Black Americans in the legal profession.

Black judges' institutional initiatives unquestionably help to promote and increase diversity in the legal profession and judiciary. Not only do they develop and nurture interest in the law among individuals from communities underrepresented in the legal profession and judiciary, but they also expose and educate individuals about career opportunities and options. Black judges are providing advocative representation by serving the Black community directly and indirectly with the types of initiatives they establish and support. Black judges are helping to develop young students and professionals who can, in the future, work in the legal profession and serve the community as it interfaces with the legal system.

CONCLUSION

In the prior three chapters, I showed how Black judges function as representatives of Black interests in their courtrooms and in the courthouse. By focusing on Black judges' community outreach and engagement, this chapter aimed to show an additional space where Black judges function as representatives of Black interests. In the interviews and surveys for this study, Black judges often remarked that their work extended beyond the individual cases. In the cases, they have a micro-level impact, but as I demonstrate in this chapter, Black judges are also having a macro-level impact. The surveys and interviews with

Black judges show the types of initiatives and organizations they have helped to establish, institutionalize, and support. Interviews, surveys, and research using court websites indicate that much of Black jurists' institutional work is clustered around three topics: adult court diversion programs and programs that offer alternatives to incarceration, programs that disrupt the youth pipeline to prison, and initiatives that connect and support black legal professionals.

Black judges' system-level work is significant because it helps reduce persisting mass incarceration in the United States. In sum, chapter 8 demonstrates that Black judges' community work qualifies as advocative representation of Black interests. These jurists' community work helps them have macro-level and long-lasting impact in the legal profession and society. Additionally, Black judges' decisions about the initiatives and organizations they establish are significant for addressing mass incarceration and representation in the legal profession.

CONCLUSION

ROBED REPRESENTATIVES IN AMERICAN COURTS AND THE FUTURE OF JUSTICE ADMINISTRATION

> Black judges can make sure they are addressing issues. You have the opportunity to transfer power. I am not even talking about giving more to Black folks than white folks. I am just saying, [be] fair but also recognize bias and when you see it, call it out . . . and just being able to be a voice and being unwilling to just accept the status quo— being unwilling to, when you got a number of cases in front of you that have these issues. Being willing to step outside the box to speak up. Being willing to convene and continue with community projects and things that show the community the legal system actually cares . . . Being able to use that power and influence, not in a bad way, but being able to use that power and influence to respond and do some of the things that can show the community that we haven't forgotten them.
>
> JUDGE HALL, a Black female judge from the South

This book's primary goal was to answer this overarching question: How and why do Black state judges represent and advocate for Black interests? To help explain why Black state judges do and might represent and advocate for Black interests, part I of the book examined the backgrounds, socialization, and identities of Black judges to assess whether an identity-to-politics link exists for them. Then, to highlight how Black state court judges represent and advocate for Black interests in their official capacity as jurists, part II of the book examined the decisions and behaviors of Black judges in order to assess the impact or consequences of their judicial work and whether an identity-to-representation link exists for Black judges.

I began this book by articulating the theory of advocative representation, which helps explain why Black judges, a highly socialized group of legal actors, might make decisions and engage in work that represent group interests that they are not technically accountable for and that they are not expected to represent. This theory is about representation in political and legal institutions that lack an expressed or widely recognized representation function. The theory maintains that political actors might represent group interests because they possess an identity-to-politics link, and that representation can exist from both intentional actions and unintended consequences related to the actors' presence and work when the actions and consequences match a group's interests. Moreover, the theory argues that self-identification as a representative is not necessary because actors do not necessarily need to see themselves as representatives of group interests for representation to have occurred or for them to be considered representatives by others. The only necessary condition for representation is a congruence of interest with an actor's behaviors and decisions.

In the context of this book on Black judges and Black representation in state courts, advocative representation theory is best understood as a function of Black judges' salient group identities, group attachments, and racial group consciousness, and it results from both their actions and the consequences of their actions that align with the legal interests of Black Americans. Assessing the existence of representation involves understanding whether and how the consequences of Black judges' actions and decisions reflect the will and interests of Black Americans. As a result, this theory helps us make sense of representation (i.e., decisions that reflect the will and interest of Black Americans) in institutions with no expressed or widely recognized representation function, such as courts. To explain why such representation would occur when there may not be an expectation for that representation nor a mandate for it, the theory submits that, if Black judges possess an identity-to-politics link and significant group attachments, they are likely to render decisions that reflect the interests of groups they are connected to because they understand the groups' interests and may even share those interests themselves. Black judges' understanding of Black Americans' legal interests is likely to influence their decisions and behaviors in courtrooms, courthouses, and broader communities across the country.

KEY FINDINGS

After presenting the overarching argument guiding this book (chapter 2), I divided the book into two parts. Part I assesses the backgrounds, socialization, and identities of Black judges to understand whether an identity-to-politics link exists for them. Having established that it does, part II examines Black judges' decisions and behavior in the courtroom as they adjudicate cases, in the courthouse as they work with their judicial peers, and in the community as they engage with community members and develop or support initiatives.

In chapter 3, I drew primarily on surveys and interviews with Black judges to examine their backgrounds, life experiences, and socialization to get a better sense of the paths by which they arrived at the bench. The chapter's primary argument is that Black judges' lives, socialization, and pathways to the court are likely to be quite varied, and yet there are likely to be important commonalities among them due to their racial group membership and living in a racialized social system. In any event, I argue that Black judges' socialization and life experiences are likely to lead to the development of a strong racial group identity, consciousness, and attachment. Chapter 3 presents some common social, educational, and professional characteristics, and thus experiences, in the backgrounds of many Black judges. Like most Black people in the United States, Black judges have had racialized life experiences, and their families and communities have racially and politically socialized them, helping them to understand Black interests and the needs of the Black community. The findings of chapter 3 are significant for the subsequent chapter in terms of the revelation that the factors that have helped many African Americans develop and preserve a racial group identity, consciousness, and group attachments are present in Black judges' lives as well.

Although the factors that have often led to the development of a strong racial group identity and consciousness are present in Black judges' lives, it is not guaranteed that every judge identifies with the racial group, feels connected and attached to it, and possesses a group consciousness that might guide their political decisions and behaviors. This is especially true because higher education and legal education in the twenty-first century occur in primarily white education institutions. Chapter 4 focuses on this topic of identity. I argue that many Black judges are likely to possess a strong racial group identity, consciousness, and attachment due to their life experiences and socialization, and most of the chapter gives voice to the group identity, consciousness, and attachments of Black judges via data from the surveys and interviews. As I expected, Black judges' responses reveal that their life experiences and socialization have led many of them to develop a strong racial group identity, consciousness, and attachment. For instance, Black judges report feeling connected to other Black Americans and the Black community at large, perceiving racial discrimination as a primary issue affecting the Black community, and feeling mobilized to work to create a more just, responsive, respectful, and receptive system of justice. Based on the findings, I concluded that many Black judges possess a strong and deep racial group identity and consciousness, are intricately attached to Black communities and people, and see themselves as playing an essential role in the system. I suspected that Black judges' group identity, consciousness, and attachment, along with their role orientation, influenced their work as judges, a topic I turned to in the four subsequent empirical chapters, which constitute part II of the book.

One of the most critical activities state court judges engage in is sitting on the bench. In our complex court system, most cases are resolved at the state court level, meaning every single state court judge plays a significant role in the legal system and the broader society. Chapters 5 and 6 focus on Black judges' work in their courtrooms, centering on Black judges' actions when they are on the bench, including how they interact with litigants and other court actors, and how they make decisions in individual cases. Drawing on surveys and interviews, these chapters highlight Black judges' narratives about their work on the bench and the rationale they employ to defend their decisions and behavior. In their responses, Black judges revealed the links between their experiences, identities, and judicial behaviors. The chapters discuss the numerous ways Black judges provide both procedural and distributive justice in their courtrooms and the finding that Black judges' actions inside the courtroom help to make the nation's state courts more just, responsive, respectful, and receptive. In other words, chapters 5 and 6 show how Black judges represent Black interests through their decisions, behaviors, and work in their courtrooms.

But judges do more than adjudicate cases. The surveys and interviews with Black judges revealed additional decisions, behaviors, and work Black judges engage in within their courthouses and broader communities. Chapter 7 focuses on Black judges playing an essential role in their local courthouse by working closely with and frequently engaging their judicial colleagues. I examine Black judges' engagement with their judicial peers by focusing on their dialogue and interactions. In their own words, Black judges highlight how they engage in collegial education by teaching their colleagues about Black people, life, and interests. This chapter shows how Black judges' peer-to-peer engagement facilitates their colleagues' development of cultural competency and racial sensitivity and how that can and sometimes does impact their colleagues' decision-making and work. This chapter reveals how Black judges are representing Black interests in courthouses across the country by diversifying the minds of jurists, especially those who lack experiential knowledge about Black people, life, and interests.

Finally, in chapter 8, I focus on Black judges' work and impact as jurists, which extend far beyond the doors of the courthouse. Chapter 8 examines some of the community and institutional activities Black judges engage in and involve themselves with when they are not adjudicating cases. Drawing on interviews, surveys, and other data, this chapter highlights Black judges' outward-facing work with their local residential community, their local court system, and the legal profession. I find three key similarities in the kind of work Black judges are involved in. Combined, Black judges' community work helps first to strengthen the connection between the court and the community so that judges can better understand local community needs and issues and support community members. Second, it helps to improve the functioning of and justice within local court systems and communities, and finally, it helps to increase diversity in the legal profession. Black judges' community outreach and institutional initiatives demonstrate their commitment to and work toward community-, institution-, and system-building, which ultimately reveal ways Black judges are representing Black interests in their outward-facing community work.

Ultimately, there are four main findings. First, many Black judges possess an identity-to-politics link, which has a profound influence on their judicial work. Second, Black judges represent Black interests in the courtroom, courthouse, and community. Black judges' actions on the bench frequently align with the interests of Black Americans. Their decisions, courtroom interactions, and emphasis on procedural and distributive justice contribute to making the state court system more responsive, respectful, and equitable. These actions reflect a commitment to justice that is informed by their unique perspectives and lived experiences. Third, Black judges' institutional impact has little to do with how they decide the legal matters they preside over. Beyond the courtroom, Black judges play an essential role in shaping the perspectives and practices of their judicial peers, as discussed in chapter 7. By engaging in peer-to-peer education and fostering cultural competence, Black judges influence their colleagues' understanding of Black communities and interests, thereby amplifying their impact within the broader judiciary. Finally, Black judges' community engagement leads to systemic reforms. Chapter 8 highlighted the outward-facing work of Black judges, including their community outreach and efforts to improve the functioning of local court systems. This work strengthens the connection between court and community, enhances public trust in the judiciary, and promotes diversity within the legal profession.

BROAD IMPACTS: IMPLICATIONS FOR REPRESENTATION AND DEMOCRACY

Because *Robed Representatives* highlights how Black state judges' identities and experiences eventually lead to their representing and advocating for Black interests, even in systems that traditionally lack an explicit mandate for representation, the broad impacts of this research extend across political, social, institutional, and academic domains. By exploring how Black state judges engage in advocative representation, or deliberately or unintentionally representing Black interests, this work reshapes our understanding of the judiciary and its role in society and helps us better understand the implications of judicial diversity for representation and democracy.

Advocative Representation in the Judiciary

Prior to the late twentieth century, Black judges were virtually nonexistent in state courts. Racism negatively impacted Black Americans' ability to obtain a legal education, and even those who graduated with a law degree struggled to access employment opportunities and networks that would propel them to the bench. As a result of the anti-Black exclusionary practices, Black Americans were generally underrepresented within the legal profession, especially in the judiciary.

The Black Civil Rights movement and Civil Rights advancements ushered diversity into the courts by increasing racial diversity within the electorate and making judicial diversity a policy priority.[1] Whereas Black judges represented less than 1 percent of all state court jurists in the mid-twentieth century, Black judges currently represent roughly 10 percent of all state court judges. While they are still slightly underrepresented, considering that Black Americans account for roughly 13 percent of the general population, Black judges are, in fact, the second most represented group of judges in state courts.

Do these Black state court judges ever represent Black interests and people? The short answer is yes, many of them do. The research presented here, especially in chapters 5, 6, 7, and 8, indicates Black judges make decisions in their official capacity as jurists in the courtroom, courthouse, and community that align with Black legal interests. Black representation can and often does occur when Black judges are present. For instance, when Black judges say evidence is inadmissible in court because it was obtained by police officers who violated someone's civil liberties, especially a Black defendant's constitutionally protected liberties, they are representing Black interests. And because Black legal interests are what they are, when Black jurists do any of the things highlighted in chapters 5–8, they are representing Black interests. This representation is occurring irrespective of the judges' intentions because, ultimately, as advocative representation theory maintains, representation is focused on outcomes and consequences, not on whether an action, behavior, or decision was intentional.

Ultimately, this book sheds light on representation occurring in the judiciary without an expressed representation function. Black judges' presence challenges traditional notions of judicial neutrality by showing that diversity strengthens judicial systems, not by introducing bias but by addressing systemic blind spots through the infusion into their work of their understandings and perspectives. Black judges enhance the judiciary's ability to represent and respond to Black communities. The research shows that Black judges are likely to understand and consider the unique legal challenges faced by Black Americans due to their life experiences, racial socialization, and group consciousness. This means that their decisions can align more closely with the interests and needs of marginalized groups, which according to advocative representation theory, qualifies as representation.

Representing Black Legal Interests Enhances American Democracy

The United States' democratic republic was founded on numerous ideals that the nation still aspires to, including equal justice and representation. A recent paper showed that Black Americans consider equal justice, community engagement, respect, protection of their constitutional rights, and judicial diversity as some of their key legal interests (Means and Lohani 2025). In other words, representing Black interests in the courts does not mean preferential treatment or favoritism and bias. It is racist to imply or suggest Black judges' representation of Black interests is intrinsically biased and prejudiced, because that ignores that Black legal interests include fairness and equal justice.[2] Indeed, Means and Lohani (2025) show that Black Americans share wanting equal justice and treatment in all legal processes, as well as fair outcomes. Thus, Black Americans have revealed that their interests are or should be *everyone's* interest insofar as what should occur in a democracy's legal system. Black judges, then, represent Black legal interests, but more generally speaking, they represent democratic legal interests.

Because Black judges represent democratic legal interests, they enhance the nation's democracy. In recent years, the courts, especially the Supreme Court of the United States (SCOTUS), have received significant media attention due to decisions they have made (Badas and Justus 2023). These SCOTUS decisions have raised serious questions about whether the courts are eroding the nation's democracy and creating a crisis of legitimacy. Judicial diversity can increase legitimacy among people interested in a judicial system that reflects the makeup of society (Scherer 2023). People advocating for judicial diversity are clearly getting more than just visual diversity; they are getting something tangible. They are getting and can expect to get more democracy as racial diversity increases, at least with Black judges, because these judges are deciding and behaving in ways that enhance the quality of the United States' democracy. With Black judges, we can expect more nuance in the face of complexity, justice, fairness, due process, challenges to assumptions about Black people and other marginalized populations, and equity. This story of Black judges representing Black interests is important for theoretical reasons as a micro story, but the story that this data tells is much bigger than the representation of Black legal interests by Black judges. A macro view of the data presented in this book is fundamentally about representation in the courts producing a more democratic system because, when all is said and done, Black legal interests of equal justice, a racially competent and sensitive legal system, judicial diversity, and addressing mass incarceration are American democratic interests, and Black judges represent those interests and uphold fundamental principles of democracy in what they do on and off the bench. Black judges are moving us closer to a fully democratic society, one in which due process and equal justice is available to all.

We know Black Americans were blocked from these roles for a very long time. Understanding Black judges' work in the context of democratic interests provides insight into why Black judges might be viewed as dangerous. Although Black judges might be stereotyped as more liberal and biased in favor of Black-related issues and people (Harris and Sen 2019), we must understand that Black judges also may be viewed as dangerous by people trying to uphold the current legal system, which has operated in classist and racist ways since its inception (Alexander 2010; Van Cleve 2016). I would argue that resistance to diversification is not just about wanting to keep the courts looking the way they have looked for centuries, void of racial and gender diversity. At the heart of the movement against increased judicial diversity is an expectation and, perhaps, understanding that diversification within the courts will help to bring those critical legal spaces closer to the American creed and democracy. Efforts to stifle or heavily police judicial diversity can be understood as attempts to prevent people who have experienced marginalization and oppression from bringing something new to the table that would be manifested in their decisions and behaviors, even if such behaviors are necessary for transforming the courts into more democratic institutions.

Community Connection: Black Judges Address Mass Incarceration

In the interviews for this study, Black judges often remarked that they have micro-level impact in deciding cases on the bench, but their work and impact extends far beyond the individual cases they preside over. Chapters 7 and 8 demonstrate that Black judges' work does indeed extend beyond adjudication of cases and that these jurists can have macro-level impact too. Black judges' work on and off the bench, at both the micro and macro levels, helps to address mass incarceration as a systemic and structural issue.

Mass incarceration refers to the fact that the United States is the world's leader in confinement and incarceration. According to a report, "today, almost 2 million individuals—disproportionately Black Americans—are incarcerated in our nation's prisons and jails."[3] This represents a 500 percent increase in the prison population since the early 1970s. Numerous factors have contributed to this staggering growth in incarceration and confinement in the United States, including the criminalization of drug use and mental illness, which both began in the last half of the twentieth century (Alexander 2010). Few could credibly argue that the United States is not a carceral state or that the carceral system does not wreak havoc in minority and impoverished communities, given the racialized nature of predictive policing in minority communities and the racial disparities in sentencing (Gottschalk 2013).

At the same time that state and federal governments were criminalizing addiction and mental illness, the country was also experiencing an increase in the number of Black judges. These Black jurists were positioned to uniquely understand the impact of mass incarceration on individual people, families, and communities, because many of them came from Black communities, had family that still lived in those communities even if they themselves did not, and were connected to those communities.[4] As insiders in the legal system, they could see how and why the appropriate response to mental health crises and drug addiction is treatment and support, not arrest, prosecution, and confinement. It makes sense then that their familiarity with and understanding of the issue of mass incarceration, including the scale of the problem and its disparate impact on Black Americans, would lead at least some of them to make decisions and behave in ways that would try to address mass incarceration from their position of power. The systemic ills in the legal system make it impossible for Black judges to address deeply structural issues such as racial bias in the legal system and mass incarceration on their own. Yet, as we have seen in this book, there are decisions Black judges can make, conversations they can have, outreach they can do, and programs they can start and support that, when considered together, enable Black judges to address, even in a small way, structural and systemic issues through individual and collective means.

Throughout part II, we see Black judges trying to address mass incarceration in many ways. In chapters 5 and 6, we see how Black judges adhere to the principles of procedural justice and distributive justice. They operate hospitable courtrooms, engage in respectful ways with criminal defendants, and approach their decision-making in a critical yet empathetic way. All these courtroom behaviors help ensure that Black Americans are treated fairly in terms of due process and the final outcome in their legal matters. Chapter 7 shows us how Black judges communicate with their colleagues in ways that help them develop and enhance their cultural competency and sensitivity, which can impact their work in the legal system. Chapter 7 underscores how Black judges' collegial teaching can reverberate throughout the legal system, and they can indirectly impact the administration of justice through the decisions their colleagues are making. In chapter 8, through an examination of some of the programs and initiatives that Black judges establish and support, we see how Black judges are working to respond to the crisis that is mass incarceration, especially its racialized nature, by trying to address issues before they become legal issues by creating youth programs and diversion programs for individuals with legal cases and by connecting and supporting future and current Black and other underrepresented legal professionals.

Often we think of the legacy of judges as being tied only to their case decisions and the way they impact jurisprudence in certain issue areas. This book urges us to consider how and why the legacy of Black judges is about more than their on-the-bench work. Their legacy is also about the ways they have impacted others via their conversations and how their initiatives in the court system and community have extended their reach. Their work can help reduce persisting mass incarceration in the United States, where bipartisan recognition exists that the United States' incarceration rates are appalling, yet bipartisan commitment to decarcerating and reducing the size and scope of the carceral system is lacking, partially because safety, "law and order," and policing are hot-button political and racial issues that politicians weaponize for electoral benefit.

Advancing Academic Conversations: Reframing the Idea of Representation, the Courts as Representative Institutions, and Judges as Representatives

By demonstrating that many Black judges represent Black interests, the book also reframes the role of the judiciary. Courts are often seen as neutral arbiters of law without a direct representational role. *Robed Representatives* challenges the traditionally limited view of the role of the courts by showing how judges' identities and socialization can influence their decisions in ways that align with the interests of groups. By representing Black interests, Black judges, in particular, contribute to a judiciary that is more empathetic, culturally competent, and responsive to systemic inequities. This work reframes the judiciary not just as a legal institution but also as a space for subtle advocacy and representation, especially for but not limited to underrepresented communities. Thus, this work also shapes broader conversations on representation occurring beyond legislatures and elected bodies and from judges. Representation can and does exist in unelected, ostensibly neutral institutions like courts.

Representation Beyond the Courtroom

As mentioned previously in this book, scholars have primarily studied the impact of salient social identities by examining judges' final decisions in cases. Scholars rarely consider representation beyond judges' final case decisions. This limits our understanding of how judges can represent group interests with any decision or action they make as a judge. Chapters 7 and 8 highlight Black judges' influence beyond the courtroom. Black judges' engagement with peers and communities extends their impact, influencing the judiciary's culture and addressing systemic inequities. This advocacy could lead to broader reforms in legal institutions and transformation or reshaping of institutional culture.

Through peer-to-peer education and discussions, Black judges introduce their colleagues to perspectives that might otherwise be absent in a predominantly white professional environment. By sharing insights into Black experiences and interests, they help other judges develop cultural competence and racial sensitivity. This influence can ripple outward, shaping decisions made by colleagues and fostering judicial practices that are more attuned to issues of systemic racism and inequality. Over time, this could lead to structural reforms in the judiciary. By improving their peers' understanding of racial and cultural issues, Black judges contribute to broader institutional change, potentially reducing bias and fostering more equitable outcomes in courtrooms across the country.

Black judges also represent Black interests in the community. Beyond their courtroom and courthouse work, Black judges often engage in outreach initiatives to address needs in their jurisdiction, the legal profession, and implementation of justice. Their community and public-facing efforts highlight the judiciary's role as a proactive force in justice, societal, and professional improvements. These activities directly and indirectly help enhance justice processes and outcomes and create pathways for underrepresented groups to enter and remain in the legal profession. Ultimately, Black judges' representation of Black interests via their collegial education efforts and establishment of and support for programs and initiatives extends their impact, influencing the judiciary's culture and addressing systemic inequities in justice administration.

Identity-Driven Decision-Making

Research has long shown that racial identity and group consciousness influence legislative, executive, and bureaucratic behavior. This book demonstrates that racial identity and group consciousness influence judicial behavior. In doing so, the work raises questions about how diversity influences the interpretation and application of law. Black judges often have a strong sense of attachment to their racial group, which shapes their understanding of justice and informs their decision-making. Their courtroom, courthouse, and community decisions and behaviors reflect an awareness of systemic inequities, even when they don't consciously see themselves as advocates. This challenges the traditional view of judicial impartiality by highlighting how personal identity and lived experience can enhance the fairness and responsiveness of judicial decisions. While some may dislike the idea that identity influences judicial decisions because it challenges mainstream views of judges and courts, this work encourages embracing judicial diversity as a strength rather than a deviation from neutrality. Black judges' decisions can set precedents that address systemic disparities, such as in sentencing or procedural fairness, thereby contributing to a more just legal system. If Black legal interests were about favoritism or bias, it would be understandable that judicial diversity be seen as troubling. But that is not the case for Black legal interests and for the representation by Black judges. Black judges representing Black interests bring us closer to our aspirations for justice administration.

POLICY RECOMMENDATIONS

Numerous policy recommendations emerge from this research, with two of the most important recommendations being policies that would increase judicial diversity and facilitate the development of cultural competency for all judges.

Increase Judicial Diversity

This study underscores the importance of diversity in judicial selection, not just for symbolic representation but for tangible impacts on fairness and justice. First, colleges and those working within the legal field should work to increase accessibility and equity in the legal profession. This would entail addressing systemic barriers to the profession such as the affordability of law school and opportunities for mentorship. Pipeline initiatives that include partnerships between the courts, law firms, and colleges are one way to address this issue. Ultimately focusing on accessibility and equity in the legal profession will lead to a strong and diverse pool of candidates from which to select judges.

Second, policymakers should use this research to justify measures and policies that prioritize and facilitate diversity in judicial selection processes at the state and federal levels. Moreover, in order to retain judges from marginalized backgrounds, court administrators should use this research to justify the creation of and support for policies and programs that can benefit underrepresented individuals in the judicial system. Over time, such recruitment and retainment policies and practices could lead to a judiciary that more accurately reflects and serves an increasingly diverse population, enhancing public confidence in the legal system.

Implement Cultural Competency Training

Black judges understand the diverse populations they serve, given their own backgrounds and life experiences, but representing Black interests should not fall exclusively on the shoulders of Black judges. Black judges' colleagues lack the backgrounds and life experiences that Black judges have had, and therefore, they may struggle to know and then represent Black interests (i.e., lack cultural competency). Although Black judges engage in collegial education in order to help their colleagues better understand the lives of the diverse populations they serve, this is significant (unpaid) labor for Black judges. In order to standardize at least some of the understandings and knowledge these Black judges possess, law schools and court administrators should require training for judges about cultural competency, implicit bias, and racial sensitivity. Most lawyers have continuing education requirements. Legal organizations should develop education programs for judges about systemic racism, social justice, and the historical context of marginalized groups' experiences in the legal system. And because collegial education is important and potentially more effective, Black judges could be called upon as experts in peer-led training that leverages their unique knowledge.

In *Black Robes, White Justice*, New York State Supreme Court justice Bruce Wright writes about judges knowing the law well but not being meaningfully trained before going to the bench: "We are handed heavy responsibilities without being tested for our intellectual or psychological ability to cope fairly and impartially" (1990, 7). He argues that such training will lead to a quality bench, one that can be impactful in terms of producing meaningful change to the system. He calls for training prospective judges "how to be humanitarians in their allegiance to jurisprudence" (9). Cultural competence training is consistent with Wright's suggestion for improved professional development available to judges. The lack of racial diversity has led to a judiciary that rarely works for Black Americans. With increased diversity and the existence of policies that try to address the competency of current judges, advances can be made. Ultimately, increasing the number of culturally competent judges can foster a more inclusive and informed judiciary.

These policy recommendations align with the overarching goal of creating a judiciary that is more inclusive, representative, and capable of addressing systemic inequities in the legal system. They also emphasize the importance of institutional reforms that not only bring diversity to the bench but also foster a culture of equity, justice, and accountability in the legal profession.

FUTURE RESEARCH ON IDENTITY AND
REPRESENTATION IN THE COURTS AND BEYOND

During a job interview in 2015, I was asked, "If Black judges represent Black interests, who do white judges represent?" This is a great question. Do, or to what extent do, white judges represent white interests? This could be expanded: Do Asian American judges represent Asian American interests? Do Native American judges represent Native American interests? Do Latino/a judges represent Latino/a interests? These are all questions that I did not answer here because they are beyond the scope of this study, but they are worthwhile questions researchers should explore and answer because our democratic system of governance includes a judiciary that is increasingly diversifying along racial lines. Although Black judges are the second largest group of jurists in the nation, there are significant numbers of Asian American, Latino/a, and Native American judges as well. We do not fully understand the ways court institutions are transforming as a result of the presence of these historically excluded groups.

This book focused on *race* and representation, analyzing data from both Black men and women judges. Future studies might take an intersectional approach to tease out the existence of gender-related differences. Specifically, how do Black women judges differ from Black men judges, if at all, in their representation of group interests? Intersectional nuances might exist, and an intersectional approach would highlight them. The work of people like Kimberlé Crenshaw, who coined the concept of intersectionality, suggests that isolating race and studying it alone might mask important gender differences (Crenshaw 1989). The theory of intersectionality maintains that, because race and gender, among other identities, overlap and intersect, these salient aspects of an individual's identity need to be examined simultaneously, not observed separately, in order to fully understand how identity affects individuals' treatment and perception in society. The theory undergirding this book project hinges on race as a salient identity for Black American judges that might influence their politics and their behavior and decisions. Perhaps gender also is salient for Black American judges, and considering whether Black male judges differ at all from Black female judges—and/or how white and Black female judges differ—might yield fascinating intragroup variances masked in the current study.

For the reasons mentioned in the introduction, this book answered the question of race and representation by looking exclusively at Black state court judges, and not at the many Black federal court judges. But we can and should explore whether Black state court judges differ from their federal counterparts. Important institutional mechanisms such as lifetime tenure suggest that judges have a bit more freedom to explicitly make decisions that represent some group interests. While their decisions could be publicly criticized and might harm institutional legitimacy, federal judges can make decisions without fear of retaliation or punishment. State court judges, by contrast, do not have lifetime tenure and must face recurring elections. Because of this electoral accountability, they may avoid decisions that could jeopardize their chances of reelection, which can lead them to issue more conservative rulings than they otherwise might. Thus, the decisions and behaviors of federal judges should be assessed to better understand whether group interests are being represented with the increase in federal judicial diversity, and if so, whether the ways in which representation occurs differ from those used by state court judges.

Finally, another direction for future research is the applicability of the theory of advocative representation beyond the court context. As I wrote in chapter 1, I developed the theory of advocative representation to help explain why representation might occur in an institution that is neither charged with representing group interests nor held accountable for representation. Black state court judges are a highly socialized group of people who are not necessarily supposed to represent group interests nor are they, or any other court actors, generally held accountable for the representation of group interests. But Black judges are likely not the only group of people in a position of power who may make decisions and behave in ways that align with some group's interests and therefore function as representatives.

This theory is unlikely to *only* describe, explain, and help us understand how and why Black state court judges decide and behave the way they do. Instead, this theory is meant to be a general one. Scholars should be thinking about representation and what it means to have people in positions of political power who may have an identity-to-representation link like Black state court judges. Court scholars need to start thinking about what it means to be a judge, and also what it means to be any other legal actor with discretion. This theory might be helpful in explaining the decisions and behaviors of other legal actors, such as police officers and prosecutors. In addition, identity-politics scholars need to look at what other groups of actors working in institutions without a widely accepted representation function might be doing that advances group interests intentionally or unintentionally.

JUDICIAL DIVERSITY IS NECESSARY BUT INSUFFICIENT

Black judges are needed for the representation of Black legal interests and increased court legitimacy among Black Americans (Scherer 2023). They enhance the system in important ways. But they are not enough. In the face of structural and institutional issues within the courts, such as bias, pervasive racial disparities in sentencing, and issues with procedural justice, many Black judges can improve our system but they cannot save it. There are too few of them, and the structural issues that are embedded in the policies and practices of the courts are too entrenched. Structural issues always require institutional responses. Individual Black judges can move the courts closer to where they should be in terms of equal justice, but they cannot solve or resolve many of the issues within the system. Yes, judicial diversity is necessary, but it is not enough to fully transform a system with deep structural inequalities.

CONCLUSION

Toward the end of writing this book, I participated in a virtual writing work-shop with Q. M. Zhang (Kimberly Chang), a writer, teacher, editor, and founder of MemoryWorks, a creative research and writing practice for writ-ers interested in making legible silences in the communities they study.[5] The workshop deeply impacted my thinking about this book and the stories it was telling, especially the silences I was trying to interpret and write into. The homework for the workshop was to bring one source important for our research and writing that contains a silence, absence, or erasure. Zhang said the source could not just be a typical academic source, but one that "holds for you both the desire to know and the impossibility of knowing." As I pondered what source I would bring that related to this study of Black judges, I could not help but think about Ted Ellis (T. Ellis) and his artwork that decorates many of the Black judges' chambers I visited in my data collection for this project.[6] This artwork is also featured on the cover of this book (see figure A.2 and figure A.3 in the appendix).

T. Ellis is a contemporary artist who thinks of himself as a "creative his-torian," recording history and educating through his artistry. His website de-scribes him as a "passionate man" who paints and creates art that represents and reflects "many facets of American life, particularly, African-American culture and history."[7] In 1993, T. Ellis created a collection of art about Black Americans in the legal profession for black lawyers and judges. The first law painting was *Justice*, which features a Black male attorney and a Black male judge. This piece was followed by *Equal Justice*, a painting that features a Black female attorney and a Black female judge.

I became familiar with T. Ellis and his Black legal artwork after seeing *Justice* and *Equal Justice* on display in numerous Black judges' chambers during my interview sessions. These are striking paintings and draw you in. They make you want to study the faces of the Black legal actors to understand what they may be thinking and saying and to examine the lighting to understand the tone of the courtroom. After I noticed their frequent presence in Black judges' chambers, I asked one judge about the paintings. With pride, the judge I was interviewing shared that the artwork was from T. Ellis's collection and recommended that I look him up and research his work. I did.

I spoke to T. Ellis by telephone twice during the writing of this book. We

FIGURE C.1: Justice.

Source: Ted Ellis.

FIGURE C.2: Equal Justice.

Source: Ted Ellis.

spoke early during the pandemic and in spring 2023. In both conversations he was incredibly supportive of the book, given his interest in producing, creating, and supporting work that will educate people about the representation of Black Americans. I knew in the middle of writing the book that I wanted one of his paintings to be the cover image.

When I asked T. Ellis what motivated him to create art featuring Black legal professionals, he shared that he was interested in increasing the visibility of this group of powerful people and celebrate their successes:

> The motivation behind creating art featuring Black legal professionals was to highlight and elevate the representation of Black individuals in positions of authority and influence, particularly in the legal profession. Growing up, I didn't often see Black lawyers, judges, or other legal professionals depicted in mainstream media or art. I wanted my work to both acknowledge and celebrate their presence, their intellect, and their significant contributions to the legal field, especially in environments where Black individuals are historically underrepresented.

T. Ellis's goals for his work were not lost on the Black judges who purchased and displayed them. I asked him to share why he thought Black legal professionals would display his art pieces in their offices, very visible public locations. He shared that he thought the pieces affirmed their presence and identity as Black judges, motivating them to continue on the path despite challenges that may come up for them.

> I believe Black legal professionals purchase and display my art in their offices because it serves as a visual affirmation of their identity and the value of their work in a space where they may often face microaggressions or feel isolated. These images affirm their place in the legal system, inspire confidence, and remind them of the historical and contemporary importance of their roles. Seeing these images daily can reinforce a sense of pride, purpose, and connection to a broader legacy of Black excellence and achievement. It provides a reminder that they are part of a lineage of lawyers and judges who have shaped and continue to shape justice in powerful ways.

But displayed art is impactful not just on the owner but also on people who come into contact with it. I asked T. Ellis to share how he thinks Black and non-Black people are affected by seeing his artwork. Did he see the artwork as likely to have a profound or insignificant effect? He shared that his work "can be a powerful, transformative experience." Then, he went on to share how different populations might experience his work:

> For Black individuals, particularly those just starting out in the legal field, seeing images of Black judges can be a source of inspiration and validation. It communicates that they too belong in these spaces and that there is a pathway to success, even in traditionally exclusionary fields. For non-Black individuals, my artwork challenges conventional notions of authority and power, reminding them that Black professionals are just as capable and deserving of these positions. It creates an opportunity for reflection on issues of racial justice, representation, and systemic inequalities. Ultimately, these images can help foster more inclusive and equitable perspectives in the legal community.

In conclusion, T. Ellis's *Equal Justice* on the cover reflects the reality, which is that courtrooms in this country are increasingly diverse. Black judges are present on the bench in many jurisdictions across the country, but we know little about them and the work they do. Yet, liberty and justice through the courts continue to be subject to those who exercise judicial power. This reality and understanding of the power of the courts undergird calls for diversification among judicial officials. Black people have had a long, turbulent relationship with the legal system, and I contend that the lack of diversity is at least part of the issue. At the state and federal levels, white men have been overrepresented among judges despite the overrepresentation of Black Americans as defendants. But racial diversification has happened in the post–Black Civil Rights movement era, leaving us with courts that better, albeit not perfectly, reflect the United States' multiracial society. This increase drives the need for research on them, but also a renewed public and scholarly interest in the representation of Black Americans in the courts has risen. This follows recent presidents' historic appointments of Black men and women to the federal judiciary, including Ketanji Brown Jackson to the Supreme Court of the United States in 2022, as well as the recent electoral success of Black judges at the state level, such as the nineteen Black women elected in 2018 to the bench in Harris County, Texas (Greater Houston), after collectively campaigning under the #BlackGirlMagic slogan.

The questions people have been asking or at least thinking about related to the increased presence of Black judges are the questions at the center of this book. This book, which engages with scholarship on political representation, racial identity, and judicial behavior, offers new insights into the lives, identity politics, and actions of Black state court judges. By chronicling Black judges' backgrounds, life experiences, socialization, group identities and attachments, and behavior, the narratives centered in the book reveal an identity-to-politics link that exists among Black judges and leads them to represent their group interests. Thus, this book unveils the existence of an identity-to-representation link for Black judges and highlights numerous previously unidentified features, including their manifestations of representation in the legal system. The book demonstrates that only through research that considers the lives, identities, and behaviors of historically underrepresented judges will we arrive at a more comprehensive understanding of the significance of racial diversity in the courts.

As we move into a future where the courts are increasingly playing a role in our political system and deciding some of the most important political and legal issues of our times, understanding how and why certain judges decide the way they do will allow us to be better advocates for judicial diversity. This work demonstrates the critical role of identity and representation in fostering a more equitable legal system and emphasizing the need for continued research about and support for diversity in judicial institutions. *Robed Representatives* provides a strong case for increasing diversity in the judiciary, and I hope we will all commit ourselves to this endeavor.

APPENDIX

TABLE A.1: Demographics of interview participants.

Pseudonym	Region	Gender	Self-identified race/ethnicity	Interview date
Smith	Midwest	Male	Black	April 4, 2014
Brown	Midwest	Male	Black	April 4, 2014
Johnson	Midwest	Female	Black	April 4, 2014
Jones	Midwest	Male	Colored/POC	April 3, 2014
Williams	Midwest	Male	African American (AA)	April 4, 2014
Davis	Midwest	Female	Black or AA	April 3, 2014
Miller	Midwest	Female	Black	April 3, 2014
Wilson	South	Male	Black	April 4, 2014
Hunter	South	Male	Black or AA	April 4, 2014
Taylor	South	Male	Black	November 8, 2013
Clark	Midwest	Male	Black or AA	December 19, 2013
White	Midwest	Female	Black	December 19, 2013
Moore	Midwest	Female	Black	December 20, 2013
Thompson	West	Male	Black	October 24, 2014
Allen	West	Female	Black	April 2, 2015
Martin	South	Male	AA	October 24, 2014
Hall	South	Female	Black or AA	October 24, 2014
Adams	South	Female	Black or AA	October 24, 2014
Terry	South	Male	Black	October 24, 2014
Wright	South	Male	Black or AA	February 16, 2013
Baker	South	Female	Black	March 15, 2013
Hill	South	Female	Black	February 16, 2013
Anderson	South	Male	Black	February 16, 2013
Lewis	South	Male	Black	February 16, 2013
Harris	South	Female	Black	February 16, 2013
Wood	South	Male	AA	February 16, 2013
King	South	Female	Black	February 16, 2013
Jackson	South	Female	Black	February 16, 2013
Lee	South	Female	AA	February 16, 2013
Green	South	Female	Black	March 8, 2013
Washington	North	Male	Black	September 20, 2019
Ingram	North	Female	Black	September 12, 2019

Source: Author.

FIGURE A.1: Map of Black judges surveyed.

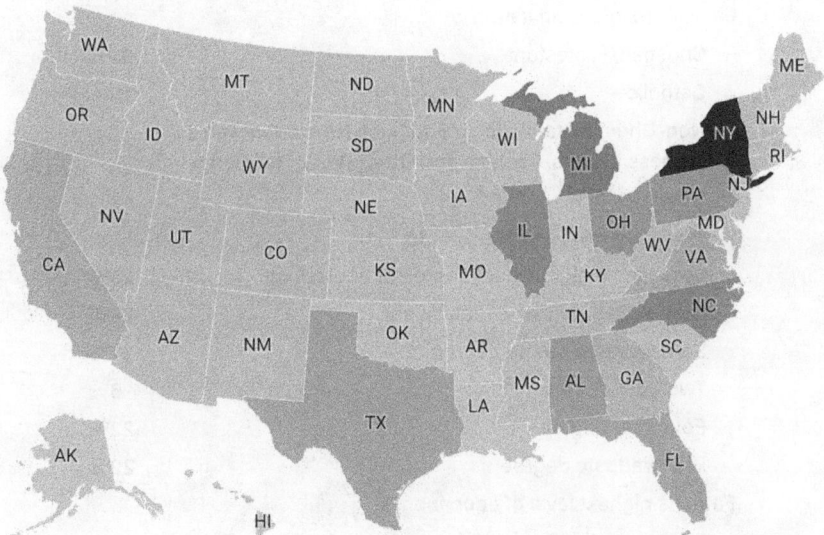

Black Judges Surveyed

Number of Judges

0   35

Created with Datawrapper

Source: Federal Judicial Center, Biographical Directory of Article III Judges.

TABLE A.2: **General background characteristics of Black judges surveyed, 2019–2020.**

Childhood	
National origin	
U.S.-born	95%
Foreign-born	5%
Family's socioeconomic class	
Poor	23%
Lower middle-class	35%
Middle-class	40%
Wealthy	1%
Other	<1%
Family's religious affiliation	
Christian/Protestant	81%
Catholic	16%
Non-Christian faiths (e.g., Buddhist, Hindu, Jehovah's Witness, Jewish, Muslim, and Other World Religions)	<1%
Other	2%
Mother's highest level of education	
Less than a high school degree or equivalent	15%
High school degree or equivalent	22%
Some college but no degree	14%
Two-year degree	6%
Four-year degree	22%
Postgraduate degree	22%
Father's highest level of education	
Less than a high school degree or equivalent	18%
High school degree or equivalent	27%
Some college but no degree	13%
Two-year degree	6%
Four-year degree	13%
Postgraduate degree	23%

Young Adult Life*	
Undergraduate education	
Public	37%
Private	15%
Ivy League	5%
Liberal arts	17%
HBCU	25%
Other	1%
Law school education	
Public	48%
Private	36%
Ivy League	2%
HBCU	13%
Other	1%
Adult (Pre-bench) Life	
Primary occupation	
Attorney	88%
Private attorney	39%
Prosecutor	41%
Public defender	13%
Government attorney	5%
"Other" attorney	3%
Law professor	0%
Political career	1%
Other: Legal career	1%
Other: Non-legal career	10%
Political ideology	
Liberal	54%
Moderate	36%
Conservative	10%

Political identification	
Democrat	62%
Independent	35%
Republican	3%
Other	<1%
Net worth	
<$50,000	2%
$50,000-$99,999	5%
$100,000-$149,999	7%
$150,000-$199,999	10%
$200,000-$499,999	32%
$500,000-$999,999	29%
More than $1,000,000	16%
Socioeconomic class	
Poor	2%
Lower middle-class	4%
Middle-class	86%
Wealthy	7%
Other	1%

Source: Taneisha N. Means, "Political Representation in State Courts Study, 2020." (2020).

NOTES

Chapter 1

1. https://www.cnn.com/videos/politics/2022/02/26/ketanji-brown-jackson-call-biden-nr-vpx.cnn.

2. https://www.pbs.org/newshour/politics/watch-live-president-biden-gives-remarks-on-the-retirement-of-supreme-court-justice-stephen-breyer.

3. Information about Allen was gathered from https://www.masshist.org/beehiveblog/2019/05/passing-the-bar-americans-first-african-american-attorney/. Information about Morris was gathered from several sources: https://www.Blackpast.org/african-american-history/morris-robert-sr-1823-1882/; https://doi.org/10.1093/anb/9780198606697.article.1100616; https://johnjburnslibrary.wordpress.com/2015/05/11/robert-morris/; https://www.courthousenews.com/the-life-legal-strides-of-boston-abolitionist-robert-morris/.

4. There are roughly 68,000 judges, justices, and magistrates in the United States. This information is available from a report by the Bureau of Labor Statistics (BLS): https://www.bls.gov/oes/current/oes231023.htm. Also, the BLS reports that out of roughly 70,000 judges, magistrates, and other judicial workers, 47 percent are women, 68 percent are white, 26 percent are Black, 1.9 percent are Asian, and 17.2 percent are Latino/a. This report was last updated January 2025 and is available here: https://www.bls.gov/cps/cpsaat11.htm.

5. States voluntarily submitted their data on judicial diversity, but some states did not submit data. Those states are represented with the palest color (i.e., light gray), which is different from a true zero (i.e., no judge works in the state). The states in the pale gray may have some Black judges, but the state's data was unavailable for analysis and creation of the figure. Nevertheless, based on George and Yoon's (2017) Gavel Gap report, the states that reported data tend to have the most Black judges. Data on state-level judicial

diversity is available here: https://public.tableau.com/app/profile/ncscviz/viz/StateCourt Organization/Demographics.

6. https://www.fjc.gov/history/judges.

7. https://www.fjc.gov/history/judges.

8. Scholars combine twentieth- and twenty-first-century racial minority judges and white female judges into one undifferentiated category to compare them to white male judges (e.g., Goldman, Slotnick, and Schiavoni 2013). Although it would be preferable to include contemporary work here that compares Black judges to white judges, that work is not available. Therefore, I present research here that shows Black judges along with white women and other racial minorities have different background characteristics and follow different paths to the federal bench.

9. Formalistic representation concerns how representatives get their authority to represent and how they are held accountable for this formal responsibility. Other theories of representation to explain the behaviors of legislators and bureaucrats relate to and in some cases have been derived from Pitkin's original four, such as passive representation, active representation, representative bureaucracy, dyadic and collective representation, and discursive representation (e.g., Dryzek and Niemeyer 2008; Mosher 1968; Weissberg 1978). While important types of representations, these forms are less relevant for this book.

10. https://www.uscourts.gov/about-federal-courts/educational-resources/supreme-court-landmarks/nomination-process/chief-justice-roberts-statement-nomination-process.

11. Furthermore, the implementation of institutional mechanisms, such as lifetime tenure and salary protection in the federal judiciary and judicial performance evaluations and popular elections in state judicial systems, suggests there is a desire to ensure judges are independent and yet held accountable (Wynn and Mazur 2003).

12. After examining the backgrounds of Black and white trial court judges on the "Metro City Bench," Uhlman (1978) concluded that pre-judicial careers of Black judges and white judges are often similar. Uhlman's conclusion was based on members of both groups being active in local politics prior to ascending to the bench and receiving high-quality legal training. Findings in recent studies, however, contradict Uhlman's conclusion and indicate there are several race-related background differences (Goldman, Slotnick, and Schiavoni 2013).

13. Racial group identity is an "awareness of belonging to a certain group and having a psychological attachment to that group based on a perception of shared beliefs, feelings, interests, and ideas with other group members," and racial group consciousness is defined as "in-group identification *politicized* by a set of ideological beliefs about one's group's social standing, as well as a view that collective action is the best means by which the group can improve its status and realize its interests" (McClain et al. 2009, 474 and 476).

Chapter 2

1. See, for example, James Madison's *The Federalist* 10, 24, and 78 (Hamilton, Madison, and Jay 2008).

2. This is similar to scholars who, with some hesitation that they were able to overcome, have adopted the language of representation in their studies of police officers, bureaucrats, and other political officials (Hindera 1993; Meier and Nicholson-Crotty 2006; Theobald and Haider-Markel 2009).

3. *Principal-agent* refers to the relationship between a principal (e.g., voters or constituents) and an agent (e.g., elected representatives). Pitkin's framework emphasizes the complexities of representation—specifically, how agents are expected to act on behalf of principals while navigating competing interests and motivations (i.e., self-interests, group interests, and external interests).

4. The concept of hiring does not relate to payment. Here, the concept of "hire" indicates authorization allowing a lawyer to act for the individual in legal proceedings.

5. https://hbr.org/2018/08/research-having-a-Black-doctor-led-Black-men-to-receive-more-effective-care; https://www.usnews.com/news/healthiest-communities/articles/2018-08-31/why-america-needs-more-Black-doctors; https://essay.vanderbilthustler.com/Black-in-medicine-the-importance-of-representation-and-support.

6. Tatum (1997) goes on to say: "How one's racial identity is experienced will be mediated by other dimensions of oneself: male or female; young or old; wealthy, middle-class, or poor; gay, lesbian, bisexual, transgender, or heterosexual; able-bodied or with disabilities; Christian, Muslim, Jewish, Buddhist, Hindu, or atheist" (18). Brown (2014) and Brown and Lemi (2021) highlight this in work on Black women legislators, which encourages researchers to do intersectional empirical work that permits representatives to talk about the different influences on their individual and collective identities. This approach, which I take in this project, helps prevent essentializing and facilitates the expression and illumination of differences and diversity among Black judges.

7. Cross's model outlines five stages of racial identity development: pre-encounter, encounter, immersion/emersion, internalization, and internalization-commitment. In the pre-encounter stage, Black people are socialized in a mostly Eurocentric culture and take in the beliefs and values associated with it, even if they live in predominantly Black neighborhoods. The encounter stage involves Black people becoming aware of racism and the significance of race in their own lives, typically brought on by an event or experience. The immersion/emersion stage is when Black people work to increase their understanding of their group's history and seek out racial group members in exploring who they are and for affirmation and support. In the internalization stage, Black people become secure in their racial identity. Finally, in the internalization-commitment stage, Black people develop closer ties to other Black people with secure racial identities and possess a sense of commitment to working with the interests and concerns of the racial group in mind.

8. Recent scholarship highlights ideological and partisan diversity within the Black population, although strong racialized social constraints and accountability mechanisms operate to maintain general political cohesion (e.g., Philpot 2009; White and Laird 2020).

9. These jurors see emancipating some clearly legally guilty Black offenders as a "moral responsibility" for their community because the problems are "not with the Black prisoners but with the state and its actors and beneficiaries," and the social and economic

costs for removing so many nonviolent Black people from Black communities are high (Butler 1995, 691).

Chapter 3

1. Other racial and ethnic groups, such as Latinos and Whites, also develop individual and group identities as a result of their life experiences and socialization (Jardina 2019; Sanchez 2006; Sanchez and Masuoka 2010).

2. Please see chapter 1 for more information about the sample. The Black judges who participated in this study are diverse with regard to their location, gender, political ideology, partisanship, and other characteristics. See table A.2 in the appendix for more information about survey respondents.

3. See table A.1 in the appendix for more information about the interview participants.

4. "Chosen family or community" is a concept that refers to intentional, close nonbiological kinship bonds and networks for love, support, affirmation, and care. It is concept used frequently in the psychology and counseling world in reference to relationships, especially among those with marginalized identities. See more information about chosen families here: https://sk.sagepub.com/ency/edvol/embed/the-sage-encyclopedia-of -marriage-family-couples-counseling/chpt/chosen-families.

5. More information on political socialization is available here: https://doi.org/10.1093 /oxfordhb/9780199935307.013.98.

6. Walker's interview is published in Associated Press, "Ebony and Jet Magazines' Photo Archive Will Go to Smithsonian," July 26, 2019, https://www.nbcnews.com/news /nbcblk/ebony-jet-magazines-photo-archive-will-go-smithsonian-n1034851.

7. Also see Means, Eslich, and Prado's (2019) discussion about the importance of connecting judges' backgrounds via biographies to their behavior to understand why judges behave the way they do.

8. Federal court judges' backgrounds and key characteristics are available via the Federal Judicial Center. This type of database does not exist at the state court level via individual court websites or via a centralized state court website.

9. Please see chapter 1 for a more detailed description of the survey and the survey respondents.

10. See table A.1 in the appendix for interviewee characteristics.

11. Tate (2004) is clear that while members of Congress are typically affluent, Black and Brown members of Congress often have considerably less wealth than their white congressional peers.

12. Over the 2014–2016 period, the average household pretax income for Black Americans was $48,871, and roughly 55 percent of Black American households rent, while approximately 40 percent own their homes. See more information about Black income and wealth here: https://ecommons.cornell.edu/server/api/core/bitstreams/8ac609f2 -a382-4829-8efa-0443367385c0/content.

13. Roughly 46 percent of the Black judge survey participants said before becoming a judge, their approximate net worth had been $500,000 or more, with 16 percent saying their pre-bench net worth had been at least $1,000,000. Thirty-two percent reported

pre-bench net worth between $200,000 and $499,999; 10 percent reported between $150,000 and $199,999; 7 percent reported between $100,000 and $149,999; 5 percent reported between $50,000 and $99,999; and 2 percent said their net worth had been less than $50,000. Black judges' net worth highlights how, before going to the bench, many of them were arguably middle-class and might even be classified as wealthy and affluent, depending on how one defines middle-class. This is consistent with the figures in table 3.1, although some might consider them wealthy instead of middle-class given their high net worth. In terms of how Black judges define their class, the overwhelming majority (93 percent) identify themselves as either middle-class or wealthy, with most identifying themselves as middle-class. Data from the surveys also reveal many Black state court judges jumped one or two class categories between childhood and adulthood—many were born into poor and lower-middle-class families, but by the time they reached the bench, they were comfortably middle-class according to themselves and their self-reported net worth.

14. The survey data shows that their parents' education levels account for those claiming to have grown up middle-class: 56 of the 109 respondents who identified their family's socioeconomic status as middle-class or wealthy said their mother or father had a bachelor's degree or higher.

15. The data also showed 37 percent of Black judges' mothers and 36 percent of their fathers had a high school degree or less than a high school degree; 20 percent of respondents said their mother's highest level of education was either some college or an associate degree; 19 percent of respondents said their fathers had either some college or an associate degree.

16. Black judges' parents' college experience and degree attainment are consistent with many of the common blue- and white-collar careers and industries that Black Americans currently work in: manufacturing, wholesale and retail trade, transportation services, health services (including home healthcare), leisure and hospitality, and food services. These careers are similar to the careers held by Black jurists' parents. When asked to share their parents' primary occupations, the most common careers for their mothers were teacher, homemaker, postal worker, nurse, social worker, administrator, office assistant, housekeeper, cook, and sales such as in retail stores and for Avon. The most common careers for respondents' fathers were carpenter, teacher or professor, attorney, postal worker, minister or pastor, laborer (such as farm worker, paper mill worker, coal miner, construction worker, railroad worker, longshoreman, or factory worker), military service member, educational administrator (such as a dean, principal, or superintendent), entrepreneur, and accounting or business. Some legacy judges also participated in this study, noting that one of their parent's primary career was as a judge. Black judges' descriptions of their parents' careers highlight gender differences: Black judges' mothers often worked in pink-collar jobs whereas their fathers mostly worked in white-collar jobs or low-skilled jobs.

17. For information regarding Black Americans' parents' education, please see the recent study by Matt Barreto, Lorrie Frasure-Yokely, Edward D. Vargas, and Janelle Wong, "Collaborative Multiracial Post-Election Survey (CMPS) 2016." The results are available here: https://latinodecisions.com/wp-content/uploads/2019/06/CMPS_

Toplines.pdf. The survey shows that 27 percent of respondents said their mother had not graduated from high school, and 30 percent said the same of their father. Thirty-seven percent of mothers had high school degrees, and 42 percent of fathers are high school graduates. Nineteen percent of mothers, and 14 percent of fathers had some college or a two-year degree. Twelve percent of mothers and 9 percent of fathers were college graduates. Finally, 4 percent of mothers and 5 percent of fathers had a post-graduate education.

18. Although two judges reported moving from neighborhoods that were less diverse (i.e., fewer Black families) to neighborhoods that were more diverse (i.e., more Black families).

19. The report is available here: https://furmancenter.org/files/NYUFurmanCenter_RaceNeighborhoods21stCentury_Aug2013_1.pdf.

20. Please see information about how Black people talk about race within their networks compared to other racial groups here: https://www.pewresearch.org/fact-tank/2019/06/25/how-often-people-talk-about-race-with-family-and-friends/.

21. For information regarding Black Americans' political participation, please see the recent study by Matt Barreto, Lorrie Frasure-Yokely, Edward D. Vargas, and Janelle Wong, "Collaborative Multiracial Post-Election Survey (CMPS) 2016." The results are available here: https://latinodecisions.com/wp-content/uploads/2019/06/CMPS_Toplines.pdf

22. Interestingly, one judge wrote on the returned survey questionnaire that they could not respond to the question regarding how active they were in politics because they were ineligible to participate due to judicial ethics.

23. For information regarding Black Americans' political participation, please see the recent study by Matt Barreto, Lorrie Frasure-Yokely, Edward D. Vargas, and Janelle Wong, "Collaborative Multiracial Post-Election Survey (CMPS) 2016." The results are available here: https://latinodecisions.com/wp-content/uploads/2019/06/CMPS_Toplines.pdf.

24. In table 3.6, the "Judges by Undergraduate Institution" numbers are from the 165 survey respondents who answered this question. The "Judges by Law School Institution" numbers are from the 164 survey respondents who answered this question.

25. While roughly 20 percent of Black judges attended HBCUs, a recent United Negro College Fund article noted that "though HBCUs make up only 3 percent of the country's colleges and universities, they enroll 10 percent of all African American students and produce almost 20 percent of all African American graduates." The article is available here: https://uncf.org/the-latest/african-americans-and-college-education-by-the-numbers.

26. HBCU attendance was also common among twentieth-century Black judges (Smith 1983).

27. The organizations with their year of founding in parentheses are Alpha Phi Alpha Fraternity (1906), Alpha Kappa Alpha Sorority (1908), Kappa Alpha Psi Fraternity (1911), Omega Psi Phi Fraternity (1911), Delta Sigma Theta Sorority (1913), Phi Beta Sigma Fraternity (1914), Zeta Phi Beta Sorority (1920), Sigma Gamma Rho Sorority (1922), and Iota Phi Theta Fraternity (1962).

28. For Wilson's article, please visit: https://www.uvm.edu/~vtconn/v17/wilson.html.

29. The survey question about primary career yielded some other interesting responses: political career, legal services, law clerk, and other. A few judge participants also spent their careers as attorneys working in several different capacities. For example, several judges mentioned being a public defender, prosecutor, or private attorney, and some judges said they had been a prosecutor and private attorney.

30. Many Black judges also noted that they had vicarious experiences with racial discrimination and were aware of prevalent racism experienced by Black Americans. I discuss this more in the subsequent chapter.

31. In the recent study by Matt Barreto, Lorrie Frasure-Yokely, Edward D. Vargas, and Janelle Wong, "Collaborative Multiracial Post-Election Survey (CMPS) 2016," an oversample of Black respondents were asked to share whether they themselves had experienced discrimination. Sixty-three percent said they experienced discrimination, and 93 percent said they felt they were treated unfairly because of their racial background as opposed to some other characteristic like gender or sexual orientation. These results reflect the prevalence of discrimination for Black Americans in the general population; Black judges are clearly not alone in being mistreated on the basis of their race. The results are available here: https://latinodecisions.com/wp-content/uploads/2019/06/CMPS _Toplines.pdf

Chapter 4

1. Judge Higginbotham's narrative in Washington (1994), 5-6.

2. This is arguably a human rights violation as well. Denying or not providing heat creates an unsafe and potentially lethal environment in a city where the average winter temperature is around freezing (i.e., low to mid 30s).

3. Chapter 3 highlights some differences between judges who served during the Civil Rights era and those who serve in the post–Civil Rights era. Twentieth-century Black judges, for instance, grew up during the U.S. Jim Crow era and legal apartheid. In contrast, current state court judges have largely grown up in a post–apartheid/Jim Crow world with affirmative action and other policies intended to offer some redress for historical racial discrimination.

4. See chapter 3. Comparing Black judges' net worth to the average Black family's net worth and household income reveals their middle-class status. Also, the chapter provides information about their educational backgrounds.

5. Fisk University is a historically Black university in Nashville, Tennessee. This quote was taken from this *New York Times* article: https://www.nytimes.com/2016/02/07/ education/edlife/black-america-and-the-class-divide.html.

6. Until now, no publicly available survey has asked Black judges about their group identity and consciousness (Smith 1983). The dearth of data is mainly a product of the costs associated with fielding surveys and low response rates by judges in projects dealing with politics and identities.

7. The U.S. Census population estimates are available here: https://www.census.gov/ quickfacts/.

8. One older male judge, Judge Jones, differed significantly from the other Black judges interviewed in how he identified racially. Although he agreed to the interview,

which he knew early on was a study of Black judges, when asked how he classified himself racially, he responded by saying "colored."

9. This respondent is referring to Tiger Woods saying he was Cablinasian, or a composite of Caucasian, Black, Indian, and Asian. See an article about Woods' racial identification here: https://www.theguardian.com/sport/2010/may/29/tiger-woods-racial-politics.

10. Gender might also be an important characteristic of Black judges' identity. When asked how important their gender was to their identity, 7 percent said it was not at all important, 6 percent said slightly, 16 percent said somewhat important, 36 percent said very important, and 35 percent said extremely important. Thus, most participants (71 percent) reported that gender was significant for their identity. Of the judges who said their gender was not at all important or only slightly important to their identity, 29 of them were men and 4 were women. Among the judges who said gender was somewhat, very, or extremely important to their identity, 130 were women and 73 were men. These results indicate an identifiable gender dynamic, with Black women judges being more likely than Black male judges to say gender is important to their identity.

11. Pew Research Center's 2021 Survey of Black Americans' summary results are available online: https://www.pewresearch.org/wp-content/uploads/sites/20/2022/04/RE_2022.04.14_Black-Identity_TOPLINE.pdf. Instead of the response option "slightly," the survey offered "A little important."

12. Additionally, the transcripts revealed that Black judges also used the pronouns *we* and *us* to refer to Black judges as a group. For example, when talking about how she thinks Black people perceive Black judges, one Black female judge from the South said, "With the Black community, I think there is a profound proudness that they feel when they see *us* at church in the community because it's someone that they know."

13. Black judges having some preference regarding where they live does not mean they do not face housing challenges. Scholars show that middle-class Black people "have more favorable residential outcomes than poor Blacks but still live in poorer neighborhoods than the majority of whites on all measures" (Pattillo 2005, 305). In other words, class and wealth do not necessarily mean that well-to-do Black people, including judges, do not have to surmount obstacles to end up in the neighborhoods where they prefer to reside.

14. The makeup of Black judges' residential neighborhoods differs from the composition of their childhood neighborhoods. Survey respondents reported living in communities that had significantly fewer Black families than their childhood neighborhoods. Currently, less than one-quarter of Black judges (22 percent) live in neighborhoods where Black families make up more than 60 percent of the residents. However, as children, more than 65 percent (68 percent) of Black judges lived in neighborhoods where Blacks were more than 60 percent of the residents.

15. The judges who reported working in court systems where more than 80 percent of their judicial counterparts are Black and who named the state where they work came from Alabama, Georgia, Louisiana, Maryland, Mississippi, and North Carolina.

16. Black Americans are overrepresented among the people who interact with the courts, especially the criminal justice system (Alexander 2010). I asked Black judges to

share what percentage of litigants appearing before them are Black. Close to 75 percent of survey respondents said that more than 40 percent of the litigants appearing in their courts are Black. I presume that despite having an opportunity to interact with a large number of Black litigants in their work, they can rarely do so in an in-depth and nuanced way. Courts are not intimate spaces where judges and litigants interact for prolonged periods in private. Moreover, judges are not technically supposed to discuss issues with litigants that are not related to the legal matter at hand. Due to the nature of their work and their need to avoid any appearance of impropriety, Black judges must be cautious when interacting with litigants. Nevertheless, even if Black judges avoid engaging in substantive discussions with litigants, I argue that those interactions are likely to be significantly different from those of non-Black judicial peers. Furthermore, the impact of those interactions is likely to be different, as well.

17. Jack and Jill of America's website is https://www.jackandjillinc.org/. The Links, Incorporated's website is https://linksinc.org/.

18. In a *New York Times* article, Samuel Fulwood, author of *Waking From the Dream: My Life in the Black Middle Class*, said about Jack and Jill of America: "Its reputation has to do with what I call the lure and loathing of being Black and middle class in a post-segregated America. We want to fit in somewhere. We aren't always accepted in the white world, and we don't believe the stereotypes of a Black world." The article is available here: https://www.nytimes.com/1998/07/19/style/feeling-isolated-at-the-top-seeking-roots .html.

19. The organization's national website is available here: https://www.naacp.org/about -us/.

20. Information about the National Bar Association is available at the organization's website: https://www.nationalbar.org/.

21. Results from the survey are available here: https://www.pewresearch.org/short -reads/2021/03/18/majorities-of-americans-see-at-least-some-discrimination-against -black-hispanic-and-asian-people-in-the-u-s/.

22. Other scholars study the linked fate of other racial minority groups, finding that members of most ethnic groups feel a sense of linked fate with their co-ethnics, however often not to the extent that Black Americans feel their fate is linked with other Black Americans (Campi and Junn 2019; Jardina 2019; Schildkraut 2020).

23. Less than 1 percent of respondents said it was only slightly important that Black people work together to address their needs. Five percent said it was moderately important.

Chapter 5

1. See Judge Pratt's LinkedIn website here: https://www.linkedin.com/in/judge -victoria-pratt-406a1a72/.

2. See Rosenberg's article here: https://www.theguardian.com/us-news/2015/jun/23/ procedural-justice-transform-us-criminal-courts?CMP=Share_iOSApp_Other.

3. See the Pew Research Center report and survey results here: https://www.pew research.org/race-and-ethnicity/2024/06/15/black-americans-mistrust-of-the-criminal -justice-system/.

4. See the Pew Research Center report and survey results here: https://www.pewresearch.org/2022/08/30/black-americans-views-on-systemic-change/.

5. See more information about the court statistics here: http://www.courtstatistics.org/__data/assets/pdf_file/0014/40820/2018-Digest.pdf.

6. This judge is referring to the numerous posters of important figures in Black history, such as Sojourner Truth and Ida B. Wells.

7. This section of the chapter has benefitted from my engagement with readings and studies recommended by Dr. Jessica Grieser, a sociolinguist who specializes in the use of African American English. Her professional website is available here: https://jessgrieser.com/.

8. Although this type of English is used commonly among Black Americans, there is still a great deal of diversity among Black people (Baugh 2018).

9. This quote is from a *Philadelphia Inquirer* article published in 2019. The article is available here: https://www.inquirer.com/news/court-reporter-stenographer-african-american-english-aave-philly-transcript-study-20190122.html.

Chapter 6

1. See Louisville's demographic information here: https://data.census.gov/profile/Louisville_city,_Kentucky?g=160XX00US2148000#race-and-ethnicity.

2. See a newspaper article about Stevens here: https://revealnews.org/article/judges-controversial-crusade-renews-diversity-debate/.

3. https://revealnews.org/article/judges-controversial-crusade-renews-diversity-debate/.

4. For an overview about race and jury selection, see Catherine M. Grosso and Barbara O'Brien, "Jury Selection and Race," *Research Handbook on Law and Psychology* (2024): 122–35.

5. For Gilbert's remarks about Judge Stevens, see https://www.abajournal.com/news/article/was_judge_right_to_dismiss_jury_due_to_lack_of_black_members_top_state_cour.

6. See more information about the U.S. jail population here: https://www.prisonpolicy.org/reports/pie2024.html.

7. See the following links to learn more about some of the issues with bail bonds companies: https://eji.org/news/analysis-reveals-how-bail-companies-profit/; https://www.themarshallproject.org/2018/07/13/petty-charges-princely-profits.

8. Paul Butler (2010) writes that despite cases that prohibit racially based peremptory challenges, "the Court has accepted clearly pretextual justifications, such as having 'the longest hair of anybody on the panel by far' or having a 'mustache and goatee type beard,' which according to the prosecutor in question, "look[ed] suspicious" and made the person "appear not to be a good juror for that fact" (1049).

9. Additionally, they are more likely to be overcharged by prosecutors and accept plea deals. Mustard (2001), for example, examined more than 77,000 federal offenders sentences and found that "Blacks, males, and offenders with low levels of education and income receive substantially longer sentences" (285).

10. In addition to race, court scholars maintain that judges' decision-making con-

cerning final case outcomes is influenced by numerous factors, especially ideology and sometimes other identity characteristics such as age and gender (Gill, Kagan, and Marouf 2019; Glynn and Sen 2015; Manning, Carroll, and Carp 2004).

11. "Respectability politics," or politics of respectability, refers to Black judges attempting to police the behavior of other Black Americans. These judges are operating as a moral authority, even personalizing the actions of Black criminal defendants and punishing what they see as transgressions not only against the law but also the race. This is what James Forman (2018) alludes to in the vignette that opens his book *Locking Up Our Own*. In the vignette, he talks about a Black judge who would "preach" to young Black defendants prior to deciding their fate.

Chapter 7

1. This chapter was originally written for inclusion in this book. With two undergraduate researchers (Joseph P. Kelly and Simon LaClair), I developed this chapter into an essay for an edited volume about judicial communication. The essay has now been published: Taneisha Nicole Means, Joseph P. Kelly, and Simon LaClair, "Judicial Communication, Collegial Education, Cultural Competency, and the Significance of State Judicial Diversity," in *Research Handbook on Judicial Politics*, edited by Michael P. Fix and Matthew Montgomery, 302–20 (Northampton, MA: Edward Elgar Publishing, 2024). While the analysis remains the same, the framing of the chapter and paper differ.

2. https://www.americanbar.org/groups/young_lawyers/projects/men-of-color/lawyer-demographics/.

3. https://www.americanbar.org/groups/judicial/conferences/.

4. See one judge program here: https://judicialstudies.duke.edu/programs/distinguished-judge-in-residence-program/.

Chapter 8

1. https://crsreports.congress.gov/product/pdf/IF/IF10503.

2. https://www.ncsc.org/__data/assets/pdf_file/0023/51719/Court-Outreach-to-Minority-Communities-Rottman.pdf.

3. These are all volunteer organizations, and judges can belong to more than one organization. In other words, these are not a substitute for each other because judges can belong to both, and the organizations complement each other.

4. These sections focus on judges that were involved in the establishment of the initiative/organization. They do not indicate participation in the broader study (i.e., interviews and surveys used elsewhere in the book).

5. Information about the Judge Larry A. Jones Drug Court is available here: https://clevelandmunicipalcourt.org/judicial-services/court-programs-services/drug-court; information about the Green Y.A.R.D. program is available here: https://www.judgelisagreen.org/court-programs.html; information about the Pipeline to Possibilities program is available here: https://www.pipelinetopossibilities.com/; information about the Scales of Justice program is available here: https://scalesofjusticeacademy.org/about/; information about the Ohio Black Judges Association is available here: https://www.news5cleveland.com/news/state/ohios-black-judges-create-association-to-address-diversity-issues

-in-states-court-system; https://obja.us/; information about Just the Beginning is available here: https://jtb.org/mission/.

6. Jones also spent fourteen years as the Cleveland Municipal Court's administrative judge, which is important because it indicates he had significant opportunities to shape the work and functioning of the court.

7. https://cp.cuyahogacounty.us/court-information/black-history-month/judge-larry -a-jones/.

8. https://www.ojp.gov/pdffiles1/nij/238527.pdf.

9. https://nij.ojp.gov/topics/articles/do-drug-courts-work-findings-drug-court -research.

10. While the war on drugs has long been over officially, the societal context in which it was born has not fully been eradicated. In Cleveland, as in many urban metropolitan areas, drug addiction continues to be an issue. Consequently, drug courts continue to operate as an institution that can support the broader local legal system and the community by addressing addiction and offering individuals with chemical dependency issues with an alternative to incarceration.

11. https://mhanational.org/issues/mental-health-courts.

12. https://www.themarshallproject.org/2024/01/19/mississippi-hinds-county-felony -court-district-attorney-judge.

13. https://www.themarshallproject.org/2024/01/19/mississippi-hinds-county-felony -court-district-attorney-judge.

14. https://www.themarshallproject.org/2024/01/19/mississippi-hinds-county-felony -court-district-attorney-judge.

15. https://history.nycourts.gov/about_period/dispensing-justice-johnson/.

16. https://www.douglascountyga.gov/433/Superior-Court---Judge-Cynthia-C -Adams.

17. https://www.stlpr.org/government-politics-issues/2018-12-31/making-history-afri can-american-women-to-head-2-of-missouris-largest-courts.

18. https://www.stlpr.org/government-politics-issues/2018-12-31/making-history-afri an-american-women-to-head-2-of-missouris-largest-courts.

19. https://www.prisonpolicy.org/reports/chronicpunishment.html#mentalhealth.

20. https://bjs.ojp.gov/content/pub/pdf/mhppji.pdf.

21. https://www.treatmentadvocacycenter.org/key-issues/criminalization-of-mental -illness.

22. Treatment Advocacy Center, *The Treatment of Persons with Mental Illness in Prisons and Jails: A State Survey.* The report is available here: https://www.treatmentadvoca cycenter.org/storage/documents/treatment-behind-bars/treatment-behind-bars.pdf. See page 6.

23. https://www.prisonpolicy.org/reports/chronicpunishment.html#mentalhealth.

24. https://www.ojp.gov/pdffiles1/nij/grants/251952.pdf.

25. According to Leah Wang (2022), substance abuse disorders often co-occur with mental illness. "A staggering half (50%) of people in state prisons who have a history of substance use disorder treatment also have a history of one or more mental health conditions. This is disproportionate overlap: According to the National Institute on Drug

Abuse, 38% of U.S. adults with substance use disorder also had one or more mental health disorders." https://www.prisonpolicy.org/reports/chronicpunishment.html#men talhealth.

26. Information concerning poverty in inner-city areas is available from the Initiative for a Competitive Inner City: https://icic.org/blog/americas-war-poverty-inner-cities-re main-front-line-2/.

27. https://www.povertycenter.columbia.edu/s/COVID-Projecting-Poverty-Monthly -CPSP-2020.pdf.

28. https://cps.ipums.org/cps/resources/poverty/PovReport20.pdf.

29. Information concerning unemployment in inner-city areas is available from the Initiative for a Competitive Inner City: https://icic.org/blog/americas-war-poverty-inner -cities-remain-front-line-2/.

30. https://www.pipelinetopossibilities.com/; https://www.diversityinc.com/four -dallas-judges-from-alpha-kappa-alpha-and-delta-sigma-theta-are-doing-their-part-to -keep-kids-out-of-prison-2/.

31. https://mckinneylaw.iu.edu/news/releases/2018/04/iu-mckinney-alumna-helps -dallas-youth-stay-out-of-her-criminal-court.html.

32. https://www.waer.org/news/2018-05-02/su-law-school-grad-judge-ending-prison -pipeline-for-youth-along-with-3-other-dallas-area-judges.

33. https://scalesofjusticeacademy.org/about/; This program was previously known as the Justice Academy for Young Women.

34. https://www.judgelisagreen.org/court-programs.html.

35. https://obja.us/about-us/.

36. https://www.clemetrobar.org/?pg=CMBABlog&blAction=showEntry&blogEn try=61798.

37. https://www.njwla.org/color-of-justice-program/.

38. Just the Beginning—A Pipeline Organization was formerly Just the Beginning Foundation.

39. https://jtb.org/.

40. Judge Williams was the first Black woman to serve in a district court in the three-state Seventh Circuit, and when she was appointed to the court of appeals for the Seventh Circuit, she became only the third Black woman to serve as an appellate judge on any federal circuit court. In 2017, Judge Williams became a senior judge on the court of appeals for the Seventh Circuit. Since she retired in 2018, Judge Williams has worked at Jones Day, one of the largest law firms in the United States, heading up its law efforts and initiatives in Africa. https://www.jonesday.com/en/lawyers/w/judge-ann-claire -williams?tab=overview.

41. https://judicialstudies.duke.edu/2021/01/judge-ann-claire-williams-part-1/.

42. The federal courts were first racially integrated in 1937, when Franklin D. Roosevelt appointed William Henry Hastie to the U.S. District Court for the District of the Virgin Islands. He remained in that position for two years until he left to become dean at the Howard University School of Law. Hastie became the first Black federal appellate court judge in 1949, when Harry S. Truman appointed him to the U.S. Court of Appeals for the Third Circuit. Hastie is, therefore, the first Black Article III judge. Judge James

Parsons became the first Black district court judge in 1961, when John F. Kennedy appointed him to the U.S. District Court for the Northern District of Illinois.

43. https://jtb.org/mission/.

44. https://jtb.org/programs/.

45. https://apps.law.wustl.edu/enewsletter/1718/Images/2021JTBSTWAnnouncement_4-15-21.pdf.

Conclusion

1. While the movement is often remembered for mobilizing and pushing for desegregation as a way to end Jim Crow, activists also fought and died while advocating and protesting for voting rights. With the passage of the Voting Rights Act in 1965, Black Americans' access to the ballot was greatly expanded and the ability to vote in elections for their preferred candidates meant many of them could have a say in who became their state judges. The primary judicial selection method in states since the early twentieth century has been via elections, which meant that Black Americans could run for judgeships and find support among a more racially diverse electorate (Engstrom 1989). We have even seen Black judges reach the bench in higher numbers in states that do not use elections to seat their jurists because of the court diversification efforts by those involved in the judicial selection process. In the late twentieth and early twenty-first centuries, individuals charged with selecting state judges have appointed judges from diverse backgrounds. Many governors, especially Democratic governors, charged with selecting judges utilized their appointment power to appoint Black judges (Hurwitz and Lanier 2003). In some states with merit selection, commissions have prioritized diversity and tried to ensure their selections for judgeships reflect society's increasing racial diversity (Torres-Spelliscy, Chase, and Greenman 2010). All in all, judicial diversity has increased in the post-Civil Rights movement era, and this has been in states using electoral and appointment selection methods (Graham 2004).

2. Yet, this is an ongoing perception that is exacerbated by racial resentment toward Black Americans (Harris and Sen 2019; Ifill 1997; Means and Unah 2025).

3. https://www.sentencingproject.org/advocacy/50-years-and-a-wake-up-ending-the-mass-incarceration-crisis-in-america/.

4. It is true that becoming an attorney and judge situates someone in at least the middle class given their formal education and baseline salaries, but we also know that segregation of the Black middle class continues despite their wealth and education (Cose 1993; Feagin and Sikes 1994; Pattillo 2013).

5. https://www.qmzhang.com/.

6. https://tedellisart.com/.

7. https://tedellisart.com/.

REFERENCES

Abrams, David S., Marianne Bertrand, and Sendhil Mullainathan. 2012. "Do Judges Vary in Their Treatment of Race?" *Journal of Legal Studies* 41, no. 2: 347–83.

Abramson, Leslie W. 2000. "The Judicial Ethics of Ex Parte and Other Communications." *Houston Law Review* 37, no. 5: 1343–94.

Abramson, Paul R. 1977. *The Political Socialization of Black Americans: A Critical Evaluation of Research on Efficacy and Trust*. Free Press.

Alexander, Michelle. 2010. *The New Jim Crow: Mass Incarceration in the Age of Colorblindness*. New Press.

Allen, David W., and Diane E. Wall. 1987. "The Behavior of Women State Supreme Court Justices: Are They Tokens or Outsiders?" *Justice System Journal* 12, no. 2: 232–45.

Allport, Gordon W. 1958. *The Nature of Prejudice*. Doubleday.

Alozie, Nicholas O. 1988. "Black Representation on State Judiciaries." *Social Science Quarterly* 69, no. 4: 979–89.

Anderson, Elijah. 2011. "The Social Situation of the Black Executive: Black and White Identities in the Corporate World." In *Covert Racism*, edited by Rodney D. Coates. Brill.

Ashenfelter, Orley, Theodore Eisenberg, and Stewart J. Schwab. 1995. "Politics and the Judiciary: The Influence of Judicial Background on Case Outcomes." *The Journal of Legal Studies* 24, no. 2: 257–81.

Astin, Alexander W. 1975. *Preventing Students From Dropping Out*. Jossey-Bass.

Austin, Sharon D. Wright, Richard T. Middleton, and Rachel Yon. 2012. "The Effect of Racial Group Consciousness on the Political Participation of African Americans and Black Ethnics in Miami-Dade County, Florida." *Political Research Quarterly* 65, no. 3: 629–41.

Badas, Alex, and Billy Justus. 2023. "Media Attention and Deliberation on the Supreme Court." *Political Research Quarterly* 76, no. 2: 757–69.

Bailey, Michael A., and Forrest Maltzman. 2008. "Does Legal Doctrine Matter? Unpacking Law and Policy Preferences on the US Supreme Court." *American Political Science Review* 102, no. 3: 369–84.

Baugh, John. 2018. *Linguistics in Pursuit of Justice.* Cambridge University Press.

Baumgartner, Frank R., Derek A. Epp, and Kelsey Shoub. 2018. *Suspect Citizens: What 20 Million Traffic Stops Tell Us About Policing and Race.* Cambridge University Press.

Beiner, Theresa M. "What Will Diversity on the Bench Mean for Justice." 1999. *Michigan Journal of Gender & Law* 6, no. 1: 113–52.

Bell, Derrick A., Jr. 1973. "Racism in American Courts: Cause for Black Disruption or Despair." *California Law Review* 61, no. 1: 165–203.

Berdejó, Carlos. 2018. "Criminalizing Race: Racial Disparities in Plea-Bargaining." *BCL Review* 59, no. 4: 1187–249.

Bobo, Lawrence, and Franklin D. Gilliam. 1990. "Race, Sociopolitical Participation, and Black Empowerment." *American Political Science Review* 84, no. 2: 377–93.

Bodenheimer, Edgar. 1947. "The Inherent Conservatism of the Legal Profession." *Indiana Law Journal* 23, no. 3: 221–35.

Bonilla-Silva, Eduardo. 1997. "Rethinking Racism: Toward a Structural Interpretation." *American Sociological Review* 62, no. 3: 465–80.

Bonneau, Chris W., and Heather Marie Rice. 2009. "Impartial Judges? Race, Institutional Context, and US State Supreme Courts." *State Politics & Policy Quarterly* 9, no. 4: 381–403.

Boyd, Christina L. 2016. "Representation on the Courts? The Effects of Trial Judges' Sex and Race." *Political Research Quarterly* 69, no. 4: 788–99.

Boykin, A. Wade, and Forrest D. Toms. 1985. "Black Child Socialization: A Conceptual Framework." In *Black Children: Social, Educational, and Parental Environments,* edited by Harriette Pipes McAdoo and John Lewis. Sage Publications.

Brazelton, Shenita, and Dianne M. Pinderhughes. 2021. "Black Federal Judges and Civil Rights in the Age of Obama." In *After Obama,* edited by Todd C. Shaw, Robert A. Brown and Joseph P. McCormick II. New York University Press.

Broockman, David E. 2013. "Black Politicians Are More Intrinsically Motivated to Advance Blacks' Interests: A Field Experiment Manipulating Political Incentives." *American Journal of Political Science* 57, no. 3: 521–36.

Brown, Nadia E. 2014. *Sisters in the Statehouse: Black Women and Legislative Decision Making.* Oxford University Press.

Brown, Nadia E., and Danielle Casarez Lemi. 2021. *Sister Style: The Politics of Appearance for Black Women Political Elites.* Oxford University Press.

Browne-Marshall, Gloria J. 2013. *Race, Law, and American Society: 1607–Present.* Routledge.

Brunson, Rod K., and Jody Miller. 2006. "Young Black Men and Urban Policing in the United States." *British Journal of Criminology* 46, no. 4: 613–40.

Brunson, Rod K., and Ronald Weitzer. 2009. "Police Relations with Black and White Youths in Different Urban Neighborhoods." *Urban Affairs Review* 44, no. 6: 858–85.

———. 2011. "Negotiating Unwelcome Police Encounters: The Intergenerational Transmission of Conduct Norms." *Journal of Contemporary Ethnography* 40, no. 4: 425–56.

Bunyasi, Tehama Lopez, and Candis Watts Smith. 2019. "Do All Black Lives Matter Equally to Black People? Respectability Politics and the Limitations of Linked Fate." *Journal of Race, Ethnicity, and Politics* 4, no. 1: 180–215.

Burke, Edmund. 1774. *Mr. Edmund Burke's Speeches at His Arrival at Bristol: And at the Conclusion of the Poll.* J. Wilkie.

Butler, Paul. 1995. "Racially Based Jury Nullification: Black Power in the Criminal Justice System." *Yale Law Journal* 105, no. 3: 677–725.

———. 2010. "One Hundred Years of Race and Crime." *Journal of Criminal Law & Criminology* 100, no. 3: 1043–60.

———. 2017. *Chokehold: Policing Black Men.* New Press.

Campbell, Angus, Philip E. Converse, Warren E. Miller, and Donald E. Stokes. 1960. *The American Voter.* John Wiley and Sons.

Campi, Ashleigh, and Jane Junn. 2019. "Racial Linked Fate and Gender in US Politics." *Politics, Groups, and Identities* 7, no. 3: 654–62.

Canon, David T. 1999. "Electoral Systems and the Representation of Minority Interests in Legislatures." *Legislative Studies Quarterly* 24, no. 3: 331–85.

Carp, Robert A., Kenneth L. Manning, Lisa M. Holmes, and Ronald Stidham. 2020. *Judicial Process in America.* CQ Press.

Carp, Robert A., and Ronald Stidham. 1998. *Judicial Process in America.* CQ Press.

Carp, Robert, and Russell Wheeler. 1972. "Sink or Swim: The Socialization of a Federal District Judge." *Emory Law Journal* 21: 359–93.

Chew, Pat K., and Robert E. Kelley. 2008. "Myth of the Color-Blind Judge: An Empirical Analysis of Racial Harassment Cases." *Washington University Law Review* 86, no. 5: 1117–66.

Chong, Dennis, and Reuel Rogers. 2005. "Racial Solidarity and Political Participation." *Political Behavior* 27, no 4: 347–74.

Clayton, Dewey M. 2010. *The Presidential Campaign of Barack Obama: A Critical Analysis of A Racially Transcendent Strategy.* Routledge.

Claytor, Cassi Pittman. 2020. *Black Privilege: Modern Middle-Class Blacks with Credentials and Cash to Spend.* Stanford University Press.

Cohen, Jonathan M. 2002. *Inside Appellate Courts: The Impact of Court Organization on Judicial Decision Making in the United States Courts of Appeals.* University of Michigan Press.

Collins, Todd, and Laura Moyer. 2008. "Gender, Race, and Intersectionality on the Federal Appellate Bench." *Political Research Quarterly* 61, no. 2: 219–27.

Cose, Ellis. 1993. *The Rage of a Privileged Class.* Harper Collins.

Crenshaw, Kimberlé Williams. 1989. "Demarginalizing the Intersection of Race and Sex: A Black Feminist Critique of Antidiscrimination Doctrine, Feminist Theory and Antiracist Politics." *University of Chicago Legal Forum*: 139–67.

Cross, William E., Jr. 1971. "The Negro-to-Black Conversion Experience." *Black World* 20, no. 9: 13–27.

———. 1991. "The Stages of Black Identity Development: Nigrescence Models." In *Black*

Psychology, 3rd ed., edited by William E. Cross Jr., Thomas A. Parham, and Janet E. Helms. Cobbs & Henry Publishers.

Cross, William E., Jr., and Peony Fhagen-Smith. 2001. "Patterns of African American Identity Development: A Life Span Perspective." *New Perspectives on Racial Identity Development: A Theoretical and Practical Anthology* 1, no. 1: 243–70.

Crowe, Nancy E. 1999. "The Effects of Judges' Sex and Race on Judicial Decision Making on the U.S. Court of Appeals, 1981–1996." PhD diss., University of Chicago.

Cullen, James. 2018. "The History of Mass Incarceration." Brennan Center for Justice, July 20. https://www.brennancenter.org/our-work/analysis-opinion/history-mass-incarceration.

Davis, Sue, Susan Haire, and Donald R. Songer. 1993. "Voting Behavior and Gender on the US Courts of Appeals." *Judicature* 77, no. 3: 129–33.

Dawson, Michael C. 1994. *Behind the Mule: Race and Class in African-American Politics.* Princeton University Press.

———. 2001. *Black Visions: The Roots of Contemporary African-American Political Ideologies.* University of Chicago Press.

De la Roca, Jorge, Ingrid Gould Ellen, and Katherine M. O'Regan. 2014. "Race and Neighborhoods in the 21st Century: What Does Segregation Mean Today?" *Regional Science and Urban Economics* 47, no. 1: 138–51.

Demuth, Stephen. 2003. "Racial and Ethnic Differences in Pretrial Release Decisions and Outcomes: A Comparison of Hispanic, Black, and White Felony Arrestees." *Criminology* 41, no. 3: 873–908.

Deo, Meera E. 2013. "Two Sides of a Coin: Safe Space and Segregation in Race/Ethnic-Specific Law Student Organizations." *Washington University Journal of Law & Policy* 42, no. 1: 83–129.

Dovi, Suzanne. 2002. "Preferable Descriptive Representatives: Will Just Any Woman, Black, or Latino Do?" *American Political Science Review* 96, no. 4: 729–43.

Dryzek, John S., and Simon Niemeyer. 2008. "Discursive Representation." *American Political Science Review* 102, no. 4: 481–93.

Du Bois, W. E. B. 1903. *The Talented Tenth.* James Pott and Company.

———. 2017. *The Souls of Black Folk.* Introduction by Vann R. Newkirk II. Restless Books.

Dworin, Ruthie. 2021. "'It's No Compassion in These Courtrooms': Exploring the Linguistic Construction of Racial Identity in Narratives of Chicago Courtrooms." Bachelor's thesis, University of Chicago.

Edwards, Harry T. 2003. "The Effects of Collegiality on Judicial Decision Making." *University of Pennsylvania Law Review* 151, no. 5: 1639–90.

Engstrom, Richard L. 1989. "When Blacks Run for Judge: Racial Divisions in the Candidate Preferences of Louisiana Voters." *Judicature* 73, no. 2: 87–89.

Erlanger, Howard S., and Douglas A. Klegon. 1978. "Socialization Effects of Professional School—The Law School Experience and Student Orientations to Public Interest Concerns." *Law & Society Review* 13, no. 1: 11–36.

Ewing, Keith D. 2000. "A Theory of Democratic Adjudication: Towards a Representative, Accountable and Independent Judiciary." *Alberta Law Review* 38, no. 3: 708–33.

Farhang, Sean, and Gregory Wawro. 2004. "Institutional Dynamics on the US Court of Appeals: Minority Representation Under Panel Decision Making." *Journal of Law, Economics, and Organization* 20, no. 2: 299–330.

Farrell, Amy, Geoff Ward, and Danielle Rousseau. 2009. "Race Effects of Representation Among Federal Court Workers: Does Black Workforce Representation Reduce Sentencing Disparities?" *Annals of the American Academy of Political and Social Science* 623, no. 1: 121–33.

Fasold, Ralph W. 1972. *Tense Marking in Black English: A Linguistic and Social Analysis.* Harcourt College Publishers.

Feagin, Joe R. 1991. "The Continuing Significance of Race: Antiblack Discrimination in Public Places." *American Sociological Review* 56, no. 1: 101–16.

Feagin, Joe R., and Melvin P. Sikes. 1994. *Living with Racism: The Black Middle-Class Experience.* Beacon Press.

———. 1995. "How Black Students Cope with Racism on White Campuses." *Journal of Blacks in Higher Education*, no. 8: 91–97.

Fenno, Richard F., Jr. 1977. "US House Members in their Constituencies: An Exploration." *American Political Science Review* 71, no. 3: 883–917.

Fleming, Jacqueline. 2001. "The Impact of a Historically Black College on African American Students: The Case of LeMoyne-Owen College." *Urban Education* 36, no. 5: 597–610.

Flick, Uwe. 2004. "Triangulation in Qualitative Research." In *A Companion to Qualitative Research* 3, edited by Uwe Flick, Ernst Von Kardorff, and Ines Steinke. Sage.

Forman, James. 2018. *Locking Up Our Own: Crime and Punishment in Black America.* Farrar, Straus and Giroux.

Frazier, E. Franklin. 1997. *Black Bourgeoisie.* Simon and Schuster.

Free, Marvin D., Jr. 1996. *African Americans and the Criminal Justice System.* Routledge.

Fries-Britt, Sharon, and Bridget Turner. 2002. "Uneven Stories: Successful Black Collegians at a Black and a White Campus." *The Review of Higher Education* 25, no. 3): 315–30.

Gaertner, Samuel L., and John F. Dovidio. 2005. "Categorization, Recategorization, and Intergroup Bias." In *On the Nature of Prejudice: Fifty Years after Allport,* edited by John F. Dovidio, Peter Glick, and Laurie A. Rudman. Blackwell Publishing.

Gau, Jacinta M. 2016. "A Jury of Whose Peers? The Impact of Selection Procedures on Racial Composition and the Prevalence of Majority-White Juries." *Journal of Crime and Justice* 39, no. 1: 75–87.

Gay, Claudine. 2001. "The Effect of Black Congressional Representation on Political Participation." *American Political Science Review* 95, no. 3: 589–602.

Gay, Claudine, Jennifer Hochschild, and Ariel White. 2016. "Americans' Belief in Linked Fate: Does the Measure Capture the Concept?" *Journal of Race, Ethnicity, and Politics* 1, no. 1: 117–44.

Gay, Claudine, and Katherine Tate. 1998. "Doubly Bound: The Impact of Gender and Race on the Politics of Black Women." *Political Psychology* 19, no. 1: 169–84.

George, Tracey E., and Albert H. Yoon. 2017. "Measuring Justice in State Courts: The Demographics of the State Judiciary." *Vanderbilt Law Review* 70, no. 6: 1887–1910.

Gibson, James L. 1978. "Judges' Role Orientations, Attitudes, and Decisions: An Inter-active Model." *American Political Science Review* 72, no. 3: 911–24.

———. 1981. "The Role Concept in Judicial Research." *Law & Policy* 3, no. 3: 291–311.

Giddings, Paula. 1988. *In Search of Sisterhood: Delta Sigma Theta and the Challenge of the Black Sorority Movement*. William Morrow.

Gill, Rebecca D., Michael Kagan, and Fatma Marouf. 2019. "The Impact of Maleness on Judicial Decision Making: Masculinity, Chivalry, and Immigration Appeals." *Politics, Groups, and Identities* 7, no. 3: 509–28.

Glynn, Adam N., and Maya Sen. 2015. "Identifying Judicial Empathy: Does Having Daughters Cause Judges to Rule for Women's Issues?" *American Journal of Political Science* 59, no. 1: 37–54.

Goelzhauser, Greg. 2011. "Diversifying State Supreme Courts." *Law & Society Review* 45, no. 3: 761–81.

Goldman, Sheldon, Elliot Slotnick, and Sara Schiavoni. 2013. "Obama's First Term Ju-diciary: Picking Judges in the Minefield of Obstructionism." *Judicature* 97, no. 1: 7–47.

Gordon, Hava Rachel, Kate Willink, and Keeley Hunter. 2024. "Invisible Labor and the Associate Professor: Identity and Workload Inequity." *Journal of Diversity in Higher Education* 17, no. 3: 285–96.

Gottschalk, Marie. 2013. "The Carceral State and the Politics of Punishment." *The Sage Handbook of Punishment and Society*, edited by Jonathan Simon and Richard Sparks, 205–41. Sage Publications.

Gottschall, Jon. 1983. "Carter's Judicial Appointments: The Influence of Affirmative Action and Merit Selection on Voting on the US Courts of Appeals." *Judicature* 67, no. 4: 165–73.

———. 1986. "Reagan's Appointments to the US Courts of Appeals: The Continuation of a Judicial Revolution." *Judicature* 70, no. 1: 48–54.

Graham, Barbara Luck. 1990. "Do Judicial Selection Systems Matter? A Study of Black Representation on State Courts." *American Politics Quarterly* 18, no. 3: 316–36.

———. 2004. "Toward an Understanding of Judicial Diversity in American Courts." *Michigan Journal of Race & Law* 10: 153–81.

Gramlich, John. 2024. "What the Data Says About Crime in the U.S." Pew Research Center. https://www.pewresearch.org/short-reads/2024/04/24/what-the-data-says -about-crime-in-the-us/.

Green, Donald P., Bradley Palmquist, and Eric Schickler. 2004. *Partisan Hearts and Minds: Political Parties and the Social Identities of Voters*. Yale University Press.

Greene, Beverly A. 1992. "Racial Socialization as a Tool in Psychotherapy with African American Children." In *Working with Culture: Psychotherapeutic Interventions with Ethnic Minority Children and Adolescents*, edited by Luis A. Vargas and Joan D. Koss-Chioino. Jossey-Bass.

Grose, Christian R. 2011. *Congress in Black and White: Race and Representation in Washington and at Home*. Cambridge University Press.

Gruhl, John, Cassia Spohn, and Susan Welch. 1981. "Women as Policymakers: The Case of Trial Judges." *American Journal of Political Science* 25, no. 2: 308–22.

Guiffrida, Douglas A. 2003. "African American Student Organizations as Agents of Social Integration." *Journal of College Student Development* 44, no. 3: 304–19.

Gurin, Patricia, Shirley Hatchett, and James S. Jackson. 1989. *Hope and Independence: Blacks' Response to Electoral and Party Politics.* Russell Sage Foundation.

Haire, Susan B., and Laura P. Moyer. 2015. *Diversity Matters: Judicial Policymaking in the US Courts of Appeals.* University of Virginia Press.

Hall, Melinda Gann. 1995. "Justices as Representatives: Elections and Judicial Politics in the American States." *American Politics Quarterly* 23, no. 4: 485–503.

Hall, Melinda Gann, and Paul Brace. 1992. "Toward an Integrated Model of Judicial Voting Behavior." *American Politics Quarterly* 20, no. 2: 147–68.

Hamilton, Alexander, James Madison, and John Jay. 2008. *The Federalist Papers.* Edited with an introduction and notes by Lawrence Goldman. Oxford University Press.

Harper, Shaun R., and Stephen John Quaye. 2007. "Student Organizations as Venues for Black Identity Expression and Development Among African American Male Student Leaders." *Journal of College Student Development* 48, no. 2: 127–44.

Harris, Allison P. 2024. "Can Racial Diversity Among Judges Affect Sentencing Outcomes?" *American Political Science Review* 118, no. 2: 940–55.

Harris, Allison P., and Maya Sen. 2019. "Bias and Judging." *Annual Review of Political Science* 22, no. 1: 241–59.

Hawkins, Billy. 1998. "The White Supremacy Continuum of Images for Black Men." *Journal of African American Men* 3, no. 3: 7–18.

Haynie, Kerry L. 2001. *African American Legislators in the American States.* Columbia University Press.

Haynie, Kerry L., and Candis S. Watts. 2010. "Blacks and the Democratic Party: A Resilient Coalition." In *New Directions in American Political Parties,* edited by Jeffrey M. Stonecash. Routledge.

Herrick, Rebekah. 2016. *Minorities and Representation in American Politics.* CQ Press.

Hettinger, Virginia A., Stefanie A. Lindquist, and Wendy L. Martinek. 2004. "Comparing Attitudinal and Strategic Accounts of Dissenting Behavior on the US Courts of Appeals." *American Journal of Political Science* 48, no. 1: 123–37.

Hindera, John J. 1993. "Representative Bureaucracy: Further Evidence of Active Representation in the EEOC District Offices." *Journal of Public Administration Research and Theory* 3, no. 4: 415–29.

Hobbes, Thomas. 2005. *Thomas Hobbes: Leviathan.* A Critical Edition by G. A. J. Rogers and Karl Schuhmann. Continuum.

Hughes, Diane. 2003. "Correlates of African American and Latino Parents' Messages to Children about Ethnicity and Race: A Comparative Study of Racial Socialization." *American Journal of Community Psychology* 31, no. 1–2: 15–33.

Hughes, Diane, and Lisa Chen. 1997. "When and What Parents Tell Children about Race: An Examination of Race-Related Socialization among African American Families." *Applied Developmental Science* 1, no. 4: 200–14.

Hughey, Matthew W., and Gregory S. Parks. 2012. "Introduction: Black Fraternal Organizations: Systems, Secrecy, and Solace." *Journal of African American Studies* 16: 595–603.

Hurtado, Sylvia. 2001. "Linking Diversity and Educational Purpose: How Diversity Affects the Classroom Environment and Student Development." In *Diversity Challenged: Evidence on the Impact of Affirmative Action,* edited by Gary Orfield. Harvard Education Publishing Group.

Hurwitz, Mark S., and Drew Noble Lanier. 2003. "Explaining Judicial Diversity: The Differential Ability of Women and Minorities to Attain Seats on State Supreme and Appellate Courts." *State Politics & Policy Quarterly* 3, no. 4: 329–52.

Ifill, Sherrilyn A. 1997. "Judging the Judges: Racial Diversity, Impartiality and Representation on State Trial Courts." *Boston College Law Review* 39, no. 1: 95–149.

———. 2000. "Racial Diversity on the Bench: Beyond Role Models and Public Confidence." *Washington & Lee Law Review* 57, no. 2: 405–95.

Jalain, Caroline I., Paul A. Lucas, and George E. Higgins. 2024. "Assessing the Effectiveness of Mental Health Courts in Reducing Recidivism: A Systematic Review with Meta-analysis." *Justice Evaluation Journal* 7, no. 2: 212–30.

Jardina, Ashley. 2019. *White Identity Politics.* Cambridge University Press.

Jensen, Jennifer M., and Wendy L. Martinek. 2009. "The Effects of Race and Gender on the Judicial Ambitions of State Trial Court Judges." *Political Research Quarterly* 62, no. 2: 379–92.

Jones, Taylor, Jessica Rose Kalbfeld, Ryan Hancock, and Robin Clark. 2019. "Testifying While Black: An Experimental Study of Court Reporter Accuracy in Transcription of African American English." *Language* 95, no. 2: e216–e252.

Kastellec, Jonathan P. "Racial Diversity and Judicial Influence on Appellate Courts." 2013. *American Journal of Political Science* 57, no. 1:167–83.

King, Kendra. 2010. *African American Politics.* Polity Press.

Klein, David E., and Gregory Mitchell, eds. 2010. *The Psychology of Judicial Decision Making.* Oxford University Press.

Knight, Jack, and Lee Epstein. 1996. "The Norm of Stare Decisis." *American Journal of Political Science* 40, no. 4: 1018–35.

Krivo, Lauren J., and Ruth D. Peterson. 1996. "Extremely Disadvantaged Neighborhoods and Urban Crime." *Social Forces* 75, no. 2: 619–48.

Kurinec, Courtney A., and Charles A. Weaver III. 2019. "Dialect on Trial: Use of African American Vernacular English Influences Juror Appraisals." *Psychology, Crime & Law* 25, no. 8: 803–28.

Labov, William. 1972. "Some Principles of Linguistic Methodology." *Language in Society* 1, no. 1: 97–120.

Lacy, Karyn R. 2007. *Blue-Chip Black: Race, Class, and Status in the New Black Middle Class.* University of California Press.

Leech, Beth L. 2002. "Interview Methods in Political Science." *PS-WASHINGTON* 35, no. 4: 663–64.

Leslie, Emily, and Nolan G. Pope. 2017. "The Unintended Impact of Pretrial Detention on Case Outcomes: Evidence from New York City Arraignments." *Journal of Law and Economics* 60, no. 3: 529–57.

Lurigio, Arthur J. 2008. "The First 20 Years of Drug Treatment Courts: A Brief Description of Their History and Impact." *Federal Probation* 72, no. 1: 13–17.

Manning, Kenneth L., Bruce A. Carroll, and Robert A. Carp. 2004. "Does Age Matter? Judicial Decision Making in Age Discrimination Cases." *Social Science Quarterly* 85, no. 1: 1–18.

Mansbridge, Jane. 1999. "Should Blacks Represent Blacks and Women Represent Women? A Contingent 'Yes.'" *Journal of Politics* 61, no. 3: 628–57.

Martinez, Andrew, Rachel Swaner, Cassandra Ramdath, and Katherine Kusiak Carey. 2023. "Police, Courts, and Corrections: Experiences of Procedural Injustice Among Black Adults." *American Journal of Community Psychology* 71, no. 1–2: 147–57.

Massey, Douglas S., and Nancy A. Denton. 2019. "American Apartheid: Segregation and the Making of the Underclass." In *Social Stratification, Class, Race, and Gender in Sociological Perspective*, 2nd ed., edited by David B. Grusky. Routledge.

Mayhew, David R. 1974. *Congress: The Electoral Connection*. Yale University Press.

McClain, Paula D., Jessica D. Johnson Carew, Eugene Walton Jr., and Candis S. Watts. 2009. "Group Membership, Group Identity, and Group Consciousness: Measures of Racial Identity in American Politics?" *Annual Review of Political Science* 12, no. 1: 471–85.

McClain, Paula D. and Steven C. Tauber. 2019. *American Government in Black and White*, 4th ed. Oxford University Press.

McGinty, Emma E., Julia Baller, Susan T. Azrin, Denise Juliano-Bult, and Gail L. Daumit. 2016. "Interventions to Address Medical Conditions and Health-Risk Behaviors Among Persons with Serious Mental Illness: A Comprehensive Review." *Schizophrenia Bulletin* 42, no. 1: 96–124.

McGowen, Ernest, III. 2017. *African Americans in White Suburbia: Social Networks and Political Behavior*. University Press of Kansas.

McGrew, Will. 2019. *US School Segregation in the 21st Century: Causes, Consequences, and Solutions*. Washington Center for Equitable Growth, October 15. https://equitablegrowth.org/research-paper/u-s-school-segregation-in-the-21st-century/.

McLean, Iain. 1991. "Forms of Representation and Systems of Voting." In *Political Theory Today*, edited by David Held, 172–96. Wiley.

Means, Taneisha N. 2018. "Race, Gender, and the Battle to Seat Constance Baker Motley, the First Black Woman Appointed to the Federal Bench." In *Race, Gender, Sexuality, and the Politics of the American Judiciary*, edited by Samantha L. Hernandez and Sharon A. Navarro. Cambridge University Press.

———. 2020. "Political Representation in State Courts Study, 2020." Unpublished survey data.

Means, Taneisha N., Andrew Eslich, and Kaitlin Prado. 2019. "Judicial Diversity in the United States Judiciary." In *Research Handbook on Law and Courts*, edited by Susan M. Sterett and Lee D. Walker, 231–45. Edward Elgar Publishing.

Means, Taneisha N., Achal Fernando-Peiris, Georgia Hahn, Joseph Kelly, Elaina Peterkin, Katha Sikka, and Sabrina Ulsh. 2023. "The Phenomenon of Autocannibalism and Black Women Judges' On-the-Bench Experiences." In *Distinct Identities*, edited by Nadia E. Brown and Sarah A. Gershon. Routledge.

Means, Taneisha Nicole, Simon LaClair, Ria Bhutani, Benjamin Fikhman, and Rory Stumpf. 2024. "Before the Robe: Diversity and State Court Judges' Paths to the

Bench." In *Open Judicial Politics*, 3rd ed., vol. 1, edited by Rorie Spill Solberg and Eric Waltenburg. Oregon State University.

Means, Taneisha N., and Tara Lohani. 2025. "Understanding 21st-Century Black Judicial Interests." Unpublished manuscript, January 1.

Means, Taneisha, and Isaac Unah. 2025. "Public Perceptions of the Fairness of Black and White Judges in Racialized and Non-Racialized Cases." *Journal of Law and Courts*: 1–24. https://papers.ssrn.com/sol3/papers.cfm?abstract_id=5142224.

Meier, Kenneth J., and Jill Nicholson-Crotty. 2006. "Gender, Representative Bureaucracy, and Law Enforcement: The Case of Sexual Assault." *Public Administration Review* 66, no. 6: 850–60.

Melamed, Jodi. 2015. "Racial Capitalism." *Critical Ethnic Studies* 1, no. 1:76–85.

Deborah Jones Merritt, and James J Brudney. 2001. "Stalking Secret Law: What Predicts Publication in the United States Courts of Appeal." *Vanderbilt Law Review* 54, no. 1: 69–122.

Middlemass, Keesha. 2017. *Convicted and Condemned: The Politics and Policies of Prisoner Reentry*. New York University Press.

Middlemass, Keesha, and Calvin John Smiley, eds. 2020. *Prisoner Reentry in the 21st Century: Critical Perspectives of Returning Home*. Routledge.

Miller, Arthur H., Patricia Gurin, Gerald Gurin, and Oksana Malanchuk. 1981. "Group Consciousness and Political Participation." *American Journal of Political Science* 25, no. 3: 494–511.

Minta, Michael D. 2011. *Oversight: Representing the Interests of Blacks and Latinos in Congress*. Princeton University Press.

Minta, Michael D., and Valeria Sinclair-Chapman. 2013. "Diversity in Political Institutions and Congressional Responsiveness to Minority Interests." *Political Research Quarterly* 66, no. 1: 127–40.

Mitchell, Ojmarrh, David B. Wilson, Amy Eggers, and Doris L. MacKenzie. 2012. "Assessing the Effectiveness of Drug Courts on Recidivism: A Meta-Analytic Review of Traditional and Non-traditional Drug Courts." *Journal of Criminal Justice* 40, no. 1: 60–71.

Mosher, Frederick C. 1968. *Democracy and the Public Service*. Oxford University Press.

Motley, Constance Baker. 1998. *Equal Justice Under Law: An Autobiography*. Macmillan.

Moyer, Laura, Allison P. Harris, and Rorie Spill Solberg. 2022. "'Better Too Much Than Not Enough': The Nomination of Women of Color to the Federal Bench." *Journal of Women, Politics & Policy* 43, no. 3: 363–75.

Mustard, David B. 2001. "Racial, Ethnic, and Gender Disparities in Sentencing: Evidence from the US Federal Courts." *The Journal of Law and Economics* 44, no. 1: 285–314.

National Treatment Court Resource Center. 2025. *What Are Drug Courts?* https://ntcrc.org/what-are-drug-courts/.

Nicholson-Crotty, Jill, Jason A. Grissom, and Sean Nicholson-Crotty. 2011. "Bureaucratic Representation, Distributional Equity, and Democratic Values in the Administration of Public Programs." *Journal of Politics* 73, no. 2: 582–96.

Oleson, James C., Christopher T. Lowenkamp, Timothy P. Cadigan, Marie VanNostrand, and John Wooldredge. 2016. "The Effect of Pretrial Detention on Sentencing in Two Federal Districts." *Justice Quarterly* 33, no. 6: 1103–22.

Olsen, Marvin E. 1970. "Social and Political Participation of Blacks." *American Sociological Review* 35, no. 4: 682–97.

Omi, Michael, and Howard Winant. 2014. *Racial Formation in the United States*. Routledge.

Outcalt, Charles L., and Thomas Edmund Skewes-Cox. 2002. "Involvement, Interaction, and Satisfaction: The Human Environment at HBCUs." *The Review of Higher Education* 25, no. 3: 331–47.

Oyserman, Daphna. 2001. "Self-Concept and Identity." In *Individual Processes*, edited by Abraham Tesser and Norbert Schwartz. Blackwell Publishers.

Painter, Nell Irvin. 2010. *The History of White People*. W. W. Norton.

Parham, Thomas A. 1989. "Cycles of Psychological Nigrescence." *The Counseling Psychologist* 17, no. 2: 187–226.

Pattillo, Mary. 2005. "Black Middle-Class Neighborhoods." *Annual Review Sociology* 31, no. 1: 305–29.

———. 2013. *Black Picket Fences: Privilege & Peril Among the Black Middle Class*. University of Chicago Press.

Peresie, Jennifer L. 2004. "Female Judges Matter: Gender and Collegial Decisionmaking in the Federal Appellate Courts." *Yale Law Journal* 114, no. 7: 1759–90.

Pfaff, John. 2017. *Locked In: The True Causes of Mass Incarceration—and How to Achieve Real Reform*. Basic Books.

Philpot, Tasha. 2009. *Race, Republicans, and the Return of the Party of Lincoln*. University of Michigan Press.

Philpot, Tasha, and Hanes Walton Jr. 2007. "One of Our Own: Black Female Candidates and the Voters who Support Them." *American Journal of Political Science* 51, no. 1: 49–62.

Pinderhughes, Dianne Marie. 1987. *Race and Ethnicity in Chicago Politics: A Reexamination of Pluralist Theory*. University of Illinois Press.

Pitkin, Hanna. 1964. "Hobbes's Concept of Representation—I." *American Political Science Review* 58, no. 2: 328–40.

———. 1967. *The Concept of Representation*. University of California Press.

Pratt, Victoria. 2022. *The Power of Dignity: How Transforming Justice Can Heal Our Communities*. Seal Press.

Reingold, Beth, Kerry L. Haynie, and Kirsten Widner. 2020. *Race, Gender, and Political Representation: Toward a More Intersectional Approach*. Oxford University Press.

Richardson, Richard J., and Kenneth Nelson Vines. 1970. *The Politics of Federal Courts: Lower Courts in the United States*. Little, Brown.

Rickford, John R., and Sharese King. 2016. "Language and Linguistics on Trial: Hearing Rachel Jeantel (and Other Vernacular Speakers) in the Courtroom and Beyond." *Language* 92, no. 4: 948–88.

Ritchie, Andrea J. 2017. *Invisible No More: Police Violence Against Black Women and Women of Color*. Beacon Press.

Robinson, Cedric J. 2000. *Black Marxism: The Making of the Black Radical Tradition.* Foreword by Robin D. G. Kelley. University of North Carolina Press.

Robinson, Marc Arsell. 2012. *The Black Power Movement and the Black Student Union (BSU) in Washington State, 1967–1970.* Washington State University.

Rocca, Michael S., Gabriel R. Sanchez, and Ron Nikora. 2009. "The Role of Personal Attributes in African American Roll-Call Voting Behavior in Congress." *Political Research Quarterly* 62, no. 2: 408–14.

Rothstein, Richard. 2017. *The Color of Law: A Forgotten History of How Our Government Segregated America.* Liveright.

Rottman, David B. 2015. *Court Outreach to Minority Communities: Methods Used, Lessons Learned, and Transitioning from Outreach to Engagement.* National Center for State Courts.

Rottman, David B., Randall Hansen, Nicole Mott, and Lynn Grimes. 2003. *Perceptions of the Courts in Your Community: The Influence of Experience, Race, and Ethnicity.* National Center for State Courts.

Sanchez, Gabriel R. 2006. "The Role of Group Consciousness in Latino Public Opinion." *Political Research Quarterly* 59, no. 3: 435–46.

Sanchez, Gabriel R., and Natalie Masuoka. 2010. "Brown-Utility Heuristic? The Presence and Contributing Factors of Latino Linked Fate." *Hispanic Journal of Behavioral Sciences* 32, no. 4: 519–31.

Sawyer, Wendy. 2020. "Visualizing the Racial Disparities in Mass Incarceration." *Prison Policy Initiative* 27: 1–11.

Scherer, Nancy. 2004. "Blacks on the Bench." *Political Science Quarterly* 119, no. 4: 655–75.

———. 2023. *Diversifying the Courts: Race, Gender, and Judicial Legitimacy.* New York University Press.

Scherer, Nancy, and Brett Curry. 2010. "Does Descriptive Race Representation Enhance Institutional Legitimacy? The Case of the US Courts." *Journal of Politics* 72, no. 1: 90–104.

Schildkraut, Deborah J. 2020. "White Attitudes About Descriptive Representation in the US: The Roles of Identity, Discrimination, and Linked Fate." In *Body Politics,* edited by Nadia E. Brown and Sarah A. Gershon. Routledge.

Seamster, Louise. 2019. "Black Debt, White Debt." *Contexts* 18, no. 1: 30–35.

Segal, Jeffrey A., and Harold J. Spaeth. 2002. *The Supreme Court and the Attitudinal Model Revisited.* Cambridge University Press.

Segal, Jennifer A. 2000. "Representative Decision Making on the Federal Bench: Clinton's District Court Appointees." *Political Research Quarterly* 53, no. 1: 137–50.

Sentencing Project. 2018. *Report to the United Nations on Racial Disparities in the U.S. Criminal Justice System.* https://www.sentencingproject.org/reports/report-to-the-united-nations-on-racial-disparities-in-the-u-s-criminal-justice-system/.

Shingles, Richard D. 1981. "Black Consciousness and Political Participation: The Missing Link." *American Political Science Review* 75, no. 1: 76–91.

Shuman, Jerome. 1970. "A Black Lawyer's Study." *Howard Law Journal* 16, no. 2: 225–313.

Simien, Evelyn M. 2005. "Race, Gender, and Linked Fate." *Journal of Black Studies* 35, no. 5: 529–50.

Sisk, Gregory C., Michael Heise, and Andrew P. Morriss. 1998. "Charting the Influences on the Judicial Mind: An Empirical Study of Judicial Reasoning." *New York University Law Review* 73, no. 5: 1377–500.

Smedley, Audrey. 1997. "Origin of the Idea of Race." *Anthropology Newsletter.* https://www.racepowerofanillusion.org/articles/origin-idea-race/.

Smedley, Audrey, and Brian D. Smedley. 2018. *Race in North America: Origin and Evolution of a Worldview.* Routledge.

Smith, Candis Watts. 2014a. *Black Mosaic: The Politics of Black Pan-Ethnic Diversity.* New York University Press.

———. 2014b. "Shifting from Structural to Individual Attributions of Black Disadvantage: Age, Period, and Cohort Effects on Black Explanations of Racial Disparities." *Journal of Black Studies* 45, no. 5: 432–52.

Smith, Drew R., and Fredrick C. Harris. 2005. *Black Churches and Local Politics: Clergy Influence, Organizational Partnerships, and Civic Empowerment.* Rowman & Littlefield.

Smith, J. Clay, Jr. 1993. "Justice and Jurisprudence and the Black Lawyer." *Notre Dame Law Review* 69, no. 5: 1077–113.

Smith, Michael David. 1983. *Race Versus Robe: The Dilemma of Black Judges.* Associated Faculty Press.

Songer, Donald R., and Kelley A. Crews-Meyer. 2000. "Does Judge Gender Matter? Decision Making in State Supreme Courts." *Social Science Quarterly* 81, no. 3: 750–62.

Songer, Donald R., Sue Davis, and Susan Haire. 1994. "A Reappraisal of Diversification in the Federal Courts: Gender Effects in the Courts of Appeals." *Journal of Politics* 56, no. 2: 425–39.

Spencer, Margaret Beale. 1988. "Self-Concept Development." *New Directions for Child and Adolescent Development* 1988, no. 42: 59–72.

Spencer, Margaret Beale, Blanch Dobbs, and Dena Phillips Swanson. 1988. "African American Adolescents: Adaptational Processes and Socioeconomic Diversity in Behavioural Outcomes." *Journal of Adolescence* 11, no. 2: 117–37.

Spohn, Cassia. 1991. "Decision Making in Sexual Assault Cases: Do Black and Female Judges Make a Difference?" *Women & Criminal Justice* 2, no. 1: 83–105.

Steffensmeier, Darrell, and Chester L. Britt. 2001. "Judges' Race and Judicial Decision Making: Do Black Judges Sentence Differently?" *Social Science Quarterly* 82, no. 4: 749–64.

Stevenson, Bryan. 2014. *Just Mercy: A Story of Justice and Redemption.* Spiegel & Grau.

Stumpf, Harry P. 1998. *Judicial Politics,* 2nd ed. Prentice Hall.

Swain, Carol Miller. 1995. *Black Faces, Black Interests: The Representation of African Americans in Congress.* Harvard University Press.

Tajfel, Henri, ed. 1978. *Differentiation between Social Groups: Studies in the Social Psychology of Intergroup Relations.* Academic Press.

Tajfel, Henri, Michael G. Billig, Robert P. Bundy, and Claude Flament. 1971. "Social Categorization and Intergroup Behaviour." *European Journal of Social Psychology* 1, no. 2: 149–78.

Tajfel, Henri, and John C. Turner. 1979. "An Integrative Theory of Intergroup Conflict." In *Organizational Identity: A Reader*, edited by Mary Jo Hatch and Majken Schultz. Oxford University Press.

Tate, Katherine. 1991. "Black Political Participation in the 1984 and 1988 Presidential Elections." *American Political Science Review* 85, no. 4: 1159–76.

———. 1994. *From Protest to Politics: The New Black Voters in American Elections*. Harvard University Press.

———. 2004. *Black Faces in the Mirror: African Americans and Their Representatives in the US Congress*. Princeton University Press.

Tatum, Beverly Daniel. 1997. *Why Are All the Black Kids Sitting Together in the Cafeteria?: And Other Conversations About Race*. Basic Books.

Theobald, Nick A., and Donald P. Haider-Markel. 2009. "Race, Bureaucracy, and Symbolic Representation: Interactions between Citizens and Police." *Journal of Public Administration Research and Theory* 19, no. 2: 409–26.

Thibaut, John, and Laurens Walker. 1975. *Procedural Justice: A Psychological Analysis*. Lawrence Erlbaum Associates.

Thornton, Michael C., Linda M. Chatters, Robert Joseph Taylor, and Walter R. Allen. 1990. "Sociodemographic and Environmental Correlates of Racial Socialization by Black Parents." *Child Development* 61, no. 2: 401–19.

Tiede, Lydia, Robert Carp, and Kenneth L. Manning. 2010. "Judicial Attributes and Sentencing-Deviation Cases: Do Sex, Race, and Politics Matter?" *Justice System Journal* 31, no. 3: 249–72.

Torres-Spelliscy, Ciara, Monique Chase, Emma Greenman, and Susan Liss. 2010. *Improving Judicial Diversity*. Brennan Center for Justice, March 3. https://www.brennancenter.org/our-work/research-reports/improving-judicial-diversity.

Turner, John C., Michael A. Hogg, Penelope J. Oakes, Stephen D. Reicher, and Margaret S. Wetherell. 1987. *Rediscovering the Social Group: A Self-Categorization Theory*. Blackwell.

Tyler, Tom R. 2001. "Public Trust and Confidence in Legal Authorities: What Do Majority and Minority Group Members Want from the Law and Legal Institutions?" *Behavioral Sciences & The Law* 19, no. 2: 215–35.

———. 2006. *Why People Obey the Law*. Princeton University Press.

———. 2007. "Procedural Justice and the Courts." *Court Review: The Journal of the American Judges Association* 44, no. 1–2: 26–31.

Tyler, Tom R., and Gregory Mitchell. 1993. "Legitimacy and the Empowerment of Discretionary Legal Authority: The United States Supreme Court and Abortion Rights." *Duke Law Journal* 43, no. 4: 703–802.

Uhlman, Thomas M. 1978. "Black Elite Decision Making: The Case of Trial Judges." *American Journal of Political Science* 22, no. 4: 884–95.

Van Camp, Debbie, Jamie Barden, Lloyd Ren Sloan, and Reneé P. Clarke. 2009.

"Choosing an HBCU: An Opportunity to Pursue Racial Self-Development." *Journal of Negro Education* 78, no. 4: 457–68.

Van Cleve, Nicole G. 2016. *Crook County: Racism and Injustice in America's Largest Criminal Court*. Stanford University Press.

Vaught, Sabina E. 2011. *Racism, Public Schooling, and the Entrenchment of White Supremacy: A Critical Race Ethnography*. State University of New York Press.

Verba, Sidney, and Norman H. Nie. 1972. *Participation in America: Social Equality and Political Democracy*. Harper & Row,

Walker, Thomas G., and Deborah J. Barrow. 1985. "The Diversification of the Federal Bench: Policy and Process Ramifications." *The Journal of Politics* 47, no. 2: 596–617.

Walton, Hanes, Jr. 1985. *Invisible Politics: Black Political Behavior*. State University of New York Press.

Walton, Hanes, Jr., Robert C. Smith, and Sherri L. Wallace. 2017. *American Politics and the African American Quest for Universal Freedom*. Routledge.

Wang, Leah. 2022. "Chronic Punishment: The Unmet Health Needs of People in State Prisons." Prison Policy Initiative. https://www.prisonpolicy.org/reports/chronicpunishment.html#mentalhealth.

Washington, Linn. 1994. *Black Judges on Justice: Perspectives from the Bench*. New Press.

Watkins, Beverly Xaviera, and Mindy Thompson Fullilove. 2000. "The Crack Epidemic and the Failure of Epidemic Response." *Temple Political & Civil Rights Law Review* 10: 371–86.

Weissberg, Robert. 1978. "Collective vs. Dyadic Representation in Congress." *American Political Science Review* 72, no. 2: 535–47.

Welch, Kelly. 2007. "Black Criminal Stereotypes and Racial Profiling." *Journal of Contemporary Criminal Justice* 23, no. 3: 276–88.

Welch, Susan, Michael Combs, and John Gruhl. 1988. "Do Black Judges Make a Difference?" *American Journal of Political Science* 32, no. 1: 126–36.

Whipple, Edward G., John L. Baier, and David L. Grady. 1991. "A Comparison of Black and White Greeks at a Predominantly White University." *NASPA Journal* 28, no. 2: 140–48.

Whitby, Kenny J. 1997. *The Color of Representation: Congressional Behavior and Black Interests*. University of Michigan Press.

White, Ismail K., and Chryl N. Laird. 2020. *Steadfast Democrats: How Social Forces Shape Black Political Behavior*. Princeton University Press.

Wilder, Curtis, and Allan Ashman. 1973. "The Black Judge in America: A Statistical Profile." *Judicature* 57, no. 1: 18–21, 24–25.

Wilkenfeld, Joshua. 2004. "Newly Compelling: Reexamining Judicial Construction of Juries in the Aftermath of Grutter v. Bollinger." *Columbia Law Review* 104, no. 8: 2291–327.

Wilson, Timothy. 1996. "Cool Like That: Exploring the World of Historically Black Fraternities and Sororities." Manuscript, University of Vermont.

Woodward, C. Vann. 2001. *The Strange Career of Jim Crow*, commemorative ed. with new afterword by William S. McFeely. Oxford University Press.

Wright, Bruce M. 1990. *Black Robes, White Justice: Why Our Legal System Doesn't Work for Blacks.* Carol Publishing Group.

Wynn, James Andrew, Jr., and Eli Paul Mazur. 2003. "Judicial Diversity: Where Independence and Accountability Meet." *Albany Law Review* 67: 775–92.

Zhu, Ling, and Meredith BL Walker. 2013. "'Too Much Too Young': Race, Descriptive Representation, and Heterogeneous Policy Responses in the Case of Teenage Childbearing." *Politics, Groups, and Identities* 1, no. 4: 528–46.

INDEX

Page numbers in *italics* refer to illustrations.

The authorized representative in the EU for product safety and compliance is:
Mare Nostrum Group
B.V Doelen 72
4831 GR Breda
The Netherlands

www.ingramcontent.com/pod-product-compliance
Lightning Source LLC
Chambersburg PA
CBHW020458270326
41926CB00008B/653